Joe Gorman is an independent journalist and author. His work has featured in the *Guardian*, the *Sydney Morning Herald*, the *Age*, the *Courier-Mail*, *Overland*, *New Matilda*, *Sports Illustrated*, *Penthouse*, and on SBS. He has made television and radio appearances on Al Jazeera, Copa90, Deutsche Welle, and the ABC, and delivered lectures, workshops, and tutorials at the Sydney Writers Festival, the Somerset Celebration of Literature, Professional Footballers Australia, and the University of Technology in Sydney. His first book, *The Death and Life of Australian Soccer*, was long-listed for the 2017 Walkley Book Award. Joe was born in Brisbane and lives in the Blue Mountains.

ALSO BY JOE GORMAN

The Death and Life of Australian Soccer

'Gorman's book is one of the best and most important written on Australian sport.' **The Age**

'This remarkable book is packed full of the characters, passion, failure and success that define Australian soccer and its place in our proud sporting culture.' **Tracey Holmes**, journalist and ABC presenter

'A dramatic narrative engrossingly told ... the story it tells of this country since World War II is more interesting and revealing about Australia than a history of any other sport could hope to be.' **Malcolm Knox**, author of *Bradman's War*

'Important and magnificent ... in my view, *The Death and Life of Australian Soccer* is the Australian sports book of 2017.' **Geoff Armstrong**, publisher at Stoke Hill Press

HEARTLAND

HOW RUGBY LEAGUE EXPLAINS QUEENSLAND

JOE GORMAN

UQP

First published 2019 by University of Queensland Press
PO Box 6042, St Lucia, Queensland 4067 Australia

uqp.com.au
uqp@uqp.uq.edu.au

Cover design by Christabella Designs
Cover photograph of the 2007 Queensland State of Origin team courtesy of the NRL
Author photograph by Jack Baxter
Index by Puddingburn Publishing Services
Typeset in 11.5/16 pt Adobe Garamond Pro by Post Pre-press Group, Brisbane
Printed in Australia by McPherson's Printing Group

The University of Queensland Press is assisted by the Australian Government through the Australia Council, its arts funding and advisory body.

A catalogue record for this book is available from the National Library of Australia.

ISBN 978 0 7022 6042 1 (pbk)
ISBN 978 0 7022 6216 6 (pdf)
ISBN 978 0 7022 6217 3 (epub)
ISBN 978 0 7022 6218 0 (kindle)

University of Queensland Press uses papers that are natural, renewable and recyclable products made from wood grown in well-managed forests. The logging and manufacturing processes conform to the environmental regulations of the country of origin.

CONTENTS

AUTHOR'S NOTE

All quotes are drawn from a mix of archival research and from interviews conducted by me between 2017 and 2019. The quotes from the archives have an endnote. Those without an endnote are from the interviews. Other sources without an endnote include off-the-record interviews and confidential documents that cannot be acknowledged. The research for this book has been funded in part thanks to scholarships from Victoria University and the Tom Brock Bequest Committee.

FROM THE PUBLIC BAR TO THE BOARD ROOM

INTRODUCTION

As practising Maroonites we can only,
for a favourable providential intercession, invoke the saints:
Saint Wally of Lang Park pray for us!
Saint Darren of Lockyer bray for us!
Saint Billy of the Back Line catch for us!
Saint Thurston of Headgear kick for us!

Dan O'Neill
The Footy Almanac[1]

Two years ago, I was in Brisbane to report on the opening match of the 2017 State of Origin series. On the Sunday before the game I ventured into South Bank, on the edge of the Brisbane River, where thousands were celebrating the inaugural Maroon Festival.

There were all the people you would expect to find at such an event: fierce young men with neck tattoos and wraparound sunglasses, Indigenous people in loud football jerseys sponsored by the Deadly Choices health program, elderly couples with their lanyards and *Sunday Mail* showbags. A woman from New Zealand sported a maroon T-shirt, with a gold rather than silver fern, emblazoned

1

with the slogan 'MarooNZ'. As proud parents snapped photos, three young children stood at the foot of an inflatable State of Origin gladiator and yelled, 'Go Queensland!'

By the time the players arrived by CityCat in the afternoon, a large congregation had gathered to welcome them onto the main stage. Throughout the day we had listened to the King, Wally Lewis, lead the 'QUEEENSLANDAAH!' cry. 'The great thing about you wonderful people who have given us such sensational support was if we got beat in the game, you'd go home disappointed but you wouldn't abuse us,' Lewis told the rapturous audience. 'You wouldn't feel embarrassed about us, and you'd turn up for the next game. You'd show that loyalty, and loyalty is the backbone of what has created success for Queensland in State of Origin.'

It would turn out to be a deeply satisfying series for Queenslanders. The Maroons' new coach, Kevin Walters, broke down with emotion at one of the press conferences. Queensland lost Game I, but Johnathan Thurston played all of Game II with a crook shoulder and kicked a late goal to take the series to a decider. Before Game III, the frontman of Brisbane band Powderfinger, Bernard Fanning, sung to the home crowd, and even without Thurston Queensland won easily.

It was Queensland's 11th series win in 12 years. It felt that year as if State of Origin rose to even greater heights, breaking the confines of rugby league and cementing its position as the defining image of the state.

There was, for the first time, a dedicated television show on Fox Sports called *Queenslanders Only*, complete with slogans to 'Make League Great Again' and for a 'QUEXIT' – a play on the populist political slogans used in the United States and England. Tickets were selling for a State of Origin-themed musical titled *Home Ground*, produced by one of Queensland's best-known writers, Hugh Lunn. In Brisbane, an A-League soccer match between the Brisbane Roar and Sydney FC had been promoted with the symbolism and the colours of State of Origin, as had Jeff Horn's boxing bout against Manny Pacquiao.

Bob Katter, the federal member for Kennedy, had even issued a press release to voice his opinion on who should play fullback in Origin I. I had visited Katter at his parliamentary office in Canberra only weeks beforehand. As I entered, he burst into a song for Wally Lewis, and then spoke at length about his life as a rugby league player, administrator, and fan. 'I don't think there's anything in Queensland that is a common talking point, not even politics, as much as State of Origin,' he explained.

And then of course there was the Maroon Festival, a four-day 'celebration of all things Queensland', operated by the Queensland Rugby League and with the imprimatur of the state government.

I began writing this book soon after that series.

My interest in rugby league is inextricably tied to my state of origin. I was born in Brisbane in the front room of an old Queenslander house. Within a few years, we had moved to the Blue Mountains, yet that didn't stop me wearing a Brisbane Broncos jersey while playing in my New South Wales backyard, or from supporting the Maroons while my friends all cheered for the Blues. I have always thought of myself as a Queenslander, even if I only lived there for the first year of my life. In part this is because all of my extended family still live north of the border. The *feeling* of being a Queenslander, though, has always been reaffirmed in me through rugby league.

My favourite memory of State of Origin is from Game III 2002, when Gorden Tallis grabbed New South Wales fullback Brett Hodgson by the collar before dragging him like a rag doll over the sideline. When Dad went to a parent–teacher night at my high school that year, he was introduced to the father of a classmate who happened to be named Tallis.

'Did you name him after Gorden Tallis?' Dad asked innocently.

Confused, the other father explained that his son was named

after the famous English composer, Thomas Tallis. Dad shrugged his shoulders – Gorden was the only Tallis he knew.

There is no doubt that rugby league, more than any other sport, allows Queenslanders to articulate themselves and their communities. If you drive into Innisfail in Far North Queensland, standing next to a lush green cane field is a welcome notice that tells visitors they are entering the hometown of State of Origin players Billy Slater and Ty Williams. Further north, the sign for Gordonvale welcomes passers-by to the 'home of NRL champion Nate Myles'.

There are streets named after rugby league players in Mackay, Toowoomba, Logan, and Caboolture, and a stretch of the Warrego Highway is named after Darren Lockyer, a former captain of the Brisbane Broncos and Queensland.

In fact, it's hard to go anywhere in Queensland without being reminded of rugby league. It is similar to soccer in Brazil, or baseball in the USA, in that it can tell you a lot about a people, a culture, and a way of being. It is more secular religion than sport. And it tends to get under your skin.

Rugby league was founded in 1895 when a group of rugby union clubs from the north of England broke away to establish their own code of football. Modifications in rules, such as the abolition of the line-out, the amount of points for kicking a goal, and the reduction of players from 15 to 13, differentiated the new code from rugby union.

The most obvious division between the two rugbys, however, was class. Between the 1870s and 1890s, debate had raged over the issue of professionalism. The Rugby Football Union, drawn from England's middle class, did not want to compensate working-class players for missing work due to match commitments or injury, and decided to drive out clubs that paid men to play.

This precipitated a split between rugby union, the game for middle- and ruling-class men, and rugby league, the game for the workingman. As Tony Collins, the author of *Rugby's Great Split*, observed, 'rugby itself was used to define class'.[2]

In Queensland, rugby league was established in 1908 as a semi-professional alternative to rugby union. The first committee consisted of high-profile defectors from union, including Michael 'Micky' Dore, Sinon 'Sine' Boland, George Watson, and John 'Jack' Fihelly. The early involvement of Fihelly, an Irish nationalist, Labor politician, and journalist for the *Worker* newspaper, was illustrative of rugby league's close association with the Australian Labor Party and Queensland's Irish Catholic population. Such an association would exist for decades to come, primarily through league's popularity in the Catholic school system.

'As a cultural phenomenon rugby league emerged from a period when the working-class was recovering from the defeats of the 1890s and reasserting itself industrially and politically,' wrote historian Andrew Moore.[3] Since then, of course, rugby league has been transformed from a workingman's game to a commercial product. There was no one defining moment when this began, but the advent of State of Origin in 1980 certainly hastened the process.

State of Origin football – Queensland versus New South Wales – is many things to Queenslanders. In 1982, Brisbane reporter Barry Dick described the contest as 'a lifeblood' for the state.[4] Three decades later, Sydney journalist Roy Masters argued that Origin 'exists to allow Queensland to puff its chest every winter'.[5]

There has long been a feeling that State of Origin is bigger than football. In 1990, the *Courier-Mail* writer Lawrie Kavanagh reflected on the passing of the 1980s. Three events, he wrote, 'played important roles in the coming of age of Queensland in general and Brisbane in particular as a major Australian city':

Those events were the 1982 Commonwealth Games, the 1988 Expo and the advent of the State of Origin rugby league competition in

1980 [...] of the three I would nominate the introduction of the State of Origin series as the most significant event of our maturity at a national level [...] The whole state is behind these players who pull on a maroon jersey on Origin night ... little old ladies who have never been to a league match, ardent fans of other codes ... anyone who takes pride in being called a Queenslander, from the public bar to the board room. That's the spirit the series has brought to this state and I hope historians don't forget it when they come to write their learned theses on Queensland through the 80s.[6]

This book is an attempt to fulfil, and also broaden, Kavanagh's request. There is a genre of academic literature dedicated to the history of Queensland, and the question of Queensland's 'difference' to the rest of Australia. None, however, properly recognises the role of rugby league in shaping the character of the state.

I believe this is partly due to the failure of Australian intellectuals to seriously examine rugby league as a social and cultural phenomenon. As the author Thomas Keneally once said: 'The conventional view from high culture is that you only meet working-class thuggery in rugby league.'[7] Little surprise, then, that this intellectual snobbery is reflected in the histories of Queensland. Only an academic, it seems, could ignore the avalanche of Queensland parochialism unleashed in the four decades since State of Origin was established, and its cultural significance to the history of the state and the nation.

The book *Made in Queensland*, published in 2009, is typical of this elitism. The authors make passing mention of rugby league, but when they comment on the appointment of author Nick Earls to be the face of a tourism campaign in 2001, rather than a 'football legend like Wally Lewis', it is lauded as 'a testament to Brisbane's growing interest in its own culture'.[8]

To which I can only wonder: is rugby league not a legitimate expression of culture? And if not, why not?

One of the enduring qualities of Queensland is that it remains the kind of place where if you know one bloke you'll soon get to know a hundred more. There is a genuine laid-back friendliness that comes, I believe, from the fact that more Queenslanders still live in regional towns than in the capital city, and also that the state is often overlooked or simply dismissed by the powers-that-be in Sydney, Melbourne, and Canberra.

Writing this book was a reminder of Queenslanders' generosity of spirit. The QRL History Committee, in particular Steve Ricketts, Greg Shannon, Greg Adermann, and John McCoy, were immensely generous with their time. The assistance from Gene Miles, the chief executive of the Former Origin Greats, was invaluable. Chris Close, Petero Civoniceva, Kerry Boustead, and Tony Currie are some of the nicest men you will meet in Australian sport.

Currie, who played professionally in Brisbane and Sydney, is a motor mechanic. His shop, Tony Currie's Tyres and More, is in Morningside in Brisbane's east. His customers, he once explained, 'know me as a Queenslander'. 'Could it work in Sydney?' he continued. 'I couldn't do this in Manly. They'd say, "There's that Canterbury player, don't buy your tyres off him!" Here, we're tribal and thankful. I used to have all my footy gear on the wall. Blokes would come looking around, and they feel they know you.'

That anecdote struck me as being so typical of the culture of the state. There are of course rivalries and tensions between people and places, but in the end there is always a higher calling for Queensland.

Apart from my interest in State of Origin, I wrote this book as a way of trying to explain the demise of the old Brisbane competition and the Foley Shield in North Queensland, and the rise of new institutions such as the Brisbane Broncos, the North Queensland Cowboys, the Gold Coast Titans, and the Queensland Cup. It also tells the stories of Arthur Beetson, Wally Lewis, Mal Meninga, and Chris Close; of Allan Langer, Peter Jackson, Trevor Gillmeister, and

Gorden Tallis; and of Darren Lockyer, Cameron Smith, Billy Slater, and Johnathan Thurston.

But rugby league in Queensland is as much about ordinary people as it is about the celebrity players. That's why, in this book, you'll hear from everyday fans like Tom Cranitch, a lifelong Brothers supporter from Brisbane; Alf Abdullah, the godfather of the Sarina Crocodiles, who attended virtually every State of Origin game between 1980 and 2015; and Professor Gracelyn Smallwood, an Indigenous activist and health worker from Townsville and a mad Cowboys fan. Their stories are, in many ways, representative of the faith of tens of thousands of Queenslanders.

Every year, when State of Origin rolls around, the so-called Queensland spirit is referred to but rarely explained. 'People in New South Wales laugh when we talk about it,' once said Paul 'Fatty' Vautin, a former player and coach of Queensland. 'They say it's a joke, but they can't understand it because they're not Queenslanders.'[9]

Perhaps that is the way it should remain: a mythical concept that is passed by osmosis from one true believer to another. Queenslanders, on the whole, are much happier *doing* things than thinking about them.

In my view, rugby league has thrived in Queensland due to its ability to reflect – and contribute to – several key features of the state's identity. Broadly, this book covers three themes: how rugby league explains Queensland's unique decentralisation; its 'coming of age' in the 1990s; and its reckoning with race and reconciliation.

This book, I hope, will allow the next generation of Queenslanders to better understand why rugby league matters to this state. It is not a complete history of the game. Rather, it is an attempt to explain and understand how rugby league has reflected and shaped the development of a modern, self-confident Queensland.

PART I

HOW RUGBY LEAGUE EXPLAINS ...
CITY AND COUNTRY

LANG PARK IN FLOOD, 1974
'THE AMOUNT OF HISTORICAL RECORDS THAT WERE LOST WAS A TRAGEDY.'
(PHOTOGRAPH COURTESY OF SUNCORP STADIUM)

HOW RUGBY LEAGUE EXPLAINS
QLD AND COUNTRY

1

THE DEFEATS WE SUFFERED

1974–1980

On the morning of Saturday 26 January 1974, residents in Brisbane woke to find large parts of their city underwater. High winds and torrential rain lashed Queensland's capital, flooding buildings and shutting down train lines, airport runways, and all major roads. As Brisbane lay at the mercy of Cyclone Wanda, one newspaper reported that the city was 'virtually brought to a halt'.[1]

It was clear that this was a state-wide disaster. In the northwest Gulf Country, a State of Emergency had already been called as airlifts evacuated hundreds of people to dry land. Maryborough, a town on the Fraser Coast, received its worst flooding in two decades. Ipswich, in the southeast, was isolated for days.

But the most damage was in Brisbane, the river city of the south, where nearly a million people lived around a snaking, murky brown passage of water.

As the banks of the Brisbane River broke and floodwaters engulfed the surrounding suburbs, residents witnessed brown snakes and children's toys and furniture and cars and boats – some unoccupied, others filled with groups of people and possessions – drifting down streets.

Entire houses were torn from their foundations and swept away. Roads collapsed, gas plants leaked noxious chlorine fumes, and factories halted production. A 62,000-tonne tanker was ripped from its moorings and tore down the river for nearly a kilometre before it ran aground. A smaller barge crashed into one of the many bridges that spanned the waterway.

Some revellers dived from Festival Hall into the water as if it were a swimming pool. Guests evacuated through waist-deep water from the Park Royal Hotel. Drinkers in shorts and thongs watched as canoes drifted past the verandah at the Regatta Hotel in Toowong.

In the six days of wild weather, 900 millimetres of rain fell in the Brisbane area, causing 16 deaths and an estimated $200 million in damages. The 1974 flood created headlines around the world and imprinted itself on the memory of the city forever.

At Lang Park, just a short walk from the banks of the Brisbane River, administration offices and dressing rooms were flooded and the playing surface was transformed into a lake. The old football ground, which was named after an advocate for Queensland's separation from New South Wales, John Dunmore Lang, had been a cemetery, a circus ground, an all-purpose recreation facility, and a parade ground during World War I. In 1957, it was leased to the Queensland Rugby League.

The Lang Park Trust, which was established in 1962, developed the oval into the best football ground in all of Queensland. The Frank Burke Stand was built with rows of wooden seats and a roof overhead. The opposite side and both ends were grassy embankments that traced the shape of a velodrome.

By 1974 Lang Park was already a shrine to rugby league, a home to the memories of ordinary men and women who witnessed beautiful and brutal acts carried out in the name of what commentator George Lovejoy called 'the greatest game of all'. Yet the invading floodwaters damaged the playing surface and destroyed many precious records belonging to the QRL. 'The amount of historical records that were lost in the flood was a tragedy,' explained Greg Adermann, a member of the QRL history committee. 'Trophies, pennants, memorabilia, minutes of meetings – all priceless.'

Gone were the records and the history, washed away as the floodwaters receded and Queenslanders struggled to rebuild the infrastructure of their suburbs and their lives. What nobody could have known at the time, however, was that a stunning new chapter would soon unfold in the history of rugby league in Queensland.

That year, Barry 'Garbo' Muir, the hard-man halfback who played representative football for Australia, was appointed coach of the state side. Despite being born on the southside of the 29th parallel, Muir always maintained that he was conceived north of the border. He also felt that previous Queensland representative sides had relied too heavily on southerners. His predecessor, Wally O'Connell, was a Sydneysider, and the captain in 1973 was John Sattler, a star prop forward who had been lured north from South Sydney. During that series Queensland failed to score a single point in three games.

Indeed, from the birth of Australian rugby league in 1908, New South Wales had consistently beaten Queensland in the annual interstate series. There had been brief moments of resurgence by Queensland – such as in the 1920s, when a golden generation of Queenslanders won five consecutive series – but since 1960, the series had belonged to New South Wales. Queensland couldn't win a thing.

Muir set out to change the mentality of an entire state. In Game I, held at the Sydney Sports Ground, Queensland lost by nine points. But in the following two games, both of which were held at a still-recovering Lang Park, Queensland managed to hold New South Wales to consecutive draws.

Many credited Queensland's new coach for the unlikely results.

One reporter decided that fans 'should say "thank you" to the State coach Barry Muir', while the president of the QRL, Senator Ron McAuliffe, said that Muir had brought 'the sort of never-say-die spirit we needed in troubled times'.[2] 'The sun still shines, even among the darkest clouds, and if you want proof of that don't look to the sun [...] just look at the Queensland Rugby League in the season of 1974,' concluded McAuliffe. 'Not only has the game in Brisbane and Queensland overcome the setbacks of the 1973 interstate series, it has also splashed through the unexpected disaster of the January floods and bounced back with its greatest series on record.'[3]

In many respects, Senator McAuliffe was typical of his generation of rugby league officials. Born in Brisbane in 1918, he had fought in the Australian Imperial Force during World War II, owned a pub in Coolangatta in the 1950s and '60s, and diligently worked his way up the hierarchies of the Labor Party and the QRL. To him, 'the workers and rugby league and the Labor Party were pretty synonymous'.[4] He ruled in the tradition of Queensland politics: drawing support from country areas, wielding power with almost dictatorial authority, nurturing a deep distrust of intellectuals and academics, and encouraging an atmosphere of parochialism.

Together, he and Barry Muir made for a formidable duo, their unshakeable commitment to the Maroon jersey only matched by their dislike of New South Welshmen. After the two drawn games at Lang Park in 1974, both men approached Game I of the 1975 interstate series in high spirits. To a Sydney reporter, Muir promised a tough, physical encounter, and said that his Queensland side was 'the original mean machine'.[5]

For New South Wales, the most feared player was Arthur Beetson, the captain of Eastern Suburbs in Sydney and one of the most respected players in the game.[6] He was a big man with a legendary appetite, messy brown hair, an easy smile, and friendly eyes. He had an uncanny ability to stand in a tackle and offload the ball to an onrushing teammate.

'Big Artie' was born in Roma and began his career in Brisbane, and so the sight of him in a New South Wales jumper didn't sit right with many Queenslanders. For years the state's best players had journeyed south to play for wealthy Sydney clubs, diminishing the stature of Queensland's local competitions and cementing New South Wales's position as the home of Australian rugby league.

The week before Game I, Muir and his players travelled north to Fraser Island for a team camp. Instead of hard training sessions, however, the players enjoyed themselves, playing pick-up games of touch football, climbing sand dunes, swimming in the clear blue water, and bonding at the bar. Upon the team's return to Brisbane, Muir promised reporters that 'the days of the big New South Wales thrashings are gone. Queensland players have finally got the message that those superstars can be beaten.'[7]

In front of more than 20,000 hopeful Queenslanders, the Maroons scored the first try and led the Blues at half-time. New South Wales brought on their star five-eighth, Bob Fulton, to arrest the Maroons' momentum, but the underrated Queenslanders were too strong. By full-time the score was 14 points to eight – a shock victory to Queensland. 'Wednesday night's win over NSW is the greatest tonic Queensland rugby league has had in years,' wrote legendary coach Bob Bax in the *Courier-Mail*. 'This could be the start of a new era in interstate Rugby League.'[8]

Yet the 'new era' did not immediately arrive. Despite leading at half-time in Game II, Queensland lost by nine points, and then lost again by one point in the third and deciding match. New South Wales held the series for yet another year.

'Perhaps I should thank Barry Muir,' mused the New South Wales captain-coach, Graeme Langlands. 'His published statements probably stirred my players better than I could have done.'[9]

Still Muir continued to trash-talk the opposition. In May 1976, during a training run before Game I at the Sydney Cricket Ground, he harangued his players and constantly referred to the Blues as 'cockroaches'. One *Daily Mirror* journalist reported that Muir's language was so colourful that it forced television crews to 'switch off their sound equipment'.[10]

Although Queensland went on to lose all three games, the 'cockroach' nickname stuck. In the decades to come, 'cockroaches' would become shorthand for New South Welshmen, used by players, coaches, supporters, and marketers alike. 'I thought that would suit New South Wales – cockroaches – because everybody hates them,' Muir later explained. 'You see a cockroach, you want to kill it. I wanted to get a bit of hate into it. That's what we had to have: a bit of hate.'

In 1977 and 1978 the Brisbane press claimed 'moral victories' in the interstate games, but nothing could halt the dominance of New South Wales. Muir soon departed as coach, replaced by a lanky ex-Queensland centre from Toowoomba, John McDonald.

Greg Veivers, who played 16 interstate games during the 1970s, later said that Muir was 'the catalyst for change in Queensland rugby league'.[11] And according to the *Courier-Mail* reporter Lawrie Kavanagh, Muir's biggest achievement was in getting his players to produce above and beyond their regular form for their clubs. To Kavanagh, New South Wales was the Goliath to Queensland's David, with the latter 'wandering around in search of a slingshot'.[12]

The sport was now at a critical juncture. While Brisbane-based soccer and basketball sides had joined their respective national competitions, in rugby league enough Queensland-bred footballers were playing in Sydney to fill an entire team. And Kerry Boustead, a show-stopping 18-year-old winger from Innisfail, was about to join the great exodus from Queensland.

In 1978, Boustead scored five tries in his first four games for Australia and three tries in as many matches for Queensland. Yet at the beginning of 1979, he agreed to terms with Eastern Suburbs in Sydney. Senator Ron McAuliffe opposed the move, and attempted to reinstate the outlawed transfer system. Why, he argued, 'should we spend thousands on coaching schemes only to see the finished product snapped up by a Sydney club without reimbursement?'[13]

The transfer fee, Boustead later explained, ended up coming out of his own pocket. 'I had to pay him to leave,' he recalled. 'I didn't have any signed agreement or anything, and he just said, "What I'll do, I'll keep you out of the game for the whole year if I have to." He said, "I'm one of the only guys who doesn't have to show up in court. So if I were you, I'd just pay the money now and go."'

After a quiet start to the season for Easts, Boustead was selected on the wing for New South Wales for Game I of the 1979 interstate series. There, he joined fellow expatriate Queenslanders Rod Reddy and Rod Morris in a 3–0 series whitewash. To make matters worse for Queensland, Boustead scored three tries for New South Wales in the third and final game.

And so the decade ended in much the same manner as it began: with New South Wales firmly in control of the interstate series, and despondent Queensland fans wondering if the tide would ever turn. The Maroons had won just twice in the past 29 matches.

Queenslanders, concluded Lawrie Kavanagh, were tired of losing their best players to New South Wales and had come to accept the fact that unless something drastic occurred, the Blues would continue winning. 'A major suggestion now,' wrote Kavanagh, 'is a state of origin series.'[14]

★

For more than a decade, Australians had looked to Queensland and decided that it was 'different' from the rest of the country. Separated from the colony of New South Wales in 1859, Queensland had developed its unique foibles and a distinctive state identity.

By the end of the 1970s, it was the only mainland state in which more people lived in rural and regional towns than in the capital city. Significantly large populations resided in self-sufficient hubs along the coast in Bundaberg, Gladstone, Rockhampton, Mackay, Townsville, and Cairns, and in inland towns such as Mount Isa, Roma, and Toowoomba. Even the city-dwellers in Brisbane spoke of living in 'a big country town'.

Decentralisation, oppressive heat, and isolation had shaped the character of its people. Queenslanders revelled in their difference and would often describe themselves as the 'last of the real Australians'. To the rest of the country, wrote Humphrey McQueen in 1979, Queensland was 'more a state of mind than a state of their nation'.[15]

All lines of inquiry about Queensland's alleged difference led to the state's ultra-conservative premier, Joh Bjelke-Petersen. A peanut farmer who had left school aged 13, Bjelke-Petersen earned his money from land-clearing in the central west, joined the Country Party, and rose to power in 1968.

Bjelke-Petersen drew his support from country Queensland, exploiting a gerrymandered electoral system that allowed the votes of rural electorates to be worth up to five times more than those in the city. His government's 'rural bias', wrote historian Jackie Ryan, 'was evident in the naming conventions of institutions such as the Queensland Ballet, the Queensland Symphony Orchestra, and the Queensland Theatre Company, all which acknowledged the state, rather than the city in which they were based'.[16]

No Australian politician would ever harness the twin forces of conservatism and parochialism as effectively as the man they called 'the hillbilly dictator'. Bjelke-Petersen's policies and public persona won the admiration of many Queenslanders while also inspiring public protest, scorn, and derision from down south. The *Australian* newspaper called him 'the undistinguished premier of Queensland'.[17] Others called him 'jackboot Joh'. The band Skyhooks sang of escaping

Bjelke-Petersen's Queensland and returning 'over the border' to New South Wales.

A streak of Queensland exceptionalism had existed since the state boundaries were first drawn, and Bjelke-Petersen laced his public statements with anti-southern rhetoric. His enthusiasm for hectoring New South Wales and Victoria and especially Canberra almost matched his strident anti-communism. When the federal government threatened to redraw Queensland's border in the Torres Strait Islands, Bjelke-Petersen even began talking about secession. Always keen to encourage overseas investment and free enterprise, he once told a Japanese trade mission: 'We are not Australians – we are Queenslanders.'[18]

While Bjelke-Petersen was not interested in rugby league – or any sport for that matter – his opposition to poker machines had a decisive impact on the game. While Queensland rugby league relied on gate takings to fund its operations, in New South Wales – where the ban on poker machines had been lifted in 1956 – Sydney clubs were able to raise greater revenue to buy players from interstate.

By 1979 there was an acknowledgement that the Sydney competition was cannibalising the game. The chairman of the Australian Rugby League, Kevin Humphreys, even announced a legal fund to help clubs outside Sydney resist the poaching of their players. It was, as many people recognised, a bandaid for a much bigger problem. The eligibility rules for the interstate series had been designed at a time when the best players mostly lived in and played for the state in which they were born, a criterion that no longer made sense for the 1980s.

In this context, the 'State of Origin' concept appealed to Queenslanders' keen sense of parochialism and injustice. Not only had southerners squirrelled away Queensland's wealth – now they were stealing Queensland's best footballers as well!

During the Bjelke-Petersen era a cloak of conservatism was thrown over Queensland society, and within this climate rugby league fit snugly into the lives of factory workers and police officers, cane-cutters and cattle farmers, coalminers and railway gangmen, boilermakers and builder's labourers, motor mechanics and meat-workers.

Barefoot children would play pick-up games in the schoolyard and on scorching hot streets. Tom Cranitch, a ten-year-old second-rower from Brisbane, had a typical Queensland upbringing: school during the day, home for afternoon tea, the creek or a mate's place until dark, then dinnertime. Weekends were dedicated to football and school holidays to the beach. Sunday mass was always observed. When his father died suddenly from a heart attack on Easter Monday 1978, his mother called the local priest before she called the ambulance. That was the first of his losses.

Every year for his birthday, one of Cranitch's older brothers would buy him a new leather rugby league ball with the Steeden logo printed on the side. Backyard games would tide them over until the weekend, which would be spent watching their club, Brothers, play in the Brisbane Rugby League competition.

'Brothers was the family team, the Catholic team,' remembered Cranitch. 'I didn't grow up thinking rugby league was a pure sport. We were like a sectarian team. I came from a very working-class family and rugby league, to me, was tough. It was spartan, it was grit, it was like dirt. It was betting rings in the outer, it was a pisser at Lang Park which was a disgrace by half-time. You could get up and shout out from the outer or from the grandstand. I grew up with that. In many ways, it helped form me as a person.'

Rugby league in Queensland was first and foremost the expression of local identities. In Brisbane there were eight first-grade clubs: Wests, Easts, Norths, and Souths; Redcliffe, Brothers, Fortitude Valley, and Wynnum-Manly.

Up north, the Foley Shield brought together representative teams from Mount Isa to Mackay in fierce competition. Many North

Queensland men built their reputations, both as a footballer and as a local identity, through this town-versus-town tournament. The Foley Shield, remarked one reporter, 'is to North Queensland what the Opera House is to Sydney'.[19]

Because of Queensland's decentralisation, and the sheer enormity of the distances between the towns, in smaller places such as Gympie or Toowoomba just four clubs would play one another repeatedly. The clubs had names that indicated a locality, such as Souths, Norths, Easts, Centrals, and Wests; or an occupation, such as Railways, or Black Stars. There were Dolphins and Sharks, Wallaroos and Kangaroos, Wattles and Waratahs, University and Collegians, All Blacks and All Whites, Swifts, Devils, Diehards, Panthers, Magpies, Rainbows, Wanderers, and Natives.

And there were Brothers clubs in towns right across the state: from Toowoomba to Townsville, Innisfail to Ipswich, Mount Isa to Maryborough. Brothers players wore the blue-and-white butcher-striped jersey and were nicknamed 'the Leprechauns', or 'the Fighting Irish'. The Brothers club in Brisbane, which by 1979 had a large social club and a home ground overlooking the Kedron Brook, was the mothership of the confraternity.

'There was never any doubt that I was going to join Brothers,' recalled league writer Steve Ricketts, who played junior football for a Brothers club in Northern New South Wales before moving to Brisbane. 'To me, I was part of the Brothers fraternity. The average bloke at a rural Brothers club wanted to come to Brisbane. This was the club that everyone wanted to gravitate to.'

One of the many players produced through the Brothers system was Wayne Bennett. A taciturn police officer, Bennett had played for a Brothers club in Toowoomba – known then as All Whites – before moving east to play for Brothers in Brisbane.

After retiring as a player, Bennett turned to coaching. In 1979, he guided Southern Suburbs to the BRL grand final against Fortitude

Valley. He sat high on the television scaffolding overlooking Lang Park, long legs dangling over the side, deep in thought as Valleys took an early lead. By half-time, the score was 9–0. Three second-half tries and two field goals made it 26–0 to Valleys at full-time.

As Valleys supporters spilled onto the field to celebrate, players from both sides struggled through the crush of people to the dressing rooms. Among these battle-weary men stood three young footballers who were, without doubt, among the most exciting prospects to ever emerge from Queensland.

The youngest was Malcolm 'Mal' Meninga, the Bundaberg-born son of a black father and a white mother, who patrolled the centres for Souths and the streets for the Brisbane City police force. The eldest was Chris 'Choppy' Close, the barrel-chested son of a Rockhampton police sergeant, who had played football in Hervey Bay, Beaudesert, the Gold Coast, and Cunnamulla before joining Valleys in Brisbane. And the most talented was Wally Lewis, a precocious lock forward who had been groomed for sporting success by a father who had coached first-grade football and a mother who excelled at netball. In the post-grand final analysis Lewis was singled out by one reporter as 'the most natural young footballer seen on Lang Park in ages'.[20]

Of these three players, the rise of Chris Close was the most startling. In Game I of the 1979 interstate series, just weeks before he made his Queensland debut, he had crawled through a hole in the fence at Lang Park to watch the game with a group of friends. After the final whistle, they had snuck into the bar to drink with the men Close would soon call his teammates.

'The heroes weren't on TV,' he said. 'They were in the community that we lived with, and they were touchable and tangible and you knew their children and you knew their families and you knew where they worked. That's what rugby league meant to me. It wasn't about being tough, it wasn't about being a hero, it was about being part of a family. Getting to know people.'

Yet by 1979 it seemed certain that Close, Meninga, and Lewis would accept offers to sign with the circling Sydney clubs. Western Suburbs were eager to bring Close down south, Meninga had been subject to transfer rumours all season, while Lewis was being tracked by three clubs – Eastern Suburbs, Manly-Warringah, and Penrith. 'Sydney's annual pillage of cash-strapped Brisbane clubs,' remembered journalist Steve Haddan, 'had become terminal.'[21]

Desperate to maintain a sense of order, the QRL invested tens of thousands of dollars to retain their young stars. Meninga stayed with Souths, Lewis remained with Valleys, and Close moved north to sign with the Redcliffe Dolphins. He married the woman he had fallen in love with in Cunnamulla, bought a house in Redcliffe, and turned his attention to the season ahead.

Although Close had heard of rumours to changes in the selection criteria for the upcoming interstate series, nobody could have foretold the enormous impact these small alterations would have on the course of his, Lewis's, and Meninga's lives, and on the future of Australian rugby league.

★

The 1980 interstate series began in predictable fashion, with New South Wales defeating Queensland in Brisbane. Mal Meninga raised the hopes of the Lang Park crowd when he crossed over for the first try after nine minutes, but an avalanche of second-half tries made it 35 points to three to the Blues at full-time.

The scoreboard might have looked better for Queensland in Game II, but the loss was harder to take as Queenslanders watched John Lang, a 19-game veteran for the Maroons, steer New South Wales to an eight-point victory. Lang, who had come out of retirement that season and moved to Sydney, superbly directed play from dummy half and repeatedly sliced through Queensland's defensive line. 'Johnny Lang, take a bow!' enthused commentator

Frank Hyde. 'You ran like a startled rabbit, you passed with the skill of a slick five-eighth [...] and you tackled with the diligence of a Canadian Mountie.'[22]

Yet the crowd at Leichhardt Oval told a far bleaker story. Fewer than 2000 supporters were witness to New South Wales's 21st series win in as many years. Even if the interstate series was not yet officially dead, it was certainly no longer worth watching. According to one reporter the match was 'as miserable as the conditions', and 'anyone who paid money to get into the ground after half-time should apply for a refund'.[23]

'State of Origin' had been percolating in the minds of Queenslanders for decades. As early as 1964, in the midst of a dark decade of losses for Queensland, journalist Jack Reardon had called for players to be selected on the basis of their state of origin, rather than their state of residence. The suggestion, according to one historian, was 'laughed out' by league officials.[24]

Yet by the late 1970s there was a ready-made example of how a State of Origin contest might work. In Australian Rules football, an underdog Western Australia side repatriated several of their Victorian-based players and defeated Victoria at Subiaco Oval in Perth.

One of the men involved in the Australian Rules State of Origin match was Barry Maranta, a Brisbane businessman and a former Brothers player. As a Queenslander, Maranta had felt the concept would apply equally as well in rugby league. After all, the rivalry and the power imbalance between Western Australia and Victoria was similar to that between Queensland and New South Wales.

Senator Ron McAuliffe was less enamoured with the idea. According to Maranta, McAuliffe expressed doubt that Sydney-based Queenslanders would compete seriously against their club teammates. 'I knew that wasn't the case for the Western Australia–Victoria game,' recalled Maranta, 'but I couldn't convince him. He said, "It'll never work."'

What's more, McAuliffe wanted Queensland to level with New South Wales not just in the interstate series but also in the flagship competitions in Brisbane and Sydney. Granting expatriate Queenslanders a Maroon jersey, he felt, would only serve as a green light for others to move south, which in turn would hasten the decline of the Brisbane competition.

Yet the senator gradually came around. In 1979, Hugh Lunn, a journalist and rugby league fan, had sat beside McAuliffe during a flight to Canberra. When McAuliffe expressed his reluctance to hand over a Maroon jersey to an 'ex-Queenslander', Lunn responded: 'There's no such thing as an ex-Queenslander, Ron. They're like Catholics. There's only ever lapsed Queenslanders.'[25]

On Wednesday 28 May 1980, McAuliffe emerged from a meeting of the ARL with historic news. Instead of a third interstate match, a State of Origin exhibition game would be held in Brisbane. 'It's a promoter's dream,' he told reporters. 'There is tremendous interest in the match.'[26]

Many in New South Wales sneered at the new format. In a poll of 100 first-grade players, conducted by Sydney's *Daily Mirror* newspaper, 54 per cent voted against the introduction of State of Origin.[27] Bob Fulton, a former New South Wales captain, called it a 'lollipop match' and predicted that it would be 'the non event of the century'.[28] Sports broadcaster Ron Casey wrote: 'To the Queensland hillbillies in Premier Joh's Bananaland, the State of Origin match might be a big deal, but to those in the land of the living, here in Sydney, it's just another match without much meaning.'[29]

Such was the strength of the Sydney competition that Fulton, Casey, and many others in the Sydney establishment were blind to the ill health of rugby league beyond the city limits. The BRL had effectively been turned into a feeder competition for the Sydney clubs, while the interstate series was little more than a selection trial for the Australian side. For Queenslanders, though, State of Origin represented the last hope to restore state pride. 'Virtually without exception, the expatriate Queenslanders are eagerly awaiting the opportunity to represent their home State and Sydney club loyalties count for nothing,' observed John McCoy, a radio commentator for 4BC.[30]

The keenest of these expatriate Queenslanders was Arthur Beetson, who at 35 years of age had achieved almost every career milestone possible. He had yet to lose an interstate series while playing for New South Wales and on several occasions had skippered the team to victory. But he had not yet pulled on the Maroon jumper of his home state. 'Of the few ambitions I have left in football, playing for Queensland is on top of the list,' Beetson told *Rugby League Week*. 'If chosen it would be one of the biggest thrills of my career. I would consider it a great honour.'[31]

Under the supervision of the QRL director of coaching, John McDonald, seven Sydney-based Queenslanders were selected: winger Kerry Boustead, halves Greg Oliphant and Alan Smith, hooker John Lang, and forwards Rod Reddy, Rod Morris, and Beetson. They were complemented by six resident Queenslanders: fullback Colin Scott, winger Brad Backer, centres Chris Close and Mal Meninga, lock forward Wally Lewis, and second-rower Rohan Hancock.

Although they mostly played club football in Sydney or in Brisbane, the members of the first Origin side originally hailed from towns and cities across the state: Ipswich, Killarney, Toowoomba, Roma, Innisfail, Townsville, Rockhampton, Bundaberg, and Brisbane. This was, in the truest sense of the word, a representative team.

The captain of this new-look Queensland side was Arthur Beetson. Before the game, he told Lewis, Close, and Meninga that although he'd never seen them play, he believed in their ability. 'The impact that Arthur had on me in those few days was enormous,' recalled

Meninga. 'I always say, to the day I die, that the environment created a catalyst for self-belief as youngsters. I'd played interstate prior, and there was never that belief. But those days, and playing in that game, we grew an arm and a leg and were ten-foot tall.'

In front of a heaving crowd of more than 30,000 people at Lang Park, Beetson ignored the pain of a broken thumb and led Queensland to a famous ten-point victory. He seemed to be involved in everything: tackling ferociously, trading blows with the New South Wales forwards, niggling in the ruck, playing a part in the build-up of both tries, and even trying a grubber kick from inside his own half. He also stiff-armed his Parramatta teammate, Mick Cronin.

'In those days if you stood in tackles someone came in over the top, and that's all he did. It might have happened twice in the game actually,' Cronin recalled years later. 'But we didn't think too much about it [...] We actually sat together the following day coming home on the plane.'[32]

Although Boustead and Close scored one try each and Meninga celebrated his 20th birthday by toe-punting seven out of seven conversions, violence was the currency in rugby league, so Beetson's willingness to roughhouse a club teammate meant that his performance would be memorialised above all the others.

As the story of his stiff-arm on Cronin got better and more extravagant in the telling, it became a kind of creation myth for the Queensland rugby league fraternity, and for the revamped interstate series. 'Watching that first game from Bundaberg, watching them run out with Arthur in the Queensland jersey, it was like the image of a sperm impregnating an egg,' recalled Dr Chris Sarra, a future commissioner of the ARL. 'When Arthur punched Mick Cronin, that was the conception of State of Origin. Something happened in that moment, and the universe was forever changed because of it.'

State of Origin would soon become the pinnacle of the rugby

league calendar, the biggest payday for the players, and one of the most-watched television programs in the country.[33]

In the decades to come, the great dilemma of Australian rugby league would be to maintain the tribalism of the sport while also expanding and restructuring the game for the commercial demands of the modern era. State of Origin was the perfect combination of these two forces. It was a commercial juggernaut with soul.

While for New South Welshmen the interstate series would remain a secondary concern to the Sydney club competition, for Queenslanders it was an opportunity for their best players to be recognised, a bulwark against the decline of their own regional rugby league competitions, and a proxy for all the state's hopes and dreams.

Because despite Queensland's booming population, there remained a feeling that to truly succeed in politics, in business, in the arts, or in sport, talented Queenslanders needed to move south to Sydney or to Melbourne. Love and loss and homesickness would become a consistent theme in the work of writers and artists from Queensland. 'I don't think my love affair with Queensland ripened into its mature madness until I came south to live,' wrote the novelist Thea Astley in 1976.[34]

In this context, the experience of welcoming home expatriate Queenslanders only increased Origin's representative appeal. Beetson soon announced that he would return to Redcliffe as a player-coach, and as the new licensee of the Moreton Bay Hotel.[35] Big Artie was finally home.

His performance in the inaugural Origin match would leave a lasting legacy for generations of Queenslanders. In attendance at Lang Park that evening was Kevin Walters, a 13-year-old schoolboy footballer from Ipswich, who would one day represent Queensland as both a player and a coach. 'I just remember the drive down, all the cars on the road from Ipswich,' Walters once said. 'We'd been down to Lang Park a bit, but you could feel this was different. There was people everywhere – it was something I'd never experienced. Dad, in his wisdom, found a hole in the fence and we just ran through like rabbits. It was an amazing night, particularly when Arthur ran out. That feeling will stay with me forever. That was when I thought, *I wouldn't mind doing that one day myself.*'

Also in attendance that night was Tom Cranitch, an 11-year-old budding rugby league fan. Still grieving the loss of his father, he had already developed an awareness that several things, in his family at least, had tribal significance. The first was the Catholic Church. Next was the Australian Labor Party. And then there was the Brothers rugby league club.

Tribalism was not a private matter for the workingmen he admired; it was expressed through commitment to institutions. A man went to his local church to be closer to God. A man joined his union and the Labor Party to fight for his class. And a man went to watch his sporting team through good times and bad. All of the institutions to which Crantich belonged – the institutions he was supposed to inherit – would soon become warped by corruption, self-interest, and mismanagement.

But in State of Origin, rugby league's newest phenomenon, Cranitch could invest in something that felt as if it had the gravity and ritual of a great institution. And most of its significance would be shaped by his fellow Queenslanders. 'I'm interested in Origin because I still remember the defeats we suffered in the 1970s,' Cranitch later explained. 'It's a historical thing. It genuinely comes out of history both from a football perspective, but also from a socio-economic perspective.

'Carved out of New South Wales, at the arse-end of the world for a long time, decentralised, having to cope on your own, being ignored when we should have been given prominence at various stages, not being considered as having any smarts about us – it's deeply rooted in all of that. Whether you're in the arts, whether you're in the football code itself, or whether you're an everyday Queenslander, it's being treated like a bunch of hicks and yokels and that feeling of second-class-ness. That's where it comes from.'

2

OUT OF THE HICKSVILLE DAYS

1981–1982

In the weeks that followed the first State of Origin match, Mal Meninga, Chris Close, and Wally Lewis returned with mixed fortunes to the Brisbane Rugby League competition.

Meninga, who had already scored more than 200 points for the season for Souths, was being aggressively pursued by five Sydney clubs. Close ruptured ligaments in his foot and was forced to hobble around on the sidelines, left leg in a plaster cast, as his Redcliffe teammates continued on without him. And Lewis had a hand in five tries as Valleys beat Wynnum-Manly to secure the minor premiership for 1980.

'Because of their youth, they just captured the imagination of the public,' remembered league writer Steve Ricketts. 'Wally with his arrogance, Mal with his potential to be a brutal weapon, and "Choppy" was the big bush kid who wasn't supposed to be able to step like he did with his big thighs. They were just so marketable. And people sensed, you know, that maybe Queensland could be a force for years to come.'

Lewis was fast approaching his 21st birthday and was a marked man; not yet 'King Wally' but already the handsome young prince of

Brisbane football. A lock forward who had previously played in the centres during schoolboys rugby union, he moved with the cocksure, straight-backed posture of a rooster, strutting across the field with his head in the air, blond locks flying, searching for the slightest gap in the opposition's defensive line.

Even without the ball Lewis was a constant presence. As opposing players rose to play the ball after a tackle, he would brazenly thrust his right foot among the tangle of legs and arms in an attempt to win back possession. He had learned this cunning, niggly brand of football from the Valleys captain-coach, Ross Strudwick, a moustachioed halfback who tested the patience of many and was nicknamed 'the Rat'.

The hard men of the Brisbane competition reacted to Lewis's prodigious talent in the only way they knew how – by flattening him.

'The violence was horrific – blokes getting their faces splattered, spear tackles,' recalled sportswriter Phil Lutton. 'Sometimes the games would remind me of watching ice hockey: when the whistle blows and the teams don't even bother playing, they just go out and fight.'

So vigorous was Lewis's treatment that at the beginning of the finals series, the *Courier-Mail* featured a front-page story with a detailed photograph of his numerous injuries: head cuts, concussions, a smashed jaw, and a nose that had been broken five times.[1]

However many opposition supporters, as well as several pre-eminent personalities in the Brisbane rugby league scene, accused him of milking the attention for his own advantage. In the hyper-masculine world of Queensland football, where respect was earned through bravery and toughness, there was no greater accusation.

Yet it was already clear that Lewis was a different breed of footballer, and that he had an outsized role in the outcome of Valleys' matches. In the major semifinal against Souths, Lewis trudged off the field with an injury after just 30 minutes with scores locked at 7–7.

Souths took full advantage and ran in three more tries to win 22 points to 14.

With Souths destined for the grand final, Valleys faced Norths in the preliminary final. Lewis was at his mercurial best, crossing over for Valleys' first try. At half-time Valleys led by four points.

Early on in the second half, Lewis chip-kicked over the defence, regathered the ball on the halfway line, pirouetted around two would-be tacklers, and dribbled a neat kick towards the try-line. He would have completed the solo effort had it not been for his flying winger, Doug Muir, who beat him in the footrace to put Valleys six points ahead. 'It was as brilliant a piece of football as has been seen on Lang Park,' enthused one reporter, 'and once again stamped Lewis as a match winner in any company.'[2]

Nine minutes later, Norths attacked down the left side and Lewis committed to a try-saving tackle on giant forward Mark Graham. The two men fell to the ground but only Graham rose to his feet. As the ball and the attention of the players swept back to centre field, Lewis remained on the turf clutching his throat. Graham, whose stray elbow had caused the damage, immediately alerted the touch judge. 'Mark was the first to ask if I was okay,' Lewis later recalled. 'I just shook my head. I couldn't get anything in.'

Valleys trainer Brian Canavan turned Lewis over on his back while Dr Tom Dooley raced across the field, black tie flapping over the shoulder of his cream suit jacket. It was clear now that this was not a Lewis boy-who-cried-wolf special. Graham's elbow had in fact caused a laryngeal spasm, which was blocking his airway.

'When I got to him,' recalled Canavan, 'he was quite anxious; he couldn't breathe. I thought, *Well, what is this?* I'd never seen this before and didn't quite know how to treat it. And just at that time, he actually relaxed, and Dr Tom Dooley arrived on the scene.'

Dooley, who was also the Valleys club president, had been at Lewis's side all season, straightening his broken noses and challenging opposing teams they felt had crossed the line from fair to foul. Now, as Dooley knelt down beside Canavan, Lewis grabbed him by the collar and spectacularly drew Dooley into giving him mouth-to-mouth. The shocking images were front-page news in both Brisbane and Sydney the next day.

Within minutes of Lewis leaving the field, Norths scored a converted try to win the match by a single point. It was a famous comeback, and a week later Norths would overcome Souths in the grand final.

Yet the heroes of the season were Brian Canavan and Dr Tom Dooley, who attended to the prodigal son of rugby league in one of the most desperate, terrible scenes ever witnessed at Lang Park. What they could not have known, however, is that by resuscitating Lewis, they were in fact breathing life into Queensland's future hopes for State of Origin.

By the beginning of the 1981 season, Wally Lewis had fully recovered and was being touted as a future Australian international. In May, after Lewis was selected for Queensland City in a trial match against Queensland Country, City coach Arthur Beetson made the fateful decision to move him from lock forward to five-eighth. The logic was that Lewis would have a better chance of being selected for the Kangaroos if he played at pivot rather than trying to dislodge the incumbent Australian lock, Ray Price. Lewis, declared Beetson, 'has every chance of being Australia's Test five-eighth this year if he puts his mind to it'.[3]

The positional change would set in motion a golden decade for Lewis, who immediately settled into the No. 6 jumper and guided City to a crushing win over Country.

The gulf in quality between Brisbane and the bush could not have been starker. Yet the irony was that many players in the 'City' squad – including Bundaberg-born Mal Meninga and

Rockhampton-born Chris Close – came from the country. Indeed, the BRL was to the rest of Queensland as Sydney was to Brisbane: sucking talented players away from their hometowns and into a big-city competition.

Senator Ron McAuliffe was well aware of the problem. On the weekend of the City–Country trial match, the Queensland Rugby League announced that a new State League competition would begin in 1982, in which the eight Brisbane clubs would compete in a seven-week tournament against six regional teams from the Gold Coast, Ipswich, Toowoomba, Wide Bay, Central Queensland, and North Queensland.

The competition, which was designed primarily to benefit the country areas, immediately received support from the city. Former state hooker John Lang said it was 'the best news I have heard all year', while 4BC commentator John McCoy wrote that he hoped the new league 'will allow country players to remain in their home centres, but still play in top company'.[4]

Of more pressing concern for most Queenslanders, however, was the looming interstate series. Although State of Origin had proved immensely popular in 1980, it was agreed that the new selection policies would be employed only for the third and final game. And so three Sydney-based Queenslanders – Kerry Boustead, Paul McCabe, and John Ribot – started for New South Wales in Game I, and the Maroons lost by eight points. Ribot, a Brisbane boy, scored both tries for New South Wales. 'This might sound silly,' Ribot remembered, 'but scoring tries *against* Queensland probably showed guys that I'm a Queenslander.'

After the Blues won Game II in Sydney, just one resident Queenslander – Wally Lewis – was considered good enough to be selected for the Australian side. He made his international debut in Sydney, helping the Kangaroos to a 40-point win over France. And yet, in what would be a sign of things to come, in Queensland there was more interest in the third and final interstate game, which was to be held under the new State of Origin selection rules. Tickets sold faster to the Origin game than to the Kangaroos Test match against France scheduled ten days later at Lang Park.

Beetson, the newly appointed Queensland coach, opted not to play and Lewis was anointed as his successor.

In an intense opening ten minutes, in which two players were sin-binned and several brawls broke out across the field, Meninga missed a penalty kick from right in front, and New South Wales winger Eric Grothe ran in a spectacular long-range try. Three more tries to the Blues, another missed penalty kick from Meninga, and a try to Queensland winger Brad Backer made it 15–5 to New South Wales at half-time.

It was Lewis who changed the match. Patrolling centre field, he received the ball 15 metres out, stepped left to find a gap in the defence, and then darted back to the right to exploit the space. From there nobody could stop him, and Meninga's resulting conversion closed the margin to five points.

Not long after the restart, Lewis put Colin Scott through a hole in the New South Wales defensive line. Scott dashed 50 metres, evaded four players, and would have scored were it not for an incredible try-saving tackle from Eric Grothe. As Scott tried to get to his feet, Grothe held onto his legs to slow down the play-the-ball. Chris Close was the first to arrive in support. One eye on the try-line, his new white boots gleaming in the floodlit evening, Close belted Grothe across the face, collected Scott's play-the-ball and dived over for the most important try of his career. As he was mobbed by his teammates Grothe stayed on the ground, clutching his face from Close's backhander.

For months Close would deal with accusations of foul play, mostly from the Sydney press. But among his own teammates and his fellow Queenslanders he was a hero. After Meninga converted a penalty try to make it 22 points to 15, completing an unbelievable comeback, Close was awarded man of the match – the second time he'd earned the title for the first two Origin games.

Close, who had grown up watching Queensland lose every year, was acutely aware that it was up to his generation – the first State of Origin generation – to set a new path for the 1980s. 'There was a lot of aftermath,' recalled Close. 'I was called a coward and gutless and a grub and everything else, but I don't apologise for one minute for what I did. I mean, what I did changed the history of our game. We won the second State of Origin game based on my decision to take control. At 22, not many young men would be willing to do that. But it meant everything to me – that moment meant everything. It was payback.'

★

By 1981 the state of Queensland, according to the *Courier-Mail*, had 'reached a decisive stage in its growth'.[5] Fuelled by a generous resources boom and a thriving tourism sector, thousands of interstate migrants continued to flock north across the border. Brisbane was preparing to host its first Commonwealth Games, and the Bjelke-Petersen government began officially promoting 'Queensland Day', to celebrate Queensland's separation from the colony of New South Wales on 6 June 1859. Across the state there were rodeos, art exhibitions, sportsman's breakfasts, and school functions. At the opening concert at Brisbane's Botanic Gardens, a singer belted out a new state anthem he had written for the occasion. The back-to-back victories in State of Origin, then, were one part of the beginning of Queensland's 1980s renaissance.

'What I vividly recall is going home that night after the first State of Origin game and thinking, *That is the greatest game of footy I've ever seen*,' remembered David Wright, a former Queensland representative who was working as a commentator at the time. 'And then the second game, which was a year later, Queensland were down 15–0 at one stage. We were down three converted tries and we came back and won it. And I remember going home thinking, *THAT'S the greatest game I've ever seen.* That's how it all started, with this huge emotional feeling for the Queenslanders.'

State of Origin was just one of several reforms that would benefit rugby league in Queensland. In 1980, after a special report into the administration of the game, the QRL had become an incorporated body with a general manager, a marketing manager, media liaisons, a streamlined committee, and a board of directors. 'The game,' announced Senator McAuliffe, 'will be run like any business.'[6]

Attracting the corporate world was an essential part of this business model. The revolutionary new state competition was christened the Winfield State League after the cigarette company provided $350,000 in sponsorship. Several of the teams featured Colonel Sanders' head on their jerseys after Kentucky Fried Chicken became a major sponsor, while other backers included breweries; car and sportswear manufacturers; and oil, mining, and pharmaceutical companies.[7]

Not only did the Winfield State League broaden the game's commercial appeal, it also helped to unify the entire state for the first time in weekly competition, complementing the dizzying, fleeting moments of unification in State of Origin.

In New South Wales, too, there was a realisation that the game needed to expand. In 1982, the Canberra Raiders and the Illawarra Steelers were admitted into the Sydney competition. But while Illawarra and Canberra were only a short drive from the city, where the majority of games would be held, in Queensland's Winfield State League the Brisbane teams would be expected to play most of the games away from home, in regional areas.

The buzzword in Sydney at the time was 'decentralisation', but it was in Queensland where that promise was turned into reality.

In the first season of the Winfield State League, matches were scheduled for 21 towns and cities, including far-flung places like Mount Isa, Ingham, Emerald, and Biloela, before a finals series played over two weekends at Lang Park in Brisbane.

Despite the huge distances the Brisbane-based players would have to travel, the coach of Easts Tigers, John Lang, noticed an eagerness to get out to the country areas. 'I have not seen players as keen to start a competition as my blokes have been to get into the State League,' he wrote in his column for the *Courier-Mail*.[8]

The new competition, remembered Wally Lewis, 'was a very important PR machine for rugby league in Queensland. It was spreading the gospel.'

Yet Lewis was set to miss the entire State League season after being served a lengthy suspension for eye-gouging. In both Sydney and Brisbane, the officialdom was desperate to clean up the image of the sport. The brutality that had for so long characterised rugby league was to be legislated out of the game through severe punishments for any man found guilty of violent play.

Many commentators found these new activist judiciaries confronting. One reporter called Lewis's suspension 'a tragedy'.[9] Another said that fans had been 'robbed'.[10]

By the time Lewis had his suspension reduced to three weeks after an appeal, he was fit and ready to travel to Mount Isa for Valleys' blockbuster Round 6 clash against North Queensland.

Mount Isa in 1982 was unlike anywhere else in Australia. The most remote inland city in the country – 900 kilometres west of Townsville, 1800 kilometres northwest of Brisbane – 'the Isa' was also one of the most multicultural. Everyone, it seemed, had come from somewhere else. People from more than 50 different nationalities lived in the sprawling desert city, attracted by the lucrative lead, silver, copper, and zinc mines.

For many, the isolation was almost unbearable. Describing a town 'dominated by the smelter chimney and its ever-belching smoke', in her book *The Copper Crucible*, novelist Betty Collins wrote that in Mount Isa there seemed to be no life, 'only mile upon stretching mile of red-brown rock, corrugated into waves and troughs like some long petrified sea'.[11]

It was not unusual to see cowboys wandering around town, or drinking at Boyd's Hotel on the corner of West Street and Rodeo Drive. 'Sport is the big thing,' observed one reporter who travelled to Mount Isa in 1980, 'and they are fiercely proud of their rugby league team.'[12]

Like many regional areas of Queensland, the health of the rugby league was dependent on the prosperity of the local industry. Most of the footballers were given good jobs in the mines, and the rugby league field, Julius Kruttschnitt Oval, was named after an American executive who had presided over the Mount Isa Mines for more than two decades.

On 26 April 1982, football fans converged upon Kruttschnitt Oval from all parts of the northwest. Also in attendance was the *Courier-Mail* reporter Lawrie Kavanagh and 4BC commentator John McCoy, who called the game from the roof of the grandstand. As temperatures soared into the high 30s, the crowd of 3000 people marinated in alcohol. A makeshift beer stall was set up in the shade of a poinciana tree, and by the end of the day it had reportedly made $4000 in sales. The driver of the cherry-picker responsible for hoisting McCoy up and down from the roof of the grandstand was soon drunk.

It was a carnival atmosphere, and North Queensland quickly led Valleys by five points. Then, as the North Queenslanders received the ball from the restart, a brawl broke out. Yet referee Barry Gomersall allowed the game to continue. 'I loved the way he handled any fights that broke out on the field,' Arthur Beetson once said. 'He'd just let 'em go until the blokes punched each other out, or looked around sheepishly and decided they'd better get on with the game.'[13]

The North Queenslanders, already accustomed to Gomersall's idiosyncratic refereeing, were the quickest to react. 'I got the ball from the scrum,' remembered halfback Paul Laffin, 'and the ball made its way out to the backs. Eddie Muller picked it up and ran 90 yards to score under the posts. That's what got us home.'

By full-time the score was North Queensland 16, Valleys 14. Wally Lewis was kept relatively quiet in what was an incredibly rough affair. However, despite the loss and Gomersall's controversial refereeing, Valleys players stayed in town afterwards to drink with the locals and sign autographs for their children. In his match report for *Rugby League Week*, McCoy described the occasion as 'an exercise in Rugby League diplomacy' and 'the day the West was won'.[14]

Barry Gomersall was a gaunt, bug-eyed North Queenslander with dark hair, a long nose that arched over a sharp moustache, and a gold chain that hung neatly between the collar of his referees jersey. His bandy legs stuck out from skin-tight shorts that made him appear impossibly thin, especially when measured against the man-mountains who surrounded him on the rugby league field. An employee for the Queensland Railways, Gomersall had presided over matches in relative anonymity until the advent of the Winfield State League. He was, in many respects, the first genuine product of the new competition. 'It was very difficult for country referees to get a top appointment before the State League,' he later explained.[15]

By the beginning of May each of the country teams had been eliminated, and Easts Tigers defeated Redcliffe in the all-Brisbane grand final at Lang Park. It was a just reward for the Easts coach, John Lang, who had publicly backed the State League concept from the very beginning.

Attention soon turned to the upcoming State of Origin series. Many people in the Brisbane competition, including Lang, were concerned with the make-up of Queensland's squad. With the Origin selection rules now expanded to cover all three interstate matches, seven Sydney-based Queenslanders were picked for Game I.

In the previous Origin fixtures in 1980 and 1981, this was welcomed due to the fact that two games were also held under the residential rules, ensuring that players who remained in Queensland would always have the opportunity to represent their state. Now, it seemed that a Queenslander would need to move to Sydney in order to be selected for the Maroons. Wally Lewis, who worked during the day at his family-owned delicatessen in Cannon Hill, expressed his displeasure in an interview with *Rugby League Week*. 'I believe Queensland would have a really great chance of beating New South Wales this season on our own merit, without bringing back the ex-patriots,' he said.[16]

After losing to a revved-up New South Wales side in Game I, the Queensland selectors picked Brad Backer, Rod Morris, and Norm Carr – each based in Brisbane – to replace Sydney-based Kerry Boustead, Bruce Walker, and Paul Vautin.

Meanwhile, Senator McAuliffe had arrived upon a dubious solution to prevent players moving south. Before Game I, he forced Colin Scott, Mark Murray, and Gene Miles to sign a 'loyalty contract' that bound them to stay in Queensland for the season following their selection for Origin. When Backer, Carr, and Morris joined the squad for Game II, McAuliffe made them do the same.

Yet the most talked-about selection was not a player but a referee – Barry Gomersall. In front of a parochial Lang Park crowd, Queensland ran in three tries to defeat New South Wales 11 points to seven, forcing the series to a decider. Queensland also won the penalty count by a fair margin, prompting one Sydney reporter to label Gomersall's refereeing 'a dreadful exhibition'.[17]

This was the first time New South Wales had been introduced to the referee they called 'the Grasshopper', but it would not be the last. For the next six years, Gomersall would frustrate and confound players, officials, journalists and supporters from down south. He formed one part of what was now an intense, all-encompassing interstate rivalry. In its first year as a three-game series, State of Origin was stalemated at one game all, 27–27 on aggregate, with the showdown to be held for the first time at the Sydney Cricket Ground.

As the excitement grew in the lead-up to Game III, tit-for-tat arguments broke out between the two states over almost everything. Sydney reporters criticised the decision to award Mal Meninga man of the match in Game II, while Ian Walsh, a former New South Wales captain and columnist for the *Daily Mirror*, accused Meninga of feigning injury. Senator McAuliffe demanded that Arthur Beetson be appointed coach of Australia if Queensland won the decider. Wally Lewis threw down the challenge to the Blues incoming five-eighth, Brett Kenny. And a neutral referee from New Zealand had to be flown in.

Queensland won the first penalty after Rohan Hancock clashed with New South Wales front-rower Royce Ayliffe. Not long after, Queensland won another penalty from which Lewis and Mark Murray laid on a try for Hancock, who grinned wildly through a mouthful of blood.

New South Wales appeared totally disjointed while Lewis was clearly in a mischievous mood. When Ray Price busted through a gap in Queensland's defence and seemed headed for the try-line, Lewis knocked him to the ground with a big front-on tackle. As Price rose to his feet, Lewis raked the ball back to regain possession, and from the next play cleared a long kick downfield to relieve the pressure. 'To me,' recalled Lewis's biographer, Adrian McGregor, 'this match was memorable because, for the first time, Wally clearly dominated play with his passing, hurling those long, space invader torpedoes which abruptly changed the whole direction of Queensland's attack and sent NSW into a scurried panic of defence.'[18]

Just before half-time, however, the Blues swept from left to right and their rookie winger, Phil Duke, crossed over in the corner. Duke, a 23-year-old from Moree, was a shock selection for New South Wales – 'one of the most stunning decisions made in more than a decade', according to one reporter.[19] An Aboriginal man who played Group 4 football for the Moree Boomerangs, he was an outsider in more ways than one. The only country footballer in the Blues squad, when he arrived at Sydney Airport nobody was there to greet him.

In the second half, with just two points separating the sides, Lewis collected the ball on halfway and kicked long into the Blues in-goal area. The awful scene that followed seemed to unfold in a wild blur: New South Wales fullback Phil Sigsworth retrieved the kick, was met by an onrushing tackler, and threw a pass in the direction of Duke, who dropped it cold. Lewis, who had now arrived on the scene, dived on the loose ball to score.

And in that brief moment of madness, during the highly charged environment of the first-ever State of Origin decider, the divergent fates of Duke and Lewis were sealed. After the match finished 10–5 to Queensland, Duke returned to Moree and never again played representative football. Lewis, meanwhile, was named man of the match and led a contingent of 11 Queenslanders to be selected in the Australian side.

*

On the eve of the 1982 BRL grand final, the *Courier-Mail* reporter Barry Dick wrote that the eventful year would 'surely go down as the most significant on record'. Queensland had won the first three-game State of Origin series, increased its representation in the Kangaroos squad, and successfully introduced the Winfield State League. The QRL 75th anniversary dinner at the glittering Tattersalls club, concluded Dick, 'underlined the growth of the code out of the Hicksville days'.[20]

The season concluded in dramatic circumstances as Wynnum-Manly, led by the Morris brothers Des and Rod, defeated Souths to secure its first premiership in three decades. More than 10,000 people celebrated for days in scenes that Arthur Lovell, the president of the club, described as 'bedlam'.[21]

But the biggest party was still to come. Eleven days after the BRL grand final, on the last day of September, Brisbane hosted the opening ceremony of the 1982 Commonwealth Games. Queensland was already the home of the Big Mango, the Big Pineapple, and the Big Cow, and now Matilda – a 12-metre-tall mechanical kangaroo – winked at the world during her lap of honour around the QEII Stadium. Brisbane, gushed one reporter, 'is on the world map forever'.[22]

Thousands of protesters, aware of the unprecedented global attention, called the event the 'Stolen-wealth Games' and demanded justice and land rights for Indigenous people, including the removal of Queensland's Aboriginal and Torres Strait Islander Protection Act, which controlled the movement of those people living in missions as well as their marriages, their employment and their finances.

Instead protesters were met with another Act – the Commonwealth Games Act – which made street marches illegal. They marched anyway, chanting, 'Joh must go!' and 'What do we want? Land rights!'

The demands received cautious approval from the *Courier-Mail*, which called the Aboriginal and Islanders Advancement Department 'an incredibly 19th century institution' and accused the Bjelke-Petersen government of having an 'Afrikaaner-type mentality' towards the Aboriginal missions.[23]

Even conservative Indigenous leader Neville Bonner pleaded with his fellow Queenslanders to listen to the protesters. 'Can you fair-minded people honestly blame my race for wanting to demonstrate peacefully and bring to the notice of the world media the absence of civil justice in this state?' he asked a gathering of journalists on the Gold Coast.[24] Bonner also appealed unsuccessfully for the protesters to refrain from marching without a permit. Torn by his responsibilities as a politician and his obligations to his people, he ended up sobbing on the floor of Brisbane's Roma Street forum as protesters were thrown one by one into police wagons.

By the 1980s the era of the black activist athlete, which had begun in the late 1960s, was effectively finished. In Australia, the most political sportsperson was Charles Perkins, who in the 1960s had played top-level soccer in Adelaide, Sydney, and in England before embarking on a career in politics. From his office in Canberra, where he ran the Aboriginal Development Commission, Perkins called Joh Bjelke-Petersen a fascist, petitioned the Queen, and labelled Queensland a police state.

In Queensland, meanwhile, the most respected sportsperson and the coach of the wildly popular State of Origin side was Arthur Beetson – an Indigenous man. He was not unaware of the problems facing his people. His mother, Marie, had been part of the Stolen Generations and had been relocated to Cherbourg – one of the missions from which many of the protesters came. Beetson had also been close friends with Kevin Yow Yeh, a lightning-fast winger of Aboriginal and South Sea Islander stock who'd died in mysterious circumstances in a prison watch house in Mackay in 1975.

Yet Beetson had an easygoing, laid-back approach to the world and, like most Queenslanders, was loath to mix politics and sport. In his experience rugby league was a great leveller – it had taken him from the bush and turned him into an Australian hero. During the early 1970s, when Indigenous activists set up a Tent Embassy on the lawns of Parliament House, Beetson was captaining his country in rugby league.

Now, as the epicentre of the Indigenous rights struggle shifted north, Beetson did not lend his voice or his reputation to the movement. 'I remember Arthur saying to me privately, back in the early 1980s, that he didn't want to get into that stuff,' one reporter recalled. '"We're all just Australians", he said.'

Meanwhile, on the streets of Brisbane, the police dismissed the protesters as 'drunk and disorderly southern black troublemakers' and locked them up in their hundreds.[25] One of the police officers on the beat was Wayne Bennett, the coach of Souths and, in the years to come, one of the most successful coaches in State of Origin.

Among the activists locked up was a young nurse named Gracelyn Smallwood, who later became a university professor and a board member of the Townsville Hospital. A descendent of South Sea Islander, Birri Gubba and Kalkadoon peoples, Smallwood had grown up in a rugby league family. 'Lots of good black and white people got together for that demonstration,' she said. 'Artie, as far as I know, always identified, but his priority was football. Watching him play, and knowing he was an Aboriginal man, gave so much self-esteem to black Australians that had low self-esteem.

'But of course, some people would say he wasn't involved in the community until after he retired. Well, I guess it would have been the same for all Aboriginal footballers. Some identified more than others. He was a big man, but let me tell you, when you reach the higher level, it's still a white world you're in … people are very nervous about political activists.'

In the end the 1982 Commonwealth Games, like State of Origin, folded neatly into an escalating sense of pride in place. Bjelke-Petersen said that he was 'terribly impressed with the way this whole operation has been carried out', the Brisbane City Council decided to bid for the 1992 Olympic Games, and at the closing ceremony Matilda the kangaroo winked at the world one last time.

Outsiders had long noted that Queensland was a place of enormous hubris: always on the verge of greatness, forever the home of the outrageous boast. What the rolling success of 1982 provided, at least to Queenslanders if nobody else, was glorious, tangible proof of their own superiority. 'The existence of these matches,' joked the *Cane Toad Times*, 'is an excellent example of the Queensland desire to at least be seen to be winning.'[26] Above all, the introduction of State of Origin enabled rugby league to surf the crest of a great wave of parochialism, and assert itself as the pre-eminent activity through which people could express their identity as a Queenslander.

'All of a sudden we were dominant,' remembered Chris Close. 'We'd gone through decades of being hammered and then, all of a sudden – hang on – we've got a rugby league team that's just conquered what would have been considered the best team in the world. That changes your mindset if you're a rugby league follower or even just a sports follower. You're going to wake up in the morning feeling different about things. And then in 1982, we got the Commonwealth Games – Brisbane put on the greatest show in the world – and it's all happening in Queensland.'

3

THE BEACON ON THE HILL

1983–1986

Mal Meninga would always line up a conversion attempt in the same way. First, he would fashion the kicking tee from a mound of dirt. Next, he would ensure that his body was square to the goalposts. Then, chin to chest, eyes focused on the ball, he would take a few steps straight back. Finally, he would run in and swing his right leg like a pendulum, the front-on action creating the appearance of an elaborate toe-punt. It was a no-nonsense approach to goal-kicking that would, more often than not, send the ball sailing majestically over the black dot.

On the first Sunday of March 1983, early on during a grand final rematch at Wynnum-Manly's Kougari Oval, Souths were awarded a penalty and Meninga went through his usual routine. Behind the goal, several Wynnum-Manly supporters hurled insulting remarks his way.

Meninga, who had been taught to always focus on football, tried to ignore the abuse and get on with the game. Moments before the half-time break, he smashed a Wynnum-Manly player with a crushing tackle, picked up the loose ball, and completed the solo effort by scoring under the posts. His conversion gave Souths an irretrievable lead.

Not long into the second half, as supporters continued to drink in the warm afternoon sun, two men from the eastern end of the ground leapt over the perimeter fence and started hitting one another. For more than five minutes several other men swarmed the field to join in, turning the impromptu amateur boxing bout into an all-in brawl.

After the final whistle, one spectator came up to Meninga and called him a 'black fag'. Finally Mal snapped, thumping his assailant before making his way to the dressing room. 'I think it was racially motivated,' he told the *Courier-Mail*. 'I've been copping it for sometime, but it was probably the first time to my face. It happened after the game and it was a personal thing, not to do with the game. The fellow who did it obviously doesn't like me, but as far as I'm concerned, I want it forgotten. It was a personal incident and I hope it won't happen again.'[1]

It had been a turbulent few months for Meninga. He had just arrived home from a three-month tour of Great Britain and France as the top point-scorer for the Kangaroos and one of the best centres in the world. But he regretted that his father, Norm, had missed seeing him play for Australia. In late 1982, before the Kangaroos squad was selected, Norm Meninga had passed away, aged 47.

'One day I was playing for Souths at Davies Park and Greg Veivers said Dad was there, watching me through the fence,' recalled Meninga years later. 'I know he was proud of me. He never showed it, though. He never told me.'[2]

In the 1960s Norm was a brilliant bush footballer who had captained teams with names such as Thangool Possums and Monto Roos; coached club, school and junior sides; and been selected for Wide Bay in representative matches against touring sides from overseas. A workplace accident in the sawmill brought Norm's career to a premature end, but for years Mal would tell anyone who would listen that his dad had missed just one grand final in 22 seasons of football.

Norm and his wife, Leona, had always wanted their four boys to look forward, not back. Marriages between black and white were taboo, and the story of Norm's family was not an easy one to tell. His grandfather was Edward Meninga, a South Sea Islander who had taken the name 'Tom Tanna' after he arrived in Queensland in 1889.

Between 1863 and 1903 more than 60,000 South Sea Islanders were brought to Queensland to cut cane in a process known as 'blackbirding'. It was relentless, back-breaking work for the indentured labourers, who were disparagingly called 'kanakas' and treated essentially as slaves. None of Edward's descendants knew for sure whether he was kidnapped, coerced, or freely chose to come to Queensland from Tanna Island in Vanuatu, but life was uncertain and difficult as he cut cane by hand for an annual salary of just £6. The white cane-cutters usually earned ten times that amount.

The discrimination softened for Edward's great-grandchildren, but still there were stories of Meninga and his brothers being excluded from junior footy trips due to the colour of their skin. Mal, though, would always view rugby league as the way to fit in. 'Where I grew up, in places like Monto, the heartbeat was rugby league,' he later explained. 'It was the social outing for the weekend. It was a point of reference for everyone in the town. Dad was highly respected in his community, and he's a black man – an Australian South Sea Islander. I grew up seeing all the good things that footy could do.'

After a childhood spent playing rugby league in regional Queensland, Mal joined the police force as a cadet. There he met Constable Wayne Bennett, the coach of Souths, who told him he could do anything he set his mind to. For the next two decades the rugby league careers of these two men would develop and mature, often in close proximity, as they rose from part-time footballers in Brisbane to heroes of their state and nation.

At the beginning of 1983 Mal was 22 years old, six feet tall, and weighed in at just under 100 kilograms. The men and women who followed rugby league watched him with a mixture of awe and fear, marvelling at his tree-trunk thighs, shaking their heads at his awesome power. Meninga was a young man ahead of his time: an early exponent of the power game that would, in the decades that followed, come to characterise Australian rugby league. The fact that he was also a goal-kicker made him an even more valuable asset: in the first five State of Origin matches, he had scored 41 of Queensland's 79 total points.

After the incident at Kougari Oval – which radio commentator John McCoy called 'one of the sorriest days ever in Queensland sport' – players, officials, and journalists all publicly supported Meninga.[3] The president of the Wynnum-Manly club backed Mal's physical retaliation, while the sports editor of the *Courier-Mail* praised him for not turning the other cheek. 'Big Mal,' he wrote, 'reacted in a way that any red-blooded Australian would.'[4]

'The really sad thing about my generation,' remembered Brothers supporter Tom Cranitch, 'was that we were taught to fear and look down on blackfellas. The stuff you would hear from the sidelines, particularly a lot of the race-based stuff, was horrific.'

While racial abuse was not new in the rough-and-tumble game of rugby league, that it had been visited upon Meninga still came as a shock to some. Queenslanders could see that he had an air of greatness. As a police officer and international footballer, he soon became a state-wide ambassador for the force and for the sport of rugby league. The president of Souths, Tony Testa, enrolled him in elocution classes, modelling courses, and paid for a set of braces to straighten his teeth. 'Let's face it, Mal is as well known in this state as Premier Joh,' Testa told *Rugby League Week*. 'Further, he's a born and bred Queenslander and despite huge offers down south in the past, has elected to stay in Queensland. If that's not a marketable Queensland product, then I don't know what is.'[5]

By the end of May 1983, Queenslanders had assumed two of the most prestigious roles in Australian rugby league. Following the sensational resignation of the ARL chairman, Kevin Humphreys, Ron McAuliffe briefly acted in the role. And Arthur Beetson, the boss of Queensland's State of Origin side, was appointed coach of the national team.

It was another step on the long road to recognition from the Sydney establishment. With power shifting north, Beetson predicted that the 1983 Origin series would be 'the daddy of 'em all'.[6]

Beetson, who had recently returned to Sydney to coach Easts, had just three Sydney residents in his starting lineup for Game I. Manly-Warringah pair John Ribot and Paul Vautin had both pulled on a Maroon jersey before, but Daryl Brohman, a 27-year-old prop forward from Penrith, was making his Origin debut and auditioning for a spot in the Australian side.

With Queensland leading after Wally Lewis's opening try, Brohman received a pass from dummy half and ran hard and straight towards the halfway line. One New South Wales forward went low, another met him front-on while a third tackler, Les Boyd, went in with a cocked elbow. Brohman's head snapped back violently and as the Lang Park crowd howled their disapproval, he lay on the turf clutching his jaw.

Referee Barry Gomersall penalised Boyd but did not send him off. Brohman, meanwhile, was less fortunate. He tried to ignore the pain of a badly broken jaw but was soon forced from the field.

It was the hit that changed rugby league. Jim Comans, once a hard-tackling forward, now a lawyer presiding over the judiciary, had already been tasked with cleaning up the game. He would suspend Boyd for 12 months – one of the longest sentences ever handed down. Later, Boyd revealed that he had been instructed by the New South Wales selectors to keep Queenslanders out of the Australian side. 'Before the game the Test selectors pulled me aside and said:

"Do what it takes, we don't care if you kill someone, we just don't want these fucking Queenslanders in our team",' he told the *Sunday Mail*.[7]

Despite New South Wales having lost four of the five State of Origin matches leading into Game I, a born-to-rule attitude continued to fester within the Sydney rugby league community. Many people still flatly disregarded the Queensland competitions and the men who played in them. Ray Price, the Parramatta and New South Wales lock, even suggested that Lewis would not hold down a first-grade spot in Sydney.[8]

Price's comments further motivated Lewis and his teammates. In Game I he scored two tries, halfback Mark Murray scored one and Mal Meninga kicked six goals from six attempts to seal a 12-point victory to the Maroons. It was an election year in Queensland, and handing out the Kangaroos medallions at Lang Park was the premier, Joh Bjelke-Petersen.

'I knew Joh and I knew the family,' said Queensland Rugby League History Committee member Greg Adermann. 'Joh was at church on Sunday while we were going to T.J. O'Neill Oval. Joh wasn't a football follower or a sport follower. But Joh as a politician milked that pro-Queensland spirit beautifully.'

After New South Wales levelled the series with a win in Game II, a decider was scheduled for the first time at Lang Park. The famous old ground, lit up by fireworks before kick-off, would be the stage for Queensland's sixth State of Origin victory in eight attempts, and the Maroons' biggest victory yet. Queensland ran in 21 points in the first half and 22 in the second to win 43–22. More startling was the fact that the Queensland squad had only two players over the age of 25.

'In 1983 State of Origin was televised for the first time in Britain,' remembered rugby league historian Tony Collins. 'I have to say, I'd never seen rugby league like it. It was as if it was from another planet:

so fast, so skilful, so intense. I was thunderstruck … it was only really when people saw State of Origin on TV that we realised how far in advance the Australian game was over the British.'

A week after Game III, as nine Queenslanders were selected for the Test match against New Zealand – under the guidance of coach Beetson – it became clear that State of Origin had truly changed Australian rugby league. For the first time, the Sydney establishment was forced to relinquish their stranglehold over the game. Their players no longer had a mortgage on the Australian jersey. It was, as journalist Adrian McGregor later recalled, 'a triumph for the triumvirate – the puppeteer McAuliffe, the guru Beetson and the battle general, Wally Lewis'.[9]

More important than any individual, however, was the underdog team spirit that seemed to drive Queenslanders to a whole new level during those all-important three games.

State of Origin had become more than just a series of football matches – it was a vivid representation of Queensland at its best and most inclusive. For where else in Queensland could an Aboriginal man be the boss, a descendant of slaves be granted such immense responsibility, and a knockabout, working-class bloke from the suburbs become the pride of an entire state?

'I think Origin became a self-fulfilling prophesy,' explained sportswriter Phil Lutton. 'In the 1970s and '80s, what did people think of Queensland? Well, it's hot. There's bananas. It's a bit backwards – full of racists and corrupt policemen. All the normal stereotypes. So what I think Origin did is almost invent a set of values for Queenslanders to treasure and to hook their teeth into.

'They kind of stumbled into this giant colossus of sport by accident – they literally had no idea what it would become. Once it started, Queensland had some heroes. Mal and Wally were God-like figures. And what do these heroes represent? Sticking up for the little guy. I'm not sure that existed in Queensland before Origin. And people thought, *Well, that's a fantastic identity to latch onto.* That has become a really powerful force for Queensland.'

★

When the Winfield State League was established in 1982, Ron McAuliffe set a five-year plan for a country side to make the finals. On the second Sunday of May 1984, North Queensland Marlins delivered the dream two seasons early.

After winning four matches in a row, the North Queenslanders defeated Brothers in Mackay to qualify for the semifinal. Local hero Dale Shearer, an 18-year-old whippet who would soon help Mackay win the Foley Shield title, crossed over for his ninth try of the season. Within 12 months he would be selected for Queensland. This, to McAuliffe, was vindication. 'I am ecstatic with the country performance,' he said. 'It has proved the success of the State League and could lead to a national league in the future.'[10]

To others, however, the State League had accelerated the demise of the regional competitions by dragging players away from their local commitments and exposing them to the selectors from richer clubs in Brisbane and Sydney.

According to historian Tony Price, the State League was good for the spectators in North Queensland, but 'the last nail in the coffin for the Foley Shield'.[11] As many as ten players from some Foley Shield teams, he wrote, would head south to play in Brisbane. The Wynnum-Manly side that defeated North Queensland in the semifinal, for instance, fielded Townsville products Gene Miles, Colin Scott, and Terry Butler, as well as Cairns-born forward Greg Dowling.

Dowling was a proud North Queenslander who'd grown up on a cane farm in Ingham. He had earned his stripes in the north, playing Foley Shield for Herbert River, Mount Isa, Townsville, and Innisfail before signing with Wynnum-Manly in Brisbane. There, he stuck close to 'Geno' and 'Scotty', worked on the wharves, drove a truck for the club sponsor, and tried as best he could to adjust to city life. 'The good thing about going to the city was the education,' he later remembered. 'We all went on to bigger and better jobs. I didn't like Sydney – it was a rat race – and I've got to admit, I struggled with Brisbane. So that's why I was rapt with the State League. Everywhere we'd go I'd take the boys out and we'd go uptown for a walk and sign autographs. We went everywhere, and I loved it. We made sure that we got out and saw the locals and said g'day.'

Yet the State League could not stop the flow of players from country to city, and in three seasons only one truly high profile player – Central Queensland hooker Greg Conescu – had moved from Brisbane to a regional side. Meanwhile, North Queensland had lost Martin Bella to Easts in Brisbane, Laurie Spina to North Sydney, Sam Backo to Canberra, and it was accepted wisdom that their newest star, Dale Shearer, would soon leave too.

The introduction of State of Origin had made many Queenslanders reconsider the structure of rugby league in their state. Why should country players, historically the backbone of the game, be forced to move to the city?

Former Easts halfback Wayne Lindenberg, who wrote a weekly column for the *Toowoomba Chronicle*, suggested that the State League introduce 'Division of Origin' whereby country sides could select their homegrown players from the Brisbane competition.[12] Others, like McAuliffe, were preparing for the introduction of a national league.[13] And Arthur Beetson, the incumbent state and national coach, was open to any suggestion that would stop city clubs bleeding the regional areas dry.[14]

A country boy at heart, Beetson understood the two-step, Brisbane-then-Sydney move that regional Queenslanders had to make if they wanted to succeed as a rugby league footballer. His own career, from Roma to Redcliffe to Balmain and then Bondi, was living proof of that fact. On 28 May 1984, his remarkable career was recognised with a life membership of the QRL. His pride in receiving such an honour, however, was soon tempered by the news that he had been replaced as the coach of Australia by Frank Stanton, the boss of New South Wales. 'I got life membership of the Queensland Rugby League,' he later remembered, 'and the boot as Australian coach.'[15]

Queenslanders could not believe it. Beetson's Maroons had the better of Stanton's Blues in the best selection trial there was – State of Origin. Indeed, the timing of the announcement, on the eve of Game I, laid bare the politics behind the decision. McAuliffe had stepped away from his caretaker role as chairman of the ARL, and so the casting vote now lay with Ken Arthurson, a New South Welshman. The Sydney establishment had clearly decided that Stanton would have the job regardless of the result of the interstate clash.

After Queensland beat New South Wales 29 points to 12 at Lang Park, pushing Beetson's Origin record to five wins over Stanton's two, Lewis publicly questioned the ARL's decision. 'It seems strange,' he said, 'that players were selected on form in the State of Origin, yet the same criterion wasn't used for the coach.'[16]

Lewis was in career-best form. After he returned from a lucrative ten-game stint in England, the British magazine *Open Rugby* declared him the best player in the world. He had left Valleys to join Wynnum-Manly and was once again the architect of Queensland's victory over New South Wales. His try, where he picked up the ball from dummy half, dived into a blindside gap nobody else could see, and placed the ball over the line, was lauded for years to come. His towering 40-metre field goal just before half-time left spectators marvelling at his all-round ability.

After he was named captain of Australia, he guided a Kangaroos outfit brimming with nine Queenslanders to victory over Great Britain at the Sydney Cricket Ground. But not even victory over the old enemy could endear him to Sydneysiders. When his name flashed on the scoreboard as man of the match, some booed and jeered loud enough for him to hear. State of Origin, once derided by those in New South Wales as a gimmick, had now become the fiercest rivalry in rugby league.

The opening fireworks had not stopped erupting over the SCG when the first fight of Game II began. On just the second tackle of the match, Queensland centre Gene Miles received the ball on his goal line and shaped to kick. Before he could get boot to ball, however, he was mauled by three New South Wales forwards. The tacklers swung their arms wildly, raining blows to his head and shoulders as he fell to the ground.

All 26 players were drawn into State of Origin's biggest brawl yet. Greg Dowling, who had grown up with Miles and was his teammate at Wynnum-Manly, was first in to thump Steve Roach. New South Wales fullback Garry Jack ran in to sock his opposite number, Colin Scott. Chris Close, never one to retreat from a scrap, lost his shirt as he wrestled with New South Wales captain Ray Price and threw wild punches at Peter Tunks. Barry Gomersall – who once quipped 'I'm there to referee the game, not fights' – waited calmly for the players to settle down. Before the first five minutes had passed, he had awarded Queensland three penalties.

The rain fell heavily, turning the turf into a muddy quagmire and restricting the creativity of both sides. Even the most skilful players dropped the ball as it slipped through muddy hands. Leading 2–0 with 25 minutes remaining, Queensland gradually worked the ball forward and commentator Jack Gibson lamented that 'all we're going to see now is some exciting two-yard runs'.

Gibson had not accounted for the dexterity of Greg Dowling, who had learnt to play sport in the wettest part of Australia. His formative years in the tropical far north had meant that playing in tricky conditions was now second nature.

On the final tackle Lewis collected the ball at first receiver and, with only five yards to the try-line, chip-kicked towards the posts.

Dowling trailed Lewis's kick like an obedient dog, and as the ball cannoned off the crossbar, he miraculously held it in his fingertips and fell over the line. Mud flew everywhere as the players celebrated the magical match-winning try.

By full-time, even the Sydney fans had to agree that King Wally was the deserving man of the match. It was his fifth such award in ten State of Origins. Queensland had now won three consecutive series, and led New South Wales eight games to two.

There were three final acts to come in what would be remembered as Lewis's greatest season. In July, he captained Australia to its third straight victory over Great Britain to wrap up the Ashes series. In August, he led the Combined Brisbane side to its first ever National Panasonic Cup triumph over Easts in Sydney. And in September, he masterminded Wynnum-Manly's 34-point victory over Souths in the BRL grand final. 'It was a good year to be part of,' remembered Lewis. 'We had the hottest side that I ever played in at Wynnum. We would out-attack and out-gun anybody. We were as good, as talented, as entertaining, as any side I played in.'

When Lewis was named *Rugby League Week*'s man of the year in August, editor Ian Heads concluded that 'no footballer in all of rugby league's 77 seasons has ever had a more extraordinary year'.[17] By now he was certainly the most marketable man in Queensland. In living rooms around the state a new television advertisement for Castlemaine Perkins, brewer of the Fourex beer, christened Wally 'the emperor of Lang Park'. The catchy jingle, arranged by the advertising agency MoJo, overlaid highlights of Lewis smashing New South Wales players to the ground and chip-kicking his way past bamboozled defenders.

Before the year was out he signed a lucrative deal with the QRL to promote the game in schools, and married his girlfriend in a ceremony that received state-wide publicity.

As Wally's star rose so did that of his state and hometown. The victory of Combined Brisbane, as well as the continued success of the Maroons, got people thinking about competing with New South Wales not just during the State of Origin series but week-in, week-out throughout the regular season.

At 66 years of age, Ron McAuliffe had retired from politics and was preparing to step away from his position as chairman of the QRL. In a few whirlwind years he had established a new statewide competition, revolutionised the corporate responsibilities of the organisation, and presided over a seismic shift in the entire structure of feeling about the game in Queensland. In an end-of-year interview with *Rugby League Week*, McAuliffe reiterated the need for a national 12-team 'Super League' that would be pegged to television and commercial sponsorships. Borrowing iconic Labor Party imagery, he proclaimed that such a league 'is the beacon on the hill'.[18]

For a game that had been traditionally controlled by a small group of insular men, to many his statements seemed outlandish. Yet not even McAuliffe himself could have foreseen the immense reforms that would, over the next decade and a half, forever change club rugby league in Australia.

★

In the first few months of 1985, the president of the United States, Ronald Reagan, was elected for a second term. The year-long coalminers' strike in England finally came to an end. A group of American artists recorded a charity single, 'We Are the World', for starving children in Africa. A dictatorship fell in Uruguay, the president-elect of Brazil died before being sworn into office, and car bombs exploded in Beirut as regional and sectarian conflicts besieged the Middle East.

In faraway Australia, Olsen Filipaina, a rampaging Samoan-Maori five-eighth, rose from the anonymity of reserve-grade football to outplay Wally Lewis in the first two Test matches between Australia and New Zealand. The response of the Australian coach, Terry

Fearnley, was to drop Greg Dowling, Mark Murray, Chris Close, and Greg Conescu for the third and final match. The controversial decision to replace four Queenslanders, interpreted by one reporter as 'an interstate slur', was the biggest flashpoint of a particularly unhinged season; a year in which civil war broke out between the states and the national interest was sacrificed at the altar of State of Origin.[19]

McAuliffe, in particular, went troppo. 'What has been happening in Beirut,' he raged, 'is nothing compared to what happened to Queensland players in Auckland.'[20]

Fearnley thought McAuliffe's response was ridiculous. After all, his New South Wales side had already wrapped up the 1985 State of Origin series after winning the opening two games. He was also concerned with the attitude of Queenslanders to the national team. After undermining Lewis's captaincy in camp, he publicly questioned why the Queenslander had turned up late to training and team meetings. 'Beating New South Wales,' Fearnley later explained, 'appears to have become more important than representing their country.'[21]

Queenslanders scoffed at the notion they were responsible for infecting the national team with interstate politics. For decades they had seen a New South Wales-stacked selection committee ignore Queenslanders in favour of overhyped Sydneysiders. And, as Lewis had suggested a year earlier, if form was the deciding factor for selection for the national team, why wasn't Arthur Beetson – the most successful representative coach of the decade – in charge of the Kangaroos?

As the squabbling continued, the third State of Origin match loomed as the Battle Royale. McAuliffe threatened to withdraw three Sydney-based Queenslanders from the Sydney competition. Extra security was hired for Lang Park. All four Queenslanders who had been dropped by Fearnley were selected for the Maroons. Before the game, McAuliffe told them they were playing for the reputation 'of Queensland itself'.[22]

At the centre of this interstate civil war was Greg Dowling. Since scoring the wonder-try in Game II of 1984, the burly front-rower had certainly made himself known. A ferocious punch-up with Kiwi prop Kevin Tamati in the first Test, which carried onto the sidelines, earned him a week's suspension and came to define the Trans-Tasman rivalry. And he was less than impressed at being dropped to the bench by Fearnley – in five Test matches for Australia he was yet to be part of a losing side.

He played Game III, as one reporter observed, 'in a state close to fury'.[23] After Queensland ran in four tries to win by 14 points, Dowling rushed to the sideline, pointed to the scoreboard, and loudly abused Fearnley. It was a regrettable way for Fearnley to end his career as a representative coach. In an effort to call détente on the interstate war, the Australian Rugby League soon brought in what became known as 'the Terry Fearnley Rule' to prevent any coach simultaneously holding both state and national jobs.

Buried beneath the acrimony was the standout performance of John Ribot. In his final interstate game, he raced down the wing to score the deciding try of the match. Playing alongside his mates in the Queensland side, he said, was 'the highlight of my life'.[24] Anticipating Ribot's retirement, McAuliffe had employed him as a development officer with the QRL. It was assumed that his popularity and business acumen would make him the perfect man for the job.

As Lewis and Meninga chaired Ribot from the field, the Lang Park crowd chanted his name, and in that happy moment, nobody could have possibly imagined the enormously divisive influence he would soon have on the direction of the game.

Ribot, who was playing club football for Redcliffe, could see that the decline of the Brisbane competition had reached the point of no return. Before the season had even been completed, reigning premiers Wynnum-Manly went bankrupt and needed to be bailed out by the QRL. Other clubs such as Valleys, Souths, and Wests were also struggling financially.

As word of yet another player exodus swirled throughout Brisbane, Mal Meninga announced that he would play the next two seasons with the Canberra Raiders, before finishing his career in England. 'Leaving Brisbane,' he told one reporter, 'has been a very hard decision to make.'[25]

Meninga, who had just turned 25, was ready for a new challenge. Tours with the Kangaroos, as well as a successful stint with St Helens, had broadened his horizons. In England the football was freer, the tactics more open and attacking, and the players much less fit than Australians.

Big Mal had hit the scene like a wrecking ball. He scored 28 tries in 31 games, guiding St Helens to a premiership and a famous victory in the Lancashire Cup final. For decades the English would remember him as the greatest import ever – even better than Wally Lewis.

'He just killed it over there,' recalled fellow Queensland centre Gene Miles. 'They couldn't handle him. He was too big, too strong, too fast. That's where his reputation started. Worldwide he was known as this big monster playing in the centres, and no one could dominate him.'

Before Meninga could leave Brisbane for Canberra, however, he had one last piece of business to attend to. In eight seasons of first-grade football he had won only a single premiership, and the record defeat Souths had suffered against Wynnum-Manly in the grand final the season prior was not long in the memory. Here was an opportunity to avenge that loss, and leave Brisbane on his own terms.

Not even a hairline fracture in his left knee could stop him from playing in what would be his final club match in Queensland. On a heavy dose of painkillers, he led a brave defensive display by Souths to narrowly defeat Wynnum-Manly by two points. Later it would be revealed that Meninga had fractured his knee in a second place and torn a medial ligament. The surgeon's table, as well as adjusting to a new club and a new city, now lay ahead. 'He'll be remembered,' predicted Souths coach Wayne Bennett, 'as a superstar.'[26]

As Meninga departed for Canberra, a pall of darkness fell over rugby league in Queensland. For the first time, the Maroons did not win a single match of the 1986 State of Origin series. Even though Wynnum-Manly won its third premiership in five seasons, newly appointed captain-coach Wally Lewis did not get paid at all for the year.

'It didn't impress us at all,' Lewis recalled years later. 'In those days you had to sign an agreement to stay in Queensland for the next two years. I remember one meeting between the players, and one of the blokes said, "We'll beat this in court seven days a week." The players considered doing it until another bloke said, "Yeah, well, it might be two years until the Queensland Rugby League is ready to fight this in court." We were in a no-win situation.'

To make matters worse, Lewis and several high-profile players were also being chased by the taxation department following new laws brought in by the federal Labor government. Desperate clubs struggled to balance the books; frustrated players departed for Sydney. 'One of the reasons I went to Canberra,' remembered Meninga, 'was your talent never got recognised until you played week-in, week-out in the New South Wales rugby league comp.'

The 1980s would be remembered as the decade in which Queensland lost much of its creative class. Writers, artists and musicians all flocked south, desperate to escape the place they regarded as an oppressive cultural backwater. Although rugby league players were rarely associated with Queensland's arts scene, their departure to Sydney was reflective of the talent drain affecting the state.

What connected football to the counter-culture was a shared frustration with the conservatism of Joh Bjelke-Petersen's National

Party government. Thirty years had passed since the introduction of poker machines in New South Wales, yet Bjelke-Petersen still refused to allow them in Queensland. It had crippled a once-proud football competition.

The wealthy clubs from down south no longer even bothered to wait until the end of the season to pinch Queensland's players. When Canterbury-Bankstown fullback Mick Potter was sidelined with injury in June, club secretary Peter Moore simply went to Brisbane and signed Queensland utility Tony Currie from Wests.

North Sydney, which had already recruited Queenslanders Gavin Jones, Les Kiss, Brett French, Martin Bella, and Terry Butler, now turned its attention to signing Gary Larson, a 19-year-old emerging star for Central Queensland in the Winfield State League.

Meanwhile, Wayne Bennett left his position as coaching director of the QRL to become the assistant coach of the Canberra Raiders. 'Before the first ball was kicked in 1987,' remembered historian Jack Gallaway, 'fifty-nine Brisbane A Grade footballers, the equivalent of four football teams, had signed contracts with Sydney clubs.'[27]

For nearly a decade, soccer had managed to run a national league that encompassed multiple states and cities. Australian Rules had established a team in Sydney and was planning further expansion into Perth and Brisbane. Even basketball had a national league. That a player like Meninga should have to move south just to prove himself as a footballer was neither sustainable nor tolerable.

Even if most enjoyed their footy down south, it remained a challenge to adapt to a new city. 'It was a shock, and probably one that I didn't handle real well,' later explained Mike McLean, a Bowen boy who joined Eastern Suburbs in 1985. 'I was easily influenced and led easily, too. It was a pretty fast life down there, and I was always up for that. It definitely affected my football, because I had too good a time.'

In the great migration from Brisbane to Sydney, Trevor Gillmeister, a no-nonsense second-rower, was another refugee. 'I drove down to

Sydney and didn't know a soul,' he remembered. 'I said to Dad, "How do you get to Bondi?" He said, "Get over the bridge, son, and then hook a left." It was a Friday afternoon and I ended up driving down Oxford Street. For a young bloke from Queensland, it was a massive shock to see blokes walking down the street holding hands. I went, *Holy hell, what's going on with this place?*

And there were other, subtler, differences, too. 'When I went to Sydney,' recalled Tony Currie, 'they bagged me because of my accent. I said, "I packed me port and jumped on a plane." They said, "A port!? That's where a ship comes in!" Togs aren't togs. A Refidex? What's a Refidex? They used to give it to me all the time. So there's another difference – we speak a different language.'

When Queensland forward Wally Fullerton-Smith signed for St George in the middle of the 1986 season, David Wright, a commentator for the ABC, realised that the Brisbane competition was fighting a losing battle. 'The penny finally dropped for me,' he remembered. 'I went on radio that Saturday morning and said, "There's only one way to stem this flow, because they'll go to Sydney and then come back and play State of Origin anyway!" They get the best of both worlds. So I became a very strong advocate of a Brisbane team joining the Sydney competition.'

The questions were when, and in what form. Many of the local clubs were wary that any new entity would hoover up all their supporters and monopolise public interest. A flurry of activity would soon follow as several consortia fought for the right to control the future of the game in Brisbane. The boardroom struggles would test old loyalties and turn workingmen into professionals, budding youngsters into superstars, and past heroes into villains.

For rugby league and the state of Queensland, times were changing fast.

4

A CHANGE OF CULTURE

1987–1989

By his own admission, at the beginning of 1987, Allan Langer was employed in a 'dead-end job' for the Ipswich City Council.[1] On weekdays he was one of the workers in the road gangs, holding stop-and-go signs, fixing gutters, watching the world slip past. On weekends he came alive, gambling on racehorses and playing halfback for the Ipswich Jets.

Located an hour's drive west of Brisbane, Ipswich was a working-class town of coal mines, railways, and the air force; a place of 'hard work and tough old blokes', as Langer described it.[2]

At 20 years of age, he stood five foot five and weighed just 68 kilograms, with snowy blond hair and an elfin face. His size always put him at a disadvantage on the football field, but as a child he had quickly learned how to duck and weave past dangerous opponents, how to break the line with a big step or a deft kick, and how to bring down much stronger men with his unusual over-the-leg tackling style.

His brothers Cliff, Kevin, and Neville had been formidable opponents in backyard footy. Three of the four siblings played Queensland schoolboys and Kevin, the second-eldest, was the captain of Wests in Brisbane. Yet Allan was the youngest and the best of the lot, and he had the good fortune of making his way into first-grade just as rugby league in Queensland was experiencing its greatest upheaval in history.

In 1986, the Ipswich Jets had been accepted into the Brisbane competition, meaning that Langer's debut season brought him up against tough opposition not only during the Winfield State League but week-in, week-out in the Brisbane Rugby League. The Jets hired Tommy Raudonikis, one of the most competitive halfbacks ever to play the game, as coach. The relationship between he and Langer would be akin to that of master and pupil, as Langer leafed through his old footy scrapbooks, peppered him with questions, and soaked up every bit of knowledge he could.

It paid off immediately. Langer was the brightest spark in an otherwise gloomy year for the BRL, taking on the responsibilities of goal-kicker, creative playmaker, even captain on a few occasions. 'He is always doing something,' observed one coach, 'a probe at the line, the chip and regather, the kick across field to pick up a flanker, the huge pinpoint bomb or simple setting up of his supports.'[3]

Langer was also fortunate that injury had forced the incumbent Queensland halfback, Mark Murray, into early retirement. 'Muppet' had long been a fixture of the Brisbane scene, and had played in almost every Origin game since 1982. In Langer's first audition for the vacant halfback spot, during Combined Brisbane's loss to Penrith in the Panasonic Cup, he was substituted with 20 minutes left on the clock. In his second audition, during a trial match between the Queensland Residents and the Sydney Maroons, he ended up on the losing side.

The overwhelming favourite for the halfback position was Laurie Spina, a North Queenslander who was in excellent form for Eastern Suburbs in Sydney and had got the better of Langer in the residents-versus-expatriates trial match. Spina was the favoured choice of the players and the coach, but Dud Beattie – a Queensland selector from Ipswich – insisted that Langer play the first game.

In the end, six resident Queenslanders were picked in the squad of 15: Wally Lewis, Gene Miles, Greg Dowling, Greg Conescu, Colin Scott, and Allan Langer. Of the six, Langer was the only rookie. As Queensland had lost six of the past seven Origin matches, at a time when almost all of the best Queenslanders had left to play in the Sydney competition, it was perhaps the biggest selection gamble in the history of the series. Picking Langer, reported Sydney's *Daily Mirror*, was proof that Queensland had taken a 'decisive step towards oblivion'.[4]

By 1987 State of Origin had been in place for seven years. A few traditions had been established in the Maroons camp. One was that Wally Lewis would drive the team bus, always at breakneck speed. Another was that if you had a problem, you went to see Dick 'Tosser' Turner, the president of the Redcliffe Dolphins and the best team manager in the business. And then there was the late-night, alcohol-fuelled bonding sessions, the card games, the easy-going friendship between residents and expatriates who enjoyed a beer and their shared identity as Queenslanders.

Allan Langer, the little Ipswich imp who loved a punt, a drink, and a laugh, overcame his initial shyness and soon fitted in well. The older players called him Alf, short for Alien Life Form, and hoped that he would be up to the rigours of representative football.

'He had to catch the rattler in from Ipswich,' remembered Gene Miles. 'He turned up with this little brown port. And honestly, you know, we'd been there for a few more years than Alf, and when he arrived in camp we thought, *This guy's not going to make it.* I was one of those doubters, and so was Wally.'

Peter Jackson, Queensland's live-wire centre, later recalled Wayne Bennett telling the senior players to look out for Langer. 'Wally had always played behind the line for Queensland,' wrote Jackson, 'but Bennett wanted him to swap with Alf because the coach was worried about NSW targeting Langer as a weak link. Fatty Vautin then piped up: "He's a Queenslander, Benny, he'll handle it!"'[5]

In an intense Lang Park atmosphere, in which beer cans were hurled at police officers and players strained to hear each other over the roar of the crowd, Queensland went down by four points after New South Wales scored a late try. But Langer, who missed just three tackles all night, was voted best on ground by his teammates. He had earned his spot.

'That Queensland side – they lost the first game, but then they won the next eight games, which had never been done,' recalled Spina, Langer's rival for the halfback spot. 'If I could have played in a team like that ... who knows? But at the end of the day, you have to feel that the best man was chosen. He just grew and grew and grew. I missed out to a better bloke.'

Like many up-and-coming Queensland footballers, Langer was keen to test himself against the best players in Sydney club football. Fortunately for him, the New South Wales Rugby League had accepted two new Queensland teams into its competition for 1988: one from Gold Coast–Tweed Heads, backed by a group of former players that included John Sattler, Peter Gallagher, and Bob Hagan; and a private consortium from Brisbane headed by local businessmen Barry Maranta, Paul 'Porky' Morgan, Gary Balkin, and Steve Williams.

Having seen off the competition of several other bids, including one fronted by Ron McAuliffe, the new Brisbane side would become the most controversial. Known in those early days as the 'Maranta syndicate', it won the licence after promising the Queensland Rugby League a range of financial benefits and sponsorships. Immediately Maranta and Morgan recruited two employees from the governing body. They poached QRL development officer John Ribot to become their club's general manager, while Maroons boss Wayne Bennett was appointed as coach.

The first player to sign was Wally Lewis, on Wednesday 10 June, at a crowded press conference in Brisbane. Gene Miles was next. Greg

Conescu, Colin Scott, and Greg Dowling soon followed. It was clear that this new Brisbane side would be stacked with battle-hardened representative players.

Following Game II of State of Origin, which Queensland won at a waterlogged Sydney Cricket Ground, Langer agreed to join the new Brisbane club. The owners initially baulked at the transfer fee demanded by Ipswich, before revising them down to a lower figure.[6]

By mid-July 1987, the Maranta syndicate had signed every one of the resident Queenslanders preparing for State of Origin Game III. And on the eve of the all-important game, the new club was launched as the Brisbane Broncos, with a garish maroon, gold, and white jersey, which purported to represent the traditional colours of Queensland, the Brisbane City Council, and the BRL competition.

Money flowed freely as Maranta promised that the Broncos would pay an unprecedented $1500 win-bonus to the players. All of a sudden Langer, who was accustomed to a workingman's wage at his local council, was a State of Origin player and a member of the hottest team in town.

On Wednesday 15 July 1987, in front of a packed house at Lang Park, he was named man of the match as Queensland defeated New South Wales in Game III of Origin. The famous victory, nine months in the making, was compared to 'the birth of a child' by team manager Tosser Turner. 'There just had to be doubts about Allan, so small, so young,' he said. 'But he has proven that he can play for Australia. And one day he will.'[7]

Next day, the front page of the *Courier-Mail* led with a photo of Langer and Wally Lewis locked in an embrace, as if to symbolise the passing of the baton from one creative genius to another. For the next decade and a half, Alf would do for Queensland in the 1990s what Wally had done in the 1980s. Unlike Lewis, however, Langer benefited enormously from the entry of the new Brisbane team into the Sydney competition. While Lewis forever faced questions about whether he would have made it in Sydney during his prime, Langer would prove himself by matching his State of Origin form with regular, dazzling displays for the Brisbane Broncos.

★

By the end of July 1987, cracks were beginning to show in the premiership of Joh Bjelke-Petersen. For six months he had embarked on the infamous 'Joh for PM' campaign, succeeding only in splitting the Liberal–National Party coalition vote at the federal election. The bluster and hubris that had once made him a folk-hero of the political Right had finally caught up with him, and for the conservative movement he was now a kind of King Midas in reverse: everything he touched turned to shit. As Labor was elected to a third successive term in office, the federal leader of the Liberal Party, John Howard, declared that Bjelke-Petersen 'must carry an enormous share of the blame'.[8]

Within weeks of the humiliating result, in which Labor actually gained four seats in Queensland, a probe into police misconduct began. Prompted by an investigation by the ABC's *4 Corners* program, as well as months of reporting by the *Courier-Mail*, the Fitzgerald Inquiry raked through a vast web of official corruption – an open secret known in Queensland as 'the Joke'. According to Matthew Condon, author of a true-crime trilogy of books about corruption during the Bjelke-Petersen era, 'the Joke' was an 'elaborate, multi-million dollar scheme of kickbacks from illegal gambling, SP bookmakers, brothels and escort services'.[9]

The 18-month-long inquiry would result in the imprisonment of a police commissioner and three government ministers, and an end to the 19-year reign of Bjelke-Petersen, who was deposed as premier before the year was out. The revelations were terribly ironic for the rugby league community, which had been brought to the brink of financial collapse in part due to Bjelke-Petersen's moral crusade against poker machines. In the end, some wondered, what had it all been for?

'We had been writing about the hypocrisy of the Queensland government,' recalled Anne Jones, a former editor of the *Cane Toad Times*. 'They were wowserish, anti-gambling, anti-prostitution, and yet you could go through the Valley and there were these places called Bubbles Bathhouse, which had gambling and girls.

'Famously, Wickham Street in the Valley was closed off by police in order to crane in a new gaming table to the top storey, and meanwhile Russ Hinze is going, "There's no gambling in the Valley!" That wowser aspect of the Bjelke-Petersen government did stop Queensland from competing in some areas.'

While clubs in Sydney had built on the profits of their lucrative slot machines, football clubs in Queensland had been forced to search for other ways to raise capital. The Brothers club in Brisbane, for instance, decided to invest in prize homes, also known as art unions, which were raffled off to the public. Instead of creating a lucrative revenue stream, however, the art unions were a disaster. By the winter of 1987 Brothers were reportedly $3 million in debt and placed in the hands of a receiver.

To some committee members, such as treasurer Noel Hall and secretary Don Munro, the manner in which these raffles were conducted typified the mismanagement of the club during the 1980s. 'At the end of 1982 a guy called Frank Melit became president,' explained Noel Hall, who served as treasurer from 1968 to 1983. 'He wanted to expand the club and do lots of things, and money was a bit short, so he organised these house raffles. I didn't like the way he was doing it – he wouldn't tell you how many tickets he'd sell, if he was going to build a house he wouldn't tell you where it was. It was difficult. So on 30 June 1983, I said, "Frank, I can't wear this, I'm resigning."'

The financial reports stopped arriving soon after, recalled Don Munro, a life member of the club. 'I said to Frank, "Listen, Frank, every year I've got to write minutes and these minutes have got to be legal." We always put up our treasury report at every meeting. I said, "Frank, I understand these things happen, but next meeting we've got to have a treasury report." So the next meeting, it didn't come. I went to the meeting and said, "There's my resignation." We'd become illegal.'

The cruel irony was that Brothers had historically been a well-run, relatively affluent club, with a network of affiliates throughout the state and one eye on the future. When the clubhouse was opened in the winter of 1971, a confident document titled 'The Spirit of Past Brothers' was produced to be read by members at the start of the new millennium. 'What I do know for certain is that whenever a man or boy pulled on the blue and white striped jersey of the Brisbane Brothers in the past 51 years, I have touched his heart and his soul,' it read.[10]

One of those men was ABC commentator David Wright, who played for Brothers during the 1970s. According to Wright, it was a club ahead of its time. 'They used to say to the former president, Doc Alroe, "How come you've got these power-points at one-metre centres along the wall?"' Wright remembered. 'Of course it was because it was set up for poker machines. Doc would say, "Oh no, we've just got short cords on our vacuum cleaners, that's why we need those power-points."

'By the time the Broncos concept came in, in 1987, Brothers were already in trouble. Had they not got into strife, caused by mismanagement in the early 1980s, I'm sure they would have been one of the key players. And actually, there's many people who would say that they would have been *the* Brisbane club. They were that strong.'

Yet from the outset there was a cold war between Brothers and the Broncos. It stemmed, primarily, from the fact that the Brothers coach, Ross Strudwick, had been overlooked by the Broncos directors for the vacant coaching position.

During the 1987 season Strudwick complained that the Broncos' spending spree was disrupting team harmony in the Brisbane competition, while Maranta made a thinly veiled swipe at Brothers' lack of cooperation with his organisation. And as the season progressed, not a single Brothers player signed for the Broncos. Instead, Strudwick organised contracts for his players with clubs in Sydney. Five first-graders, including the captain Trevor Bailey, ended up signing for St George – Strudwick's old side.

Bailey, 25, had been at the club since his junior days and had been prepared to finish his career with Brothers until the financial crisis hit. For a brief period, after being told they might not get paid at all, the first-grade side began betting on the outcome of their own games as a way of earning money for an end-of-season trip. 'It was probably an illegal bookmaker,' recalled Bailey. 'In one game, I got taken off with about ten minutes to go, and there was a journo on the sideline. Tony Rea kicked this field goal to go one point ahead of our margin. Nobody knew this but us, and we've gone berserk. The journo said, "What's going on?", and I said, "Mate, we backed ourselves!" And then I thought, *Oh shit, I shouldn't have said that.*'

By the end of August, Brothers beat Norths twice in two weeks; first to secure the club's first minor premiership in 17 years, and then again to reach the grand final. Employing Strudwick's revolutionary 'slide defence' to full effect, Brothers, concluded one reporter, 'have played the most thoughtful and disciplined football in Brisbane'.[11]

Winter gave way to spring, and with the Broncos set to enter the Sydney competition, there was a sense of finality to the last rounds of the 1987 BRL season. In the lead-up to the grand final, *Rugby League Week* published a dramatic front page with nine Brothers players decked out in Parramatta, St George, and North Sydney jerseys – the clubs they would join in 1988. It was, as the headline suggested, the 'last tango in Brisbane'.[12]

On the afternoon of Sunday 20 September 1987, Brothers were led out onto Lang Park by an eight-year-old mascot, Bradley Jacobs, who was dressed in a bright green leprechaun outfit and top hat – a throwback to the club's Irish Catholic roots. The players bravely absorbed ten minutes of pressure from a fired-up Redcliffe side before Bailey, in his last-ever game for Brothers, crossed over for the first try of the match. From there, the Brethren ran in five more tries to win by 18 points. As Bailey hoisted the trophy aloft, his teammate Steve Carter lifted the happy young leprechaun mascot onto his shoulders.

Despite the off-field drama, Brothers had managed to win both the reserve-grade and first-grade titles. Chairman Frank Dolan promised reporters that the club was 'looking to the year 2000' and hoped that there would be a Brothers club in Brisbane for their little mascot to play for in the future.[13] Yet as the Brothers faithful crammed into the clubhouse to celebrate into the early hours of the morning, what should have been the start of a glorious new era instead became a long, painful hangover. Within a few years, Brothers would be forced from its leagues club and home ground – which were eventually demolished to make way for townhouses – and the football side was reduced to a shadow of its former self.

The situation facing Brothers was a powerful metaphor for the collapse of the BRL. For Barry Maranta, a Brothers old boy who was now heading up the Broncos, there was never any intention to adversely affect Brothers or any other club. Still, he was aware that big changes were necessary to rejuvenate the game. 'We wanted the BRL to be successful,' he remembered. 'Gary Balkin played for Brothers and Souths; Porky Morgan played for Toowoomba and Norths, I think it was; I played for Brothers and Steve Williams played for Wests and Redcliffe. But none of us *went* to rugby league. Rugby league was not promoted in any way shape or form … I mean, it was moribund.'

In the end, the only Brothers players to join the Broncos in 1988 were Joe Kilroy and Brett Le Man, while the rest split up for good. For supporters such as Tom Cranitch – who had not even been born the last time that Brothers had won a premiership in 1968 – the demise of his club left a bitter aftertaste to what should have been a memorable year.

'The 1988 Broncos team was a corporate structure, privately owned, and right from the word go you could tell they had no intention of respecting the heritage of the thing,' remembered Cranitch. 'They wanted a new marketing arrangement. And they did the right thing in the end, because they knew where the market was heading.'

To a remarkable degree, the decline of the old style of Queensland politics coincided with the decline of the traditional world of rugby league. The end of Joh Bjelke-Petersen's long reign as premier would soon be followed by the collapse of the BRL competition.

At the beginning of 1988 the city of Brisbane was caught in rugby league purgatory. Other sports were moving in. The Brisbane Bears, a newly established Australian Rules club, had set up shop on the Gold Coast, while in basketball, the Brisbane Bullets were drawing crowds of 10,000 people a game.

Yet the Brisbane Broncos had to resolve a far more complex set of circumstances than the Bears or the Bullets. It would need to negotiate the divided loyalties of the existing rugby league supporters, as well as capturing the attention of the latent community of sports fans in Southeast Queensland.

The Broncos directors studied the success of the National Football League in America and were impressed by a financially viable organisation underpinned by professional marketing and dazzling match-day entertainment. 'We never ever wanted to treat the Broncos as anything more than a business,' later recalled Broncos director Porky Morgan. 'The intention was to create a really good side under private enterprise lines to make sure that there are sufficient funds there to develop what we thought was the way football should be run.'[14]

Over the next decade and a half, all the football codes in Australia would experience profound changes in their relationship to supporters and to the general public. Football would soon become a privatised product, beholden to the family-friendly expectations of the entertainment industry. In many ways, the Broncos began this gentrification of Australian sport. The rough-and-tumble world of Brisbane club football – the brawls at 'Bash-up Park', the crude verbal tirades from the 'chook pen' at Kougari Oval, the stinking urinals of Lang Park – were almost prehistoric compared to the Broncos' vision for rugby league.

Adrian McGregor, a journalist and biographer of Wally Lewis, once observed that rugby league clubs were in fact workingmen's clubs, with their social and cultural values 'fixed in an Australia which existed between 1930 and 1960'.[15] 'When the Brisbane Broncos run on to Lang Park [...] for their inaugural Sydney premiership match,' predicted McGregor, 'their toughest task will not be to defeat Manly-Warringah, but to drag rugby league into the 21st century.'[16]

Maranta admitted that none of his fellow directors would take their wives to hyper-masculine rugby league matches. Instead, they decided to civilise rugby league by separating Lang Park into drinking and dry sections, while Maranta told reporters that wives and kids were welcome, as well as dads.[17]

At the Broncos' first trial match at Lang Park in February, an overexcited ground announcer heckled the Canberra Raiders over the PA system, blasted neighing horse noises, and a brass band struck up a tune whenever an opposition player lined up a conversion attempt. This kind of confected atmosphere was, as more than a few people noted, taken straight from the artificial bombast of American sport.

But on the first Sunday of May 1988, more than 17,000 Queenslanders witnessed the Broncos beat the defending premiers, Manly-Warringah, by 34 points. Standing on the terraces at Lang Park that evening, Brothers fan Tom Cranitch was impressed by the scoreline but unconvinced by the occasion. He was 17 years old, obsessed with rugby league, very parochial about his city and his state, and yet he left Lang Park reaffirmed in his loyalty to Brothers, and never returned to another Broncos game. To him the Broncos did not faithfully represent the rough, tribal game he had grown up with. 'I wanted to like the Broncos,' he later explained, 'but I couldn't do it. I couldn't really find any club that I identified with in the Sydney competition. Apart from Origin, I stopped watching rugby league from about 1989 to 1998. I just couldn't bring myself to watch footy. Brothers were the love of my life.'

Yet for many more Queenslanders, the Broncos were like an extension of the state side. Wayne Bennett was coach of both teams; the Broncos general manager, John Ribot, had only recently been farewelled from the Maroons; and the Emperor of Lang Park, Wally Lewis, carried his genius from State of Origin to club football.

The inaugural Brisbane Broncos were an attractive bunch: Gene Miles, Colin Scott, and Greg Dowling appealed to North Queenslanders, while Terry Matterson, the goal-kicker recruited from Easts in Sydney, was a kind of psychological salve for those who remembered the countless players Easts had pilfered from Queensland over the past two decades.

Bryan Neibling and Greg Conescu were stalwarts of the Brisbane competition, while on the flanks were Michael Hancock, a 17-year-old sensation from Stanthorpe, and handsome Indigenous flyer Smokin' Joe Kilroy, a member of the Black Uhlan's motorcycle gang and one of the coolest men in Australian sport.

And the playmaker in the No. 7 jumper was Allan Langer. For a new franchise that hoped to spread rugby league's appeal, he was a revelation. Anyone who had been put off by the raw brutality of rugby league was now comforted by the fact that Langer, who looked like a small child, could mix it with the best. When 'Alfie' received the ball, onlookers could not stop a grin spreading across their face. Children flocked to him at club functions and open days. Mothers and grandmothers simply adored him. According to one reporter, 'New York's Madison Avenue advertising district could not have manufactured a more appealing product than Langer is already.'[18]

What the Broncos were attempting to do, in effect, was end the class prejudice that existed towards rugby league and reach out to new audiences. 'There was a real bad feeling towards rugby league,' recalled Barry Maranta. 'I played golf at Royal Queensland and no-one would talk to me because I was a leaguie! Serious. I didn't go to a GPS school and I played rugby league, so I was *persona non grata*!'

Maranta and his fellow directors set about transforming the mud, sweat and beers approach of clubs in the 1970s into a corporate franchise that would be all things to all men – and women. 'The first thing we decided, in trying to get bums on seats, was why deny yourself half the marketplace?' explained Maranta. 'We went out of our way to get women immersed with us from day one. Our No. 1 Bronco supporter, and in fact jersey-holder, was Sallyanne Atkinson, who was the lord mayor of Brisbane at the time.

'The first game that we played against Manly, Sallyanne was the one that kicked the ball off, and notoriously her shoe went further than the ball. It became quite a thing, and was publicised in the media, because rugby league was considered not a game for women to go to – they went to the rugby union. We changed that, virtually from game one.'

★

In Sydney there was also an atmosphere of change and renewal. The NSWRL had just recorded a profitable year, an exhibition State of Origin match had been played in the USA, and plans were being made to take a competitive Origin fixture to the virgin territory of Melbourne. The game was now firmly committed to expansion.

Part of the modernisation process included Sydney clubs moving from charming, but often dilapidated suburban grounds to new all-seater stadiums. In 1986 Easts had said goodbye to the old Sydney Sports Ground in Moore Park, and in 1987 South Sydney farewelled Redfern Oval. In 1988, Australia's bicentennial year, a new stadium was unveiled on the spot where the old Sports Ground once stood. Easts and Souths both moved in.

The Sydney Football Stadium should have been a great gift to rugby league, offering a rectangular 42,000-seat home, but it was immediately unpopular. Fans associated the SFS with increased ticket prices, were disappointed by its lack of atmosphere, and complained that the unusual roof offered little protection from the elements.

On Tuesday 17 May 1988, the first State of Origin match was played at the new stadium. With tickets selling for $32 each, just 26,000 spectators turned up, leaving wide bays of empty seats at both ends. And despite Queensland missing Wally Lewis for the first time in the history of State of Origin, the performance by the Blues was as flat as the atmosphere.

Crestfallen at Queensland's unlikely victory, former New South Wales skipper Ray Price predicted that the SFS would be 'the biggest white elephant this city has seen' and recommended that the third match should be moved to Parramatta Stadium.[19]

There were no such concerns for Game II at Lang Park. Here was a ground that seemed to blend in seamlessly with the surrounding suburbs, from the pubs of Caxton Street on one side to the bright lights of the iconic Castlemaine Perkins Brewery on the other. Country Queenslanders looked forward to making the pilgrimage to Lang Park while Brisbane residents felt privileged to call it their home. It was old-fashioned, distinctive, like one of those historic timber Queenslander houses on stilts.

To a generation of Queensland representative players, Lang Park had been the home of the big occasion, a site of raw masculinity, but also a place for fun and mischief. Chris Close, one of Queensland's heroes in the 1980s, had climbed through a hole in the fence just weeks before making his representative debut. The Broncos up-and-coming five-eighth, Kevin Walters, had done the same with his brothers on the night of the first State of Origin match. Others, such as Wally Lewis and Tony Currie, had grown up messing around with family and friends who lived close by.

'I was a hot chips seller at Lang Park,' remembered Currie. 'I used to do many, many Cup games on a Wednesday night in the cold, selling my hot chips. So I was brought up with Lang Park. I lived in Hale Street, which was a stone's throw away. Me and my mates all played at Wests, and we'd cut a hole in the fence and jump through. We'd climb the light towers, get toilet paper, tie it up and let it roll all the way down, climb back down and light it. Or we'd play night footy – we'd jump the fence and play footy with a thong or a can of Coke.'

With its low slung terraces and long bench seats, Lang Park helped ease the transition between the old world to the new. It was one of those rare football grounds where a parochial home crowd could still influence the outcome of a match.

'I played at Lang Park,' remembered Bob Katter, the federal member for Kennedy. 'The games I played there were third grade, but if you did something good … the roar! It set your adrenaline running something fearsome. It was a primitive place, thousands of people could pack in there, standing room only. It was our home ground.'

Even before kick-off in Game II, the partisan crowd had begun hurling their yellow cans of Fourex beer onto the field. The players ran out in their maroon jumpers, Queensland flag stitched on their chests, as bright red fireworks crackled overhead. The stands shook as supporters brayed at the Blues, hurled insults at the referee, and stomped their feet with excitement.

But New South Wales scored the first try, and with 20 minutes left on the clock led 6–4. When Queensland hooker Greg Conescu dived on a loose ball, he was isolated among a crowd of Blues players and punched by front-rower Phil Daley.

Realising Conescu's discomfort, Wally Lewis raced over to help out and soon several players were trading blows. The referee tried to restore order by sending Conescu and Daley to the sin-bin for ten minutes and Lewis for five, but sections of the crowd had already turned feral. The ref had sin-binned the King.

The noise was deafening and more beer cans rained from the terraces, some empty, some dangerously full. Sideline reporters and cameramen shielded their heads and headed for safety. After the restart, the chant of 'QUEENS–LAND!' rang around the ground and 23-year-old centre Peter Jackson came up with an intercept and sprinted towards the try-line. He was brought down right in front of a bay of overexcited supporters and, as the referee awarded Queensland a penalty, the beer cans began to rain down once more.

Four tackles later, Sam Backo dived over the line to put Queensland two points in front. From there, the Maroons never looked back, winning Game II by ten points and Game III by 16 points. It was the first time that Queensland had won all three State of Origin matches, and Slammin' Sam Backo, playing in his first Origin series, was awarded man of the match for Games II and III.

Backo, the son of Evelyn Scott, a legendary Indigenous activist from North Queensland, was an unstoppable prop forward with a walrus moustache and an old-school attitude. He had grown up in Ingham but had played most of his senior football in Canberra. When the media questioned his eligibility for State of Origin, he responded angrily that he was a proud Queenslander. 'The only good thing to come out of New South Wales,' he quipped, 'is the road north.'[20]

By season's end, he, Dale Shearer, Peter Jackson, and Tony Currie all agreed to move home to join the Brisbane Broncos. Queensland's rugby league renaissance looked set to continue into the 1990s.

The biggest event of the year was not State of Origin, or even the arrival of the Brisbane Broncos, but the World Expo '88. The Expo was a six-month-long bicentennial event held in Brisbane which attracted millions of visitors to experience a wide range of activities, cultures and cuisines. For many, the Expo marked the end of the conservative Bjelke-Petersen era, in which pubs shut their doors early, cultural sites were demolished to make way for apartment blocks, and the arts were relegated to a secondary concern. Just like the 1982 Commonwealth Games, it would be remembered as yet another milestone in Brisbane's never-ending coming of age.

'Prior to the Expo the city heart was deserted outside working hours,' remembered academics Janice Caulfield and John Wanna. 'Brisbanites feel that the city eventually "came alive" around the time of the Expo festivities, resulting in a relaxation in public regulations and new policy approaches to city life.'[21]

In this new, progressive Brisbane, the Broncos began to establish itself as part of the cultural landscape of both the city and the state. The game's newest team also tested the rules of the competition and the patience of the Lang Park Trust. At one home match, during the half-time break the players rested at the northern end of the ground behind a banner emblazoned with the club's major sponsor, Power's Brewery, while dancing cheerleaders waved placards that spelled P-O-W-E-R-S. This cheeky bit of advertising was in contravention of the marketing arrangements that the Lang Park Trust had with Castlemaine Perkins, brewers of the famous Fourex beer and a longtime sponsor of the QRL.

The chairman of the NSWRL, Ken Arthurson, later claimed to have 'no respect at all' for the Broncos management. In hindsight, Arthurson explained, the Broncos should have been expelled from the competition. 'They just kept breaking the rules, to suit themselves, fuelled by the greed and avarice of big business at its worst,' he wrote.[22]

In total, the Broncos won 14 games, lost eight, and narrowly missed the finals series. It was something of an anticlimax after the stunning opening round victory over Manly-Warringah, but wherever the new team went they energised the competition and introduced the interstate rivalry to club football.

At the Dally M Awards in Sydney, Wally Lewis was recognised as the best five-eighth, while Allan Langer was named best halfback. Coach Bennett felt it had been a successful first season. 'One thing I would like to change about the Broncos operation is our fans,' he wrote in his column for the *Courier-Mail*. 'You are too polite.'[23]

Three days after the Broncos season ended, on 16 August 1988, Ron McAuliffe passed away in an intensive care unit at St Andrews Hospital in Brisbane. He was 70 years old.

In the days leading up to his death he had made arrangements for his funeral, telling the manager of the Lang Park Leagues Club to 'bring a band in here and put plenty of booze on to blast me away'.[24] And so they did, as a five-piece jazz band entertained hundreds of guests at Lang Park. It was a fitting farewell. Almost everybody, it seemed, had at least one fond memory of the man who the *Australian* newspaper called 'Mr Rugby League'.[25] An avalanche of anecdotes spewed forth about McAuliffe: the Rat of Tobruk, the businessman, the senator, the swashbuckling sporting identity.

Of course, McAuliffe's influence had been on the wane for some time. When the licence for a team in Brisbane was being fought for in 1987, he fronted a losing bid – something that would have been unimaginable just a few years earlier, when he was at the height of his powers. What Barry Maranta and his fellow directors at the Brisbane Broncos found, while they were lobbying for the licence, was that McAuliffe had actually become quite unpopular throughout Brisbane and the regions.

Indeed, the establishment of the Broncos and the decline of the Brisbane competition remained a sore point for McAuliffe. Where the BRL was once the dominant sporting story for newspapers and radio and television bulletins, suddenly the old clubs found themselves thoroughly eclipsed by the Broncos.

'I went to see Brothers play Redcliffe in the 1987 grand final, and it was packed,' remembered Greg Mallory, the author of *Voices from Brisbane Rugby League*. 'Then I went to the grand final in 1988, it was Valleys and Ipswich, and there were 13,000 people there. They reckon there was more than 35,000 in 1987. So that's dramatic – it's a whole change of culture.'

Yet unlike in Victoria – where the demise and relocation of traditional Australian Rules football clubs was met with public backlash, mournful editorials in daily newspapers, and reverential histories – in Brisbane people simply moved on. The BRL was colonised by the Broncos and the Sydney competition. Still, for those lamenting the loss of old loyalties, solace could always be found in State of Origin. And it was Ron McAuliffe who would be forever remembered as the man who ushered in rugby league's showpiece event.

'Without McAuliffe's introduction of the State of Origin series in 1980 I am convinced Queensland could not be nearly the vibrant, winning Expo state it is today,' wrote *Courier-Mail* reporter Lawrie Kavanagh in his obituary for McAuliffe.

Queensland's success in State of Origin since 1980 has been an inspiration to Queenslanders in all walks of sport and life. The series has taught us all that we can win against the odds, standing on our own two feet. Sure the players have done the job, but we've all benefitted from the experience of success. And it was that old wizard McAuliffe who gave them, and us, the chance at equality and ultimate success. He's left a legacy that will ensure the name McAuliffe lives as long as there is a Queensland.[26]

★

From the moment the colony of Queensland gained independence from New South Wales, with Brisbane as its capital, tension had existed between the regional centres and the metropolis. The state's wealth was derived primarily from its agricultural and mining industry in the country areas, while political power was always wielded from Brisbane. Rugby league was a link between city and country.

For many country Queenslanders, rugby league was more than just a game – it was a way of life. Long before he was appointed to the Australian Rugby League Commission, Dr Chris Sarra used football to integrate into communities in the Darling Downs. 'It was just good to be connected,' he remembered. 'I was a phys. ed. teacher at the school, but I think people respected that I didn't perceive myself as above them, or too good to hang out with them, or whatever. This was in 1988. In 1989 I played in Dalby. And that was good for the same reasons – you're playing against the fathers of kids you are teaching. The kids would read about you in the paper, or you'd come to school all busted up, and it'd give you something to talk about. You became part of the fabric of the community.'

Further north, in places such as Mackay, Townsville, Mount Isa, and Cairns, ran a deep vein of resentment towards those in the southeast. From as early as the 19th century, some had called for North Queensland to secede and go its own way as an independent state. And North Queenslanders never forgot the 'Brisbane Line' – an alleged plan to abandon northern Australian in the event of a Japanese invasion during World War II.

Distance and the constant drain of wealth and talent from north to south were the main points of discontent. The major hub of the north, Townsville, was further away from Brisbane than Brisbane was from Sydney, and many North Queenslanders detested their government and legislators being located so far away. 'When a wheelright makes a wheel, does he put the hub on the rim?' asked one separatist in 1893.

> Yet the people of Queensland have placed their administrative engine, the hub of their Government, in the extreme corner of a territory of 670,000 square miles [...] What would you think of a man who told you the circulation of the blood would be more perfect if the heart were placed in the big toe?[27]

The structure and feel of North Queensland rugby league was always different to the southeast, which was ruled by an inner-city competition in Brisbane. In the north, each regional competition was backed by the local industry, and fed into the town-versus-town Foley Shield. In Mount Isa, for example, the four clubs – Wanderers, Black Stars, Brothers, and Town – provided players to the Foley Shield team. Footballers such as the Daisy brothers Vern and Frank, who might have been jeered at club level, became legends when they were elevated to the Foley Shield.

'The Daisy brothers were simply the best,' remembered Professor Gracelyn Smallwood, an Indigenous activist and health worker from Townsville. 'They would draw a crowd – black and white – for the Foley Shield. I remember my grandparents said, "We're all one mob, all countrymen." And we were so proud. Not just of those two deadly brothers, but of all the black footballers ... they were like the black stallions.'

Vern Daisy, an Indigenous man from Palm Island, was your quintessential North Queenslander. In the late 1960s, he had moved to Mount Isa to work in the mines. The plan was to stay for 12 months. He ended up staying for 30 years. 'Mount Isa was the toughest comp outside of Brisbane football at the time,' he later recalled. 'I didn't want to leave the north, but at the time there was players leaving. Well, I didn't like the idea. Much later in life Jack Gibson, the coach of Parramatta, offered me to come down. I told him, "No, Jack, thanks for the offer, mate, but I don't like the city."'

Vern played in what was billed as his last big-time Foley Shield match in September 1987. Lining up alongside his brother, Frank, he inspired Cloncurry to victory over Proserpine in the B-grade final. Vern put on an exhibition of football, entertaining the crowd with his one-hand passes, and was given a standing ovation as he was chaired from the field.

'Vern was a pretty rough, tough son-of-a-bitch,' said Greg Dowling, who had played alongside him in Mount Isa and was in attendance for the final. 'He was probably the most feared guy in North Queensland back in the day. Feared not just for his aggression but also his playing skills. Without a doubt, I couldn't think of a footballer who had more of an influence on a game of football than Vern did ... wherever he went the winning rate would have to be up in the 90 per cent.'

Although Vern continued to play at a lower level, his departure from top-flight football symbolised the end of an era where North Queenslanders could – if they so desired – remain in their hometown, secure a decent job for life, enjoy a good standard of football in the Foley Shield, and become near-enough to household names. 'We used to get 10- to 12,000 people to a Foley Shield final in Townsville,' recalled Alf Abdullah, a secretary of the Sarina Crocodiles. 'Trainloads used to come down from Mount Isa. People would go from Mackay, they'd all flock in to Townsville, you'd go to Magnetic Island in the morning and then come back for the football.'

However for a younger generation of players, such as Vern Daisy's nephew, Scott Prince, rugby league was now in a state of flux.

Moreover, the population of areas such as Mount Isa, where Prince was playing junior football, were in decline. Working conditions had worsened, and the lure of football in Brisbane and Sydney, where professional contracts and big money were increasingly on offer, was more than anything one could hope to earn playing footy in the diminished Foley Shield. In other words, people's focus and aspirations became much less localised.

The only resolution to this conundrum was to enter a side from the north in an expanded Sydney competition. Four years before his death, Ron McAuliffe had floated the idea for a side based out of Townsville to enter a national league, while several North Queensland greats, such as Rod Reddy, had also suggested such a move.

On Saturday 13 May 1989, tickets to the Panasonic Cup match between the Brisbane Broncos and the Parramatta Eels went on sale in Townsville. At 7 am a long line of enthusiastic locals, some dressed in footy shorts and thongs, others wearing wide-brimmed Akubra hats, waited for the rugby league club to open. Standing four abreast, the queue stretched more than 500 metres around the block from Redpath Street to the Grammar School. By the end of the day 14,000 tickets had been sold. 'The Broncos phenomenon,' reported the *Townsville Bulletin*, 'has united Queensland on a scale not even cyclone and flood appeals could manage.'[28]

Temporary spectator facilities were hastily erected at the Townsville Sports Reserve, the spiritual home of North Queensland football. The attendance for the Panasonic Cup clash was reported at 16,000, although some said it might have been double that, if only the old ground could have accommodated the immense congregation of people. It was Queensland's biggest rugby league crowd for a match outside of Brisbane, and a fireworks display thanked the city on behalf of the NSWRL. The Broncos, encouraged by the partisan crowd, ran in seven tries to win by 36 points.

It was the match that changed North Queensland rugby league

forever. Before he returned to Sydney, Ken Arthurson, the chairman of the NSWRL, told *Townsville Bulletin* reporter Doug Kingston that he could envision a North Queensland side entering the competition within a few years.[29] 'All we need now,' wrote Kingston, 'is for the Townsville City Council and the State and Federal Governments to back the move by financing improvements at the Sports Reserve. It's going to take a team effort, but I've got no doubt that it will happen.'[30]

In the next eight weeks, the Brisbane Broncos would win the Panasonic Cup title – securing the club's first piece of silverware – and Queensland again completed a clean sweep in the State of Origin, taking the unbeaten streak to six games.

In the space of a decade, the Maroons had won 18 Origin matches and lost just nine. In the process, Queenslanders witnessed a generation of young men become heroes and the birth of an underdog legend that would inspire many more generations to come.

The state's premier football league and many of its pioneer clubs had all but collapsed, and the regional competitions – including the Foley Shield – were contracting. Yet the State League was here to stay, as well as the new professional clubs in Brisbane, the Gold Coast, and eventually the North Queensland Cowboys in Townsville. The localism of the BRL and the Foley Shield would soon to be eclipsed by the arrival of a national competition.

The player drain, as well as the tyranny of distance and decentralisation, were now being addressed and exciting new opportunities were emerging for Queenslanders throughout the state. Young men such as Allan Langer were proof of that.

PART II

HOW RUGBY LEAGUE EXPLAINS ...
QUEENSLAND'S COMING OF AGE

LANG PARK IN 1999
'LANG PARK HAS GIVEN BRISBANE AND QUEENSLAND AN IDENTITY.'
(PHOTOGRAPH COURTESY OF SUNCORP STADIUM)

5

THE COPERNICAN REVOLUTION

1990–1992

On the first Tuesday of February 1990, Arthur Beetson jogged onto Lang Park dressed in maroon shorts, long socks, and a size 56 jersey, with a rugby league ball tucked under his arm. A group of children in club jerseys tried to tackle him to the ground. Just like the days of old, Big Artie refused to be felled. 'At my weight,' he quipped, 'I could have squashed a kid.'[1]

Watching on were more than 300 guests including the new state premier and rugby league tragic, Wayne Goss. The ceremony, which was organised by a television network and the Queensland Rugby League, celebrated the selection of 17 'Origin All-Stars' from the past decade. The players were a roll-call of Queensland heroes, hailing from all parts of the state: Kerry Boustead, Gene Miles, Greg Dowling, and Dale Shearer from the north; Mal Meninga and Chris Close from central Queensland; and Gary Belcher, Allan Langer, Paul Vautin, Wally Fullerton-Smith, Greg Conescu, Rod Morris, Mark Murray, Tony Currie, and Bryan Niebling from the southeast. Beetson, Roma's favourite son, was picked despite his humble protests, while the captain was the Emperor of Lang Park – Wally Lewis.

Ken Arthurson said that Lewis had been the difference between

Queensland and New South Wales during the 1980s, and predicted that he would retain the captaincy of Australia in 1990.[2] It was the start of Lewis's testimonial year, and even before a ball had been kicked the QRL and Power's Brewery contributed nearly $100,000 to his testimonial fund.

Yet his position at the Brisbane Broncos was already under threat. Having turned 30 in the off-season, Lewis had been sacked as captain and shifted to lock forward to make way for the new halves pairing of Allan Langer and Kevin Walters. It was 'one of the bravest decisions in the history of sport in Australia', argued league writer Steve Ricketts.[3]

'I always felt that when Wally was on the field, whatever team he was captaining had a chance,' Ricketts later explained. 'I just felt that he could play on forever. But it became obvious when he hit 30, 31, that he hadn't looked after himself that well. He didn't have the flexibility. Whatever sports science was available I don't think Wally availed himself of it. He just relied on his natural instinct.'

Following trial matches in Toowoomba, Cairns, and Bundaberg, the Broncos hosted Canterbury-Bankstown in a pre-season match at Lang Park. Brisbane's first try was scored by hooker Kerrod Walters. Three minutes into the second half, Kerrod's twin brother, Kevin, crossed over. And after Allan Langer scored the third try, the match finished 32 points to six to the Broncos.

The combination of Langer and the Walters twins had been first spotted at the Ipswich Jets in the mid-1980s. In fact, there were five Walters brothers – Brett, Andrew, Steve, Kevin, and Kerrod – and they had been just as formidable at backyard footy in Ipswich as the Langer brothers Cliff, Kevin, Neville, and Allan.

When he was young, Kevin Walters had idolised Wally Lewis from afar. 'When I signed with the Broncos,' he recalled, 'I was hoping just to get a few games and maybe fill in when Wally was injured and work my way into the team when he retired.' Now, as Lewis's body began to give way to the rigours of more than a decade of first-grade football,

Walters found himself ushering in Lewis's least memorable season.[4]

The sacking of Lewis as Broncos captain would cause a long rift between him and Gene Miles, cement coach Wayne Bennett as the ultimate authority at the club, and mark the beginning the end of Wally's time at the Broncos. 'There was probably three or four choices,' Miles remembered. 'There was Greg Dowling and myself from the older brigade, and Kevvie Walters and Allan Langer. I put my hand up and said, "Listen, I think Wally will accept the captaincy coming to me more so than giving it to Alf or Kevvie, seeing that we had played so much footy together." We were great mates, so I thought Wally would accept that no problem, you know, we'll get on and play. How wrong I was.'

In the first seven rounds, a frustrated Lewis started just three matches for the Broncos and strained his hamstring, which sidelined him for the first match of State of Origin. Queensland lost Game I and then the series. 'In the first match, Queensland looked like a ship without a rudder,' observed Greg Dowling. 'I suppose you could say Wally has been like a rudder without a ship.'[5]

But while Queensland struggled the Broncos continued winning. By the end of August, Kevin Walters had not missed a single match and, in the semifinal against Manly-Warringah, he and Peter Jackson – the only two men who had pulled on Wally's No. 6 jumper all season – scored a try each to put the Broncos one win away from the grand final.

Bennett's decision to axe Lewis was further vindicated at the Dally M Awards, where Kevin Walters was named players' player and Gene Miles best captain. And just days before the preliminary final, the Broncos directors told Lewis that he would need to take a pay cut to remain at the club in 1991. 'It was like the Copernican Revolution,' Barry Maranta told Wally's biographer, Adrian McGregor. 'Everyone thought the sun revolved around the Earth. The Broncos do not revolve around Wally Lewis.'[6]

A new decade lay ahead, one that would have no time for sentiment or loyalty. Football clubs were now constrained by the realities of the salary cap and the need to make long-term business decisions. By year's end, after being released by the Broncos, Lewis would agree to move south to join the Gold Coast Seagulls. It was the start of his long farewell to rugby league.

One fan letter, published by the *Courier-Mail*, summed up a feeling shared by many Queenslanders:

> Wally, thanks a million, mate, for the hours of watching pleasure you have given me since I first saw you turn out for Fortitude Valley. Thanks for the tries you have scored; the dummies you have thrown; the tackles you have made; the kicks that have found touch; and all the footballers you have made look like champions by putting them through gaps. Thanks for being a Queenslander through and through.[7]

Time stands still for no man, though, and in Lewis's absence 'the Ipswich connection' – as the Walters brothers and Allan Langer came to be known – laid the foundation for what would be a breakthrough period for the Brisbane Broncos.

Between 1990 and 1992, the Broncos would truly capture the imagination of the city and the state.[8] Hayley Lewis, a 15-year-old swimmer from Brisbane who had just returned home from the 1990 Commonwealth Games with five gold medals, gushed over the Broncos and told reporters that she was dying to meet Langer.[9]

In the end, the Broncos would bow out in the preliminary final, but learn a valuable lesson in the process. No player – not even King Wally – was bigger than the club.

Despite all the tumult and controversy, the Broncos had pulled the biggest crowds of the competition, achieved a record-breaking winning streak of 11 games, introduced youngsters Willie Carne and Paul Hauff to first grade, and uncovered a sensational Indigenous centre, Steve Renouf, in reserve grade. Six Broncos players, including the Walters brothers and Langer, earned selection for the end-of-year Kangaroos tour. 'In many ways,' remembered Bennett, '1990 was the beginning of the Broncos.'[10]

★

After more than a decade of top-flight football, Kerry Boustead decided to call time on his career in 1990. He had a wife and three young children, a nice house, a bottle shop, and a good job in the insurance industry. The country boy from Innisfail was well and truly settled in Sydney. Yet when he was offered the role as promotions manager for the bid to establish a Winfield Cup team in North Queensland, he couldn't refuse.

It didn't matter that the job offered half the money he was on, or that he would have to overturn his family's comfortable lifestyle. He was a loyal North Queenslander consumed by one overriding desire: to build a professional club which would provide opportunities for future generations of players from the north, so they wouldn't need to make the same move he did as a young man.

Things did not begin well. The Bousteads' first trip to Townsville was interrupted during the layover in Brisbane, where they were informed that theirs were standby tickets, and that someone else had paid full price and taken the seats. While their luggage continued to Townsville, Kerry and his wife, Leigh, were forced to stay overnight in Brisbane until the flight the next day. Leigh turned to her husband, unimpressed by the delay. 'These blokes,' she said, 'are a bunch of cowboys.'

The fiasco, as well as his wife's comment, would stick in Kerry Boustead's memory for the next two years as he worked quietly towards establishing the North Queensland Cowboys.

From the outset, Boustead was determined that the Cowboys would be a professional outfit that would represent the whole of

North Queensland, not just Townsville. He would drive thousands of kilometres to Mackay, to Cairns, and across to Mount Isa – often stopping at Julia Creek and Cloncurry along the way – to make sure everyone felt included in the project.

In 1991, Townsville was home to 114,000 residents, while Cairns, Mackay, and Mount Isa added another 166,000 people. The distance between these centres put North Queensland, an enormous but sparsely populated region, at a tremendous disadvantage.

Establishing a professional football team was no easy task, especially when the case for inclusion would ultimately be decided by Sydney powerbrokers. Yet Boustead had developed good relations with the establishment down south. During his career in Sydney he had played for both Eastern Suburbs and Manly-Warringah – two clubs closely associated with New South Wales Rugby League supremos John Quayle and Ken Arthurson.

Doug Kingston, the former sports editor of the *Townsville Bulletin*, believed that Boustead commanded such respect off the field because he had proven himself on it. 'Not only was he a great player, he was also a brave player,' remembered Kingston. 'I've seen him tackle guys twice his size and drive them over the sideline. He punched above his weight. People in North Queensland admire that sort of thing.'

Like many northerners, Boustead had little faith in the Brisbane-based administration of the QRL. When the governing body decided to support the inclusion of a second club from Brisbane – the team that would later become the South Queensland Crushers – he denounced its behaviour as 'unethical'. In an article for the *Townsville Bulletin*, he likened competing against the rival bid to 'betting against a racehorse owned and raced by the stewards', and queried how the QRL could finance a team of its own.[11]

During the first decade of State of Origin, one of Queensland's great strengths was the tight-knit culture fostered by the players. There had been rivalries among the Brisbane clubs, of course, as well as between the regional towns, but unlike New South Wales the interests of the state had always been of paramount concern. In that context, a large part of Origin's appeal in Queensland was its intensely narrow focus: it allowed Queenslanders, fired by their little-brother resentment, to put aside their differences and work towards the common goal of beating New South Wales. Quite simply, there was no bigger prize.

Even when the Broncos entered the Sydney competition, they quickly became a *de facto* Queensland club, not least because the Gold Coast side had spent its early years based across the border in Tweed Heads. Yet as two more Queensland bids jostled to become the next side to join the Sydney competition, some feared that narrow club interests and geographic rivalries would disrupt state unity. In an interview with *Rugby League Week*, Broncos utility Tony Currie called a QRL-backed side a 'ludicrous business practice' that might cause the demise of Origin.[12]

Meanwhile, Boustead had run-ins with the Broncos hierarchy from the very beginning. 'I used to go down to Brisbane and I'd be sitting in a restaurant talking to a sponsor,' he later recalled, 'and if Porky Morgan or one of the others was there, they'd abuse me. They'd make out that North Queensland were never going to get a start, and it was a joke, and why are you talking to these sponsors? They wanted Queensland to themselves.'

Another factor threatening to divide the Queensland rugby league community was the appointment of Graham Lowe, a New Zealand-born coach who had taken over the Maroons following the sacking of Arthur Beetson. Lowe was also the coach of Manly-Warringah and had masterminded the renaissance in New Zealand football during the mid-1980s, as well as Wigan's revival in the English competition.

Not since 1973, when New South Welshman Wally O'Connell guided Queensland to three defeats without scoring a single point, had a non-Queenslander coached the Maroons. Lowe, however, had the advantage of being from New Zealand, not New South Wales, as well as the fact that he had guided Norths Devils from fifth place in 1979 to Brisbane premiers in 1980.

Yet even this association with the Brisbane Rugby League was not enough to convince many Queenslanders. After all, the founding principle of State of Origin was to provide an opportunity for their boys to prove themselves against New South Wales, without outside assistance. Wally Lewis, one of Lowe's staunchest advocates, could see the tension brewing. 'When he was appointed, people had the shits,' he remembered. 'They said, "He's not a Queenslander." There was a bit of a sharp division.'

The state of Queensland, as many historians and sociologists observed, had long nourished a streak of xenophobia. The former state premier Joh Bjelke-Petersen had worn it almost as a badge of honour. 'They call us rednecks and other names in the south,' he said in 1977.

> If it is so bad here why are we the fastest-growing state? Why is it so many of them come here to live and work? Half our unemployed are southerners, enjoying the sun. I couldn't care less what they think of us. One day Queensland will be the greatest state in Australia.[13]

And yet, despite Queensland's parochialism, interstate migrants – or 'southerners', as they were called – were a key aspect of the state's identity. In the decade to 1991, Queensland experienced the fastest rate of population growth of any state in the country, and between 1986 and 1991 three-quarters of those migrants came from either New South Wales or Victoria.

Three of the Queensland's pre-eminent rugby league reporters – Steve Ricketts of the *Courier-Mail*, Tony Durkin of *Rugby League Week*, and Wayne Heming of *Australian Associated Press* – were actually from New South Wales. Heming was born in Sydney, moved to Brisbane in 1979, and covered every Origin series from 1980 to 2015. 'When I came here,' he explained, 'I was the new kid on the block. Steve Ricketts was reporting here, Barry Dick, David Falkenmire, Bernie Pramberg. I'd come from Sydney where I was competing with Peter Frilingos, Ray Chesterton, Ian Heads, Ray Hadley – top-ranked journos.

'These journos up here put their hand out like a friend and helped me. In Sydney? You ask any other journo and it's, "Sorry mate, can't help you." Straight away I felt welcome in Queensland; it was all like a family. That spread through to the players. They were more humble. So I just adapted very quickly and thought, *Gee, I like this*.'

Already there was an established tradition of accepting the honorary or adopted Queenslander. The captain of the state cricket team, Allan Border, was later inducted as one of the 150 'icons' of Queensland despite being born and raised in Sydney. Glenn Lazarus, a New South Wales prop forward, would spend six seasons with the Brisbane Broncos and later be elected to the Senate in Queensland. Perhaps the best-known honorary Queenslander, however, was the cane toad. Since it was introduced to the Little Mulgrave Creek in 1935, Queenslanders had developed a love–hate relationship with the imported pest.

The first 100 toads were let loose in Gordonvale, a sugar town just south of Cairns, to eradicate the cane beetle which had ruined many harvests. The repulsive, toxic toads ignored the beetles but began to kill much of the native wildlife, all the while multiplying and spreading across the state. The creatures soon become an accepted part of life in Queensland. In the *Townsville Bulletin*, for instance, there was a regular column titled 'Cane Toad', while in Brisbane, the *Cane Toad Times* – a satirical, political newspaper – took its name because of the 'repulsion it evoked, the feeling of fear and loathing that typified being twenty-something in the Deep North'.[14] In Sarina, 300 kilometres north of Rockhampton, a fibreglass statue of a cane toad – modelled on other 'big' tourist attractions such as Coffs Harbour's Big Banana and Nambour's Big Pineapple – was nicknamed 'Buffy' by the locals.

In 1988 the documentary *Cane Toads: an unnatural history* became a cult classic, showcasing the various ways in which the cane toad had become a distinctive Queensland symbol. 'The Queenslanders are terribly protective of them,' one man told the filmmakers, adding: 'They regard them with a sort of perverted reverence.'[15]

Nowhere was this reverence more evident than during the State of Origin series. Since the early 1980s, Barry Muir's 'cockroach' nickname for New South Welshmen had been matched with a cane toad mascot for Queensland. Within a few years, the catch-cry 'cockroaches versus cane toads' had become as readily associated with Origin as 'state versus state, mate versus mate'.

The exact origins of the cane toad symbol were never clear. According to Mike Benson, who worked in marketing for the QRL, the idea did not come out of Queensland. 'We experimented with a mudcrab, gave him muscles and a mean look and all that, but the public took little interest,' Benson once told the *Courier-Mail*.

> Then we played around with a red stag idea, but that sank without a ripple. We spent a fair amount of money researching and were still looking when the cane toad started to emerge out of New South Wales. The rumour is that some member of the public was spotted wearing a home-drawn t-shirt depicting a toad being bashed by a cockroach. A marketing company picked up the theme and our symbols were born.[16]

In 1987, when the QRL held a residents-versus-expatriates trial match, Brisbane-based players wore a maroon-and-white jersey with a cane toad logo, while Sydney-based players wore a blue jersey with a cockroach logo. Yet unlike New South Welshmen, who generally rejected the cockroach nickname bestowed upon them, Queenslanders took pride in their association with the cane toad. 'They're synonymous with us, aren't they?' Mal Meninga later explained. 'They are a bit of a pest. You can run over them, beat 'em up and they just keep coming back. It suits our mentality. It's what you get with Queenslanders.'[17]

Throughout the 1980s Wally Lewis, the undisputed leader of Queensland's cane toad army, had been the biggest pest for New South Wales. In the decade leading up to 1991, he had missed just two State of Origin matches, and when he took the field Queensland won far more often than not.

As the Maroons went into camp for the 1991 series, Lewis and Meninga were the last remaining link to the original squad that ran out with Arthur Beetson in 1980. Unlike Mal, who had moved to Canberra, Wally had played his entire career in his home state. This, almost as much as his prodigious talent, had elevated him to God-like status. Here was living proof that a Queenslander could stay at home and become the best in the world at their trade.

Lewis, wrote Roy Masters, 'gave the Maroons respectability at a time the meanderings of Joh, the excesses of the White Shoe Brigade and the revelations of the Fitzgerald Inquiry were rendering the Deep North a laughing stock'.[18]

But his knees were shot, his left arm still recovering from a break earlier in the season, and people could see that his Origin career was drawing to a close. He still had a little more to give, however, and in Game I the Lang Park crowd chanted his name as he guided Queensland to a two-point victory.

When a brawl started in Game II at the Sydney Football Stadium, he squared up to New South Wales enforcer Mark Geyer, who was much younger, stood a head taller and weighed in ten kilograms heavier. Queensland lost the game, but the vision of Lewis and Geyer snarling at one another reverberated around the two states, reaffirming Lewis as a hero among his people. This was an image Queenslanders could identify with: a little guy standing up to the big guy, never taking a backwards step despite the inherent disadvantage.

With the series level at one game each, and the scores locked at 18–18, Game III at Lang Park would be the decider. Several former New South Wales players criticised Lewis for his part in the brawl during Game II, while the QRL decided to erect high fences around the 'Pig Pen' in front of the Fourex bar and sell the rest of the punters beer in plastic cups. 'They were just concrete terraces at the two ends,' remembered Brisbane sportswriter Phil Lutton. 'We would always sit up in the terraces, no seats, and there was the sheer hatred of anyone with the New South Wales jersey on. And it wasn't joking – people with blue jerseys would walk down the front to go to the toilet and people would literally get up and pelt them with drinks. It was rough. It was old-school. I loved it.'

Yet as the excitement grew, Lewis and his wife were informed that their one-year-old daughter, Jamie-Lee, was profoundly deaf. Important though State of Origin was to Lewis, his family were his 'chosen ones'. He promptly informed team manager Dick 'Tosser' Turner that this would be the last time he would pull on a Queensland jumper. 'It's good to hear that, mate,' Lewis recalled Tosser saying, 'because if you didn't tell me, I'd be telling you it's time.'

Before kick-off, they relayed the news to the rest of the squad. Then, as the players ran down the tunnel and onto the field, the Lang Park gallery bowed theatrically to their captain, chanted his name, and waved banners that read 'WALLY: STILL KING' and 'HAIL KING WALLY'. Many of them had donned specialised 'Toad Warrior' T-shirts with a cane toad emblazoned on the front, while others held aloft stuffed cane toads dressed in maroon jumpers. The toads, which had been produced by two Townsville tannery workers, were an instant hit.

The Blues scored first, but trailed by four points at half-time. After the break, however, two tries to New South Wales allowed them to regain the lead and the momentum. Lewis stood shell-shocked in his own in-goal area, hands on his hips, eyes staring into the distance. The score was 12–8 to New South Wales and time was running out.

From Queensland's next set of six, New South Wales fullback Greg Alexander collected Lewis's grubber kick and expertly rushed the ball out of danger and up to the halfway line. Then Queensland conceded a penalty from a scrum.

But the Maroons were not yet finished. After bravely defending their own line, Willie Carne dashed down the wing to relieve pressure. Queensland were then awarded a penalty after Allan Langer was dragged down by Brad Fittler, giving them perfect field position to attack.

After four hit-ups took Queensland to within metres of the try-line, the ball travelled like a hot potato through the hands of Steve Walters, Peter Jackson, Allan Langer, Paul Hauff, and Mal Meninga. Standing in the tackle, Meninga spun around and returned the ball to Langer, who found Dale Shearer on the left with a long, looping pass. Shearer pinned his ears back and galloped over to level the scores. It was a classic never-say-die Queensland try. Meninga, who had missed his first three attempts at goal, now converted from the sideline to make it 14 points to 12.

The crowd had barely stopped cheering when a voice from above crackled around the ground: 'This is Wally Lewis's 30th and final State of Origin game.' The Lang Park scoreboard flashed a message of thanks to its Emperor and with just ten minutes left to play, the result should never have been in doubt. As the fans counted down the seconds, Lewis rose from a tackle and played the ball one last time. 'It's all over!' yelled match commentator Ray Warren, as Lewis was mobbed by his teammates. 'Queensland take out the '91 series – easily the best series in Origin history!'

A sideline reporter pulled Wally out of the scrum of celebrating Maroons and asked him to confirm his retirement. 'Yeah, that's it, mate,' Lewis responded, his voice warbling with emotion. 'I got a little girl to look after now. I love her very much.'

It may not been a vintage performance from Wally – he looked like a bank manager who had tripped down a flight of stairs: left eye swollen, moustache askew, his receding hairline tangled and dripping with perspiration – but his sheer presence, as always, had fused a bond between fans and players. 'That third game, you felt like the crowd was pushing you down the oval,' remembered Queensland's rookie second-rower Mike McLean. 'That was Wally.'

Two days later, the *Courier-Mail* reporter Lawrie Kavanagh – who had publicly called for the introduction of State of Origin way back in 1979 – thanked him for giving Queenslanders confidence to take on the world. 'I believe the least we can do to honour Lewis,' wrote Kavanagh, 'would be a bronze statue of the man erected at Lang Park by public subscription.'[19]

It was not the first time Kavanagh had called for such a statue to be built, but Lewis's emotional exit from State of Origin created the urgency to get it done. Following a campaign by the *Courier-Mail*, the public raised $10,000 for a local sculpture company to build a 175-kilogram, 2.5-metre-tall bronze Wally. 'Some donations were as large as $100 but the majority were between $5 and $20,' wrote Adrian McGregor. 'The appeal was no corporate jaunt; it was funded by the very smallest, rank and file rugby league fan.'[20]

★

Before Lewis could retire for good there was time for one final farewell to his favourite football ground. On the last Sunday of March 1992, he led the Gold Coast Seagulls onto Lang Park against his old club, the Brisbane Broncos. The crowd stood and applauded as King Wally strode out of the tunnel, blue-and-white butchers striped jersey tucked in, white socks pulled right up to the knee.

In four seasons the Gold Coast had won just one game against the Broncos, but by half-time the underdogs led by six points. The Emperor of Lang Park was at home in his kingdom.

'Lewis' 32-year-old right leg,' observed one reporter, 'seemed to launch kicks in general play further than in recent years, carried along by a wave of goodwill.'[21]

Yet after being crunched by former teammate Kerrod Walters, Lewis was forced from the field for most of the second half. When he returned, the Seagulls led 18–16 with nine minutes left to play. Before Lewis could reassert his authority on the game, Allan Langer crossed over to seal the victory for Brisbane. 'There have been better exits for me from Lang Park,' Lewis conceded after full-time.[22]

It proved difficult to say goodbye. Five weeks later, in the first State of Origin game since Lewis's retirement, Queensland went down to New South Wales in Sydney. The selectors asked him to pull on the boots for Game II in Brisbane but Wally, who was enjoying spending more time with his family, declined the offer.

Yet he was still the King, and as his statue emerged theatrically from a giant, purpose-built crown before kick-off, the Lang Park crowd roared their approval. Tacky though the ceremony may have been, the statue would assume almost religious significance to Queenslanders on their annual pilgrimage to Lang Park. In time, as Lang Park was redeveloped into Suncorp Stadium, bronze Wally would be shifted from the terraces to the stadium's entrance. 'Usually when you go to the footy and you're meeting someone, you'll say at Gate A,' explained Greg Adermann, the communications manager of Suncorp Stadium. 'The most common thing we hear is: "I'll meet you at Wally." You go out the front on game day and see people getting their photos and congregating around Wally. It's not Gate A or Gate D or the railway station or at a pub. It's: "I'll meet you at Wally."'

Queensland gave bronze Wally a perfect christening by winning Game II, but lost the series a fortnight later. It was the beginning of a three-year losing streak – the longest Queensland had experienced in the State of Origin era – as the Maroons struggled to find a replacement for their captain.

There were no such problems for the Brisbane Broncos, however. In the second half of the season, the Broncos lost just once to claim the minor premiership – 25 points ahead of Lewis's last-placed Seagulls. Having moved out of King Wally's shadow, the Broncos were now also ready to leave behind the most treasured piece of real estate in Queensland rugby league. Frustrated by the Lang Park Trust's strict commercial regulations, which prevented them from selling Power's beer, the Broncos made a deal with Jim Soorley, the newly elected lord mayor of Brisbane, to move to the council-owned QEII Stadium.

Soorley, a plain-speaking former Catholic priest, had swept into City Hall with a promise to revitalise Brisbane. He said that he would make the river blue again, and promised to cut his own salary if elected. His unorthodox campaign won the support of the public and caught the incumbent lord mayor, Sallyanne Atkinson, by surprise. For weeks after the election she refused to believe she had been beaten.

'In those early years,' remembered one reporter, 'Soorley overhauled Brisbane's public transport, introduced civilised restaurant by-laws, protected Brisbane's skyline from overdevelopment, cleaned up the Brisbane River, introduced a City Cats ferry system, and generally gave the city some style and zing.'[23]

Others, such as Brothers supporter Tom Cranitch, found him aloof and arrogant. In the early days of Soorley's reign, Cranitch had been interviewed for a job as his speechwriter and research officer. As a member of the Labor Party and a recent university graduate, he had stepped into the mayor's office quietly confident of his chances. 'His first question to me, after a deadpan silence, was: "Are you a winner?"' Cranitch recalled years later. 'Still to this day, I think, *What a wanker*. Seriously. He ended up being a fantastic lord mayor, but automatically my skin crawled.'

In the Broncos, Soorley could see a winner. In many ways, they were made for one another. The club's upstart, aspirational attitude, and its fight with the old hierarchies of the QRL, mirrored his own battles with the entrenched interests of the state Labor Party machine.

The Broncos' decision to leave Lang Park may have been met with shock and outrage among rugby league supporters, including Premier Wayne Goss, but not from Soorley. 'I was on the side of sense,' he said. 'The City owned [QEII] Stadium; we ran it for all the other sports, and we were losing money. It was a *de facto* state facility, but we as a city were subsidising it, and it was going downhill fast. So Porky [Morgan] and I talked about going out there, we did a bit of work, and he said, "Alright, we'll go."'

For all the Broncos' backroom braggadocio, the football side had developed a hard edge after five seasons in the Sydney competition. This was widely attributed to Trevor Gillmeister, the nuggety club captain who didn't miss a single game all season. In a team of superstars he was old-school grit. He was not a big man, but was respected across the competition for his superb tackling technique and quiet bravery. Gillmeister, wrote one reporter, 'represents that hard edge and the consistency that had been lacking from the free-flowing Broncos of the past'.[24]

The team left for Sydney to play in its first grand final with the state of Queensland firmly behind them. A farmer from the Darling Downs seeded his paddock so that the grass grew with the words 'BRONCOS TO WIN'. Channel 9 televised *Broncos: Bound for Glory*, a documentary about the formation of the club to its first grand final appearance. Hundreds of Queenslanders from all parts of the state sent well-wishes to the Broncos' office. And by train, car, and aeroplane the supporters – including the lord mayor and the state premier – followed their team south.

Sensing the profundity of the occasion, one editorial in the *Courier-Mail* claimed the grand final against St George could be seen as 'the old pitched against the new, the traditional against the modern, the past against the future'.

> It is not too fanciful to suggest that Brisbane is a city of the future and Sydney, well, its best years are behind it. Consider, for example, the huge population growth around Brisbane. Consider, too, the changes in Brisbane in the last decade, of which the Broncos are an important part.[25]

It took just ten minutes for the Broncos to score the first points, as Langer ran the ball on the last tackle, combined brilliantly with Gavin Allen, and scored under the posts. From there the visitors never lost the lead, scoring four more tries to win by 20 points. The fourth try, scored by the Broncos' mercurial centre Steve Renouf, was one of the greatest of all time.

It happened on the 60-minute mark: Langer received the ball from dummy half, five metres out from his own in-goal line. He spun the ball wide to Renouf, who stepped off his left foot to evade one tackler and sprinted 95 metres to score, leaving a trail of would-be tacklers in his wake. For many onlookers, this was the defining image of the Brisbane Broncos – a majestic, attacking team that sought to entertain from start to finish. 'That was a typical Broncos team try,' Renouf later explained.[26]

There were other memorable moments and standout performances, too. Second-rower Alan Cann jinked and stepped like a fullback for his two tries, while Gillmeister, claimed Wally Lewis, was the 'unsung hero' of the final. 'Gilly's defence was something else,' he said. 'He must have had 100 tackles up by half-time.'[27]

The players returned to Brisbane next day to a jubilant throng of Queenslanders. 'The deafening noise,' observed one reporter, 'almost lifted the roof off the Ansett terminal.'[28] Gillmeister walked into the mob with his grandfather, Ted, a veteran of World War II. 'He was over the moon,' recalled Gillmeister. 'The thing that sticks in my head, when we got off the plane, there were streamers everywhere and hundreds and hundreds of people, and my grandfather tapped me on the shoulder and said, "Trev, how good's this? I tell you what, this is better than winning the war!"'

If the 1980s was Queensland's renaissance, the 1990s marked the beginning of Queensland's period of modernity. And the Broncos were the sporting symbol of that transition. Unlike Queensland's Origin side, which competed just three times a year, the Broncos were a permanent, week-to-week proposition that Queenslanders could believe in and be proud of.

In the days following the grand final, a wave of congratulations letters arrived at the *Courier-Mail*. 'I am not a Broncos fanatic,' read one, 'but the way those boys danced The Cockroach Crunch was magnificent. No wonder so many people reported sick on Monday with "Broncitis".'[29]

Confidence swept through Brisbane. Mayor Soorley handed the Broncos the keys to the city. Alfie Langer crowd-surfed like a lead singer at a rock concert. 'Hey Hey We're the Broncos', a song recorded by The Ipswich Connection – a band comprising Langer and the Walters twins – topped the Queensland charts. And former Bronco Tony Currie expected rugby league's newest team to win three or four of the next five premierships. 'The Broncos,' he wrote, 'have thrown down the challenge to the other 15 teams in the Winfield Cup to match their level of skill or face an era of domination.'[30]

Over the course of the next decade, as the city shed its small-town mentality and emerged as an expansive, sophisticated metropolis, the Brisbane Broncos would play finals football every season, win four more premierships, and lead an off-field revolution that would shake the very foundations of Australian rugby league.

6

ON THE SHELL OF A MUDCRAB AND THE SKIN OF A MANGO

1993–1996

From the moment he broke into the Brisbane competition, Peter Jackson was expected to become a superstar. *Rugby League Week* heralded him as 'one of the personality players of Brisbane football', while others compared him favourably to former greats of the game.[1] By 1986 he had won a premiership with Souths and been selected for the Queensland State of Origin side.

Like Mal Meninga, Jackson was a tall, strapping police officer and centre. He was classically handsome with dark hair, a strong jaw, and a wiry frame. A tremendous all-round sportsman, as a teenager he had excelled at athletics and represented his country in schoolboys rugby union. Although raised in a middle-class household and educated at a private school, 'Jacko' had a larrikin streak that endeared him to the blue-collar boys of rugby league. He was the life of the room and the footy field, partying and training harder than anyone.

His wild personality, as well as his mischievous grin, also made him very popular with women. He had met his wife, Siobhan O'Brien, in October 1985 at the Brothers Leagues Club in Innisfail. Peter was there as a member of the touring police rugby league side; Siobhan, from a working-class Irish Catholic family, was there because her father said grace for the team before dinner.

The weekend prior she had watched Jacko play in the BRL grand final between Souths and Wynnum-Manly and thought, *Wow, this guy is amazing.* But he looked even better from across the room of her hometown leagues club. Siobhan waltzed over, introduced herself, and asked if he knew a friend of hers who also played for Souths.

'Sure do,' Jacko responded. 'Here, hold these.'

Handing Siobhan his glass of bourbon and half-finished cigarette, he requested 'Walking on Sunshine' by Katrina and the Waves and asked her to dance. They hit it off immediately. By the time Jackson moved to Canberra, in 1987, he and Siobhan were an item – the perfect Queensland union of northern country girl and southern city boy. 'I thought Siobhan was madder than him, to be honest,' recalled Mike McLean, who was there on the evening they met. 'She held her own. I think that's what people loved about them both.'

Many Queenslanders believed Jackson had the talent to fill the shoes of Wally Lewis. Jacko himself had set a goal not only to take Wally's spot, but to one day captain the Kangaroos. In 1988, he scored two tries in his debut match for Australia and replaced an injured Lewis in Game I of Origin. 'He was the ultimate team man,' recalled Lewis. 'It was a painful experience missing that game, and I remember at the end I wrapped my arms around him – we were all celebrating – and he said, "You want your jersey back?" I said, "No, mate, it's yours." He said, "Oh, okay, well, the next time you're wearing it, try not to let it down!" I got a giggle out of that.'

In two seasons with the Brisbane Broncos, Jackson failed to nail down a starting spot, so in 1991 he signed with North Sydney. Already a heavy user of marijuana, he knew that the lifestyle waiting for him in the big city was a risk. Yet the lure of Norths, where he was offered the chance to finally establish himself as a five-eighth, overrode those concerns. In his mind, this was the first step to earning back that

Queensland No. 6 jumper. 'I want that spot bad,' Jackson told one reporter in 1992. 'There is no doubt in my mind that I'm the man for the job.'[2]

Injuries, as well as recurring headaches, worked against him. At the beginning of 1993, he told reporters that the headaches were the result of leaking cerebral fluid from his spine. Siobhan, however, believed that Peter's lifestyle was also a contributing factor. 'I remember getting on a plane to see his father in Brisbane, and Peter couldn't even hold his head up,' she recalled. 'He was in so much pain – I suspect his cocaine use may have caused the headaches.'

During this time, Lex Marinos, an actor, radio presenter, and North Sydney supporter, went on fishing trips with Jackson and noticed another side to his friend. 'We talked a bit about footy,' he recalled, 'but the thing about the fishing that I loved was that Peter was really quiet. It was a time when he wasn't going at 100 miles an hour. That was when he was at his most unguarded, and where I learned more about him than at any other time.

'What became really apparent was his level of insecurity. His sense of identity was really fragile. Peter was at that stage where he knew the end was just a season or two away, and he was really concerned that once he stopped playing, would he still have an identity? Would people still like him? Did they only like him because he was a footballer? And once that was taken away … what was he?'

As Jacko languished on the sidelines for North Sydney, his former club soared to even greater heights. On Sunday 28 March 1993, the Brisbane Broncos hosted Parramatta at its new home ground. More than 50,000 people turned up to QEII, which had been rebranded as ANZ Stadium and decked out in Broncos colours and Power's Brewery advertisements.

It hardly mattered that the first match ended in a loss: a week later, 46,000 people were on hand to witness the Broncos beat Canberra, and by the end of the regular season nearly half-a-million people had clicked through the turnstiles at ANZ, at an unprecedented average of more than 40,000 spectators per game. Later it would be revealed that thousands of free tickets were distributed around Brisbane each week, but the crowds were impressive nonetheless. The Broncos directors wanted a full stadium every other weekend to show their sponsors that they were backing a go-ahead business.

The move to ANZ Stadium allowed the club to open more than 150 corporate boxes, which in turn allowed businesspeople to mingle at games. By 1993 a Broncos home game was the place to watch good football, to take the wife and kids on a day out, to hold a work function, and to build a profile in the world of corporate Queensland. 'Before the season started, we would get the box-holders in and we would tell everyone that they had to network with one another to build their businesses,' recalled Broncos director Barry Maranta. 'There was a networking group ... Top State, they called themselves. And I'll never forget it, because in '91 they awarded the Broncos the top business – not the top football club, the top *business* in Queensland.'

At the centre of the Broncos bonanza was club captain Allan Langer, who didn't miss a single match all year. Even before the season began, the weekend magazines of both the *Australian* and the *Sydney Morning Herald* published feature stories about his rise to prominence. His face and his name were plastered on everything from packets of bread to motor vehicles, land and home packages to muesli bars, Alfie dolls to discount alcohol. In one television advertisement for an insurance company, Langer passed the ball to a young blond-haired child who scored under the posts. The state premier, Wayne Goss, fielded questions from reporters about a possible career for Langer in politics. Just about everyone in Queensland seemed to be a fan of Alf. 'If Lang Park was Wally World,' reported the *Courier-Mail*, 'Brisbane's new home looks set to become Alfieland.'[3]

Here were the results of the one-team, one-town structure

that the Broncos had so cleverly exploited. Meanwhile, in Sydney – where 11 Winfield Cup sides fought for sponsors and public attention – relocation, amalgamation and extinction were front-of-mind concerns.

According to figures reported in the Sydney press, the Broncos' turnover in 1993 was $11.77 million – more than the combined turnover of Manly-Warringah and Canterbury-Bankstown.[4] Money and success fostered arrogance within the Broncos management and surly resentment from the Sydney powerbrokers. During the 1993 season, the NSWRL had flagged concerns with the dimensions of ANZ Stadium while some Sydney clubs complained about Langer's tackling style. And when the Broncos sold its own match program in direct competition with *Big League*, the official magazine of the New South Wales Rugby League, the club was accused of breaching the league's merchandising rules.

Brewing beneath each of these petty disputes was an off-field interstate rivalry. 'Sellers of *Big League*,' observed one reporter, 'claim a State of Origin contest developed on the day between the rival hawkers, with distributors of the Broncos' magazine yelling, "Buy the Queensland program. Don't buy the NSW one."'[5]

Tensions were further inflamed when John Quayle, the general manager of the NSWRL, refused to move future grand finals to Brisbane. In Brisbane a crowd in excess of 50,000 people – more than the capacity of the Sydney Football Stadium – could be virtually guaranteed. Even though Queensland had squared up to New South Wales on the field, many Queenslanders felt as if they were still seen as interlopers in Sydney's competition.

In the grand final, held at the SFS on the final Sunday of September 1993, the Broncos ran in three tries to defeat St George for a second consecutive year. Some wondered if the Broncos could break St George's record of 11 consecutive premierships, which was achieved between 1956 and 1966.

'This is a privately owned business,' explained Broncos chairman Paul 'Porky' Morgan. 'It relies on corporate support and bums on seats. The only way we are going to get that is to keep winning. So we HAVE to keep winning. A dozen premierships is just a start.'[6]

Once again, the team returned to Brisbane to celebrate with thousands of ecstatic supporters and one very happy lord mayor. The Broncos had come to embody the image of Brisbane that Jim Soorley wanted to project to the nation: confident, professional, ambitious, but also stylish and beautiful. 'I had a lot to do with the Broncos,' Soorley remembered. 'I went down to the 1992 final on their plane, and came back on their plane. The same in 1993. We had a huge big stadium set up in King George Square for both those victories. It was part of the life and energy of the city ... I think it was a reflection of the sense of change and maturity that was going on.'

Buried beneath the euphoria of the Broncos' back-to-back premierships was Peter Jackson's final game. It had been a frustrating season for Jacko. He made just three first-grade appearances for North Sydney, and on each occasion he was on the losing side.

At 29 years of age, with injury concerns and a media gig lined up, Jackson went out in style. In the reserve-grade grand final against Newcastle, held before the main event at the SFS, he had landed a field goal to win the match by a single point. Despite having a year to run on his contract with Norths, and interest from several other clubs, after the game he hinted at retirement. 'There comes a day,' he told one reporter, 'when you finish with one part of your life and get on with another.'[7]

*

At the end of 1993 the chief executive of the Brisbane Broncos, John Ribot, went on a research trip to North America. He visited professional sporting clubs and theme parks to harvest the latest ideas about sports marketing, stadium management, and so on.

In the new year, the Brisbane Broncos took control of the London Crusaders in the English second division, and renamed the club the London Broncos. In 1988 Brisbane had been the first privately owned rugby league side in Australia. Now, it was the first to take ownership of a team in a foreign competition. 'The Brisbane Broncos is, and will always be, our number one priority,' promised Ribot, 'but for any business to succeed, it must continue to expand.'[8]

In England, the big five soccer clubs had just formed the English Premier League, a breakaway competition from the 104-year-old Football League. In doing so, the new competition was able to negotiate its own commercial arrangements. The television company BSkyB, which was owned by Australian media tycoon Rupert Murdoch, had acquired the broadcast rights. By establishing the Premier League, English soccer entered a new age of fabulous wealth and global popularity.

Ribot had similar visions for rugby league. He believed the game could be taken to new audiences, that it could be administered in a far more professional manner, and that it could provide better pay and conditions for the players. He believed that it could be big business.

But he also felt the NSWRL, which had voted him off its premiership committee and opened an investigation into the Broncos' salary cap payments, was punishing that kind of entrepreneurial thinking.

'Our game was always going to be changed,' Ribot later explained. He found a kindred spirit in Ken Cowley, the chief executive of the Murdoch-owned News Limited. At the beginning of the 1994 season, Ribot sent a report for his 'Super League' concept to Cowley. Even though most people were blissfully unaware of Ribot's plans, from that moment on the game faced an uncertain future as a divide opened between the business-as-usual approach of the rugby league establishment and the new, corporate agenda of the Super League upstarts.

Barry Maranta would tell Sydney officials that rugby league resembled the medieval system. 'They were the lords of the manor, we were the serfs, and we were told which paddock we could plough,' recalled Maranta.

'The revolution had to happen in one form or another,' remembered Tony Currie. 'The players were beginning to get disgruntled.' Currie had played his last game for Australia on a tour of New Zealand in 1989. 'I can remember us at the airport after we won the series 3–0. We were in economy, and more officials and wives and hangers-on in their green blazers were waiting to fly first-class.'

Yet for all the frustration with the governing body, the game was committed to expansion. In 1994, a State of Origin fixture was again taken to Melbourne, and four new teams were preparing to enter the competition in 1995. The biggest beneficiary of expansion was Queensland, with one side to be based in Brisbane, and another in Townsville.

While the Brisbane Broncos had been plotting world domination, for two years Kerry Boustead had been quietly working on a limited budget to build the North Queensland Cowboys. He had rounded up support from Mackay to Mount Isa and even Papua New Guinea, brought local sponsors on board, organised thousands of signatures from the public, and secured the lease of the Willows Paceway in Townsville.

In June 1991, he had coached North Queensland to victory in the State League; proof, he told reporters, 'that there is an abundance of raw talent in the north'.[9] And later that year, he and former *Townsville Bulletin* sports editor Doug Kingston flew to Sydney to present the bid to the NSWRL on a stagecoach paid for by the Castlemaine Perkins Brewery. Boustead, dressed as a cowboy, rode shotgun while Kingston, at the back, fired a cap gun into the air. 'That stagecoach,' remembered Kingston, 'was the first time we got recognised by the Sydney media. I knew we had to do something – if you just walk up to the New South Wales Rugby League headquarters with a bunch of petitions and the bid, who cares? I knew from working in the media that you had to have something that was a bit different.'

At the meeting, they presented Ken Arthurson and John Quayle with a feast of mudcrab sandwiches and Bowen mangoes, donated by diehard rugby league supporters from North Queensland. So impressed were Arthurson and Quayle that they asked if they could take the last two mangoes home for their wives.

That meeting, as well as Boustead's good standing in the game, helped secure North Queensland's position in the competition. 'It could even be said,' wrote Kingston in 1995, 'that the Cowboys got into the Winfield Cup on the shell of a mudcrab and the skin of a mango.'[10]

The Cowboys tapped into the underdog spirit of the Queensland rugby league community, as well as the anti-metropolitan sentiment that had existed for generations. Many country Queenslanders gave up their affection for the Broncos and realigned themselves to the Cowboys. Dr Chris Sarra, who would later become an Australian Rugby League commissioner, was one such fan. The Broncos, he remembered, were a little too slick and corporate for his liking. 'I was living in Cairns when the Cowboys started, and what really appealed to me was that Kerry Boustead was driving it, and he was part of Queensland State of Origin. They felt more grassroots, working-class, they were bushies. They were underdogs, too, whereas Brisbane – I went to their first game and they flogged Manly! The Cowboys were a different proposition; they had to be gritty and they had to work.'

That dictum applied equally to everyone in the club, from the chairman and the CEO, to the players, the coaching staff, and the supporters. With the help of construction giants Joe Goicoechea and Laurence Lancini, as well as willing local tradesmen and some of the players, the old Willows Paceway was gradually converted into a proper football ground. Much of the labour was volunteer and costs were kept to a minimum. Rather than purchasing million-dollar floodlights, for example, they re-wired the existing racetrack lights onto makeshift towers. The old horse stables became the room for post-match functions. Andrew Whittington, who had been signed from the Gold Coast to play in the forward pack, was appointed head groundsman. His fellow players helped lay the turf on the hills that supporters would soon cheer from.

Although the stadium was very basic and located out in the boondocks of Thuringowa – Townsville's neighbouring city – the manner in which it took shape gave many of the locals a proprietorial interest in the future of the club. What's more, it allowed the place to maintain a true sense of character, reminiscent of the old tin-shed country grandstands of the Foley Shield days. 'The Cowboys,' declared the mayor of Townsville, Tony Mooney, 'have arrived at the right time.'[11]

On Saturday 11 March 1995, halfback Laurie Spina led the Cowboys onto the field that North Queensland built. Dressed in a baggy jersey of grey, white, yellow, and blue, he let the cheers of more than 20,000 supporters wash over him. The Cowboys lost to Canterbury-Bankstown, but Spina could sense that they had captured the imagination of the north.

Spina had spent eight seasons in New South Wales during the 1980s, but always remained a North Queenslander at heart. When a Sydney reporter asked him where he got his speed, he responded, 'If you had Vern Daisy chasing you, you'd be quick too!' And at every club, whether it be North Sydney, Eastern Suburbs, or Cronulla-Sutherland, he would only sign a contract on the condition that he be allowed to return to Ingham for three months during the off-season.

Now that he was at home on his family cane farm, Spina would meet his teammate Craig Teitzel in Ingham and drive the 240-kilometre round-trip for Cowboys' training sessions. 'We used to order our feed at the Yabulu servo, eat on the way home, get home probably 9:30 at night,' Spina later recalled. 'He was a butcher in Tully, and I was getting up early on the farm, back to work, and then repeat four times a week.'

Yet the thousands of kilometres were all worthwhile, even if only so he could run out in front of such phenomenal home crowds every other weekend. 'That first game, it was raining, the grass was slipping down on the hills, and there was mud everywhere,' he said. 'I'm true-blue: North Queensland's the best place, wonderful people, and to represent them was very special. We weren't on huge money, there was not a lot of star power in the team, but Kerry always said we had to build, you know – the talent was in North Queensland.'

One of the young locals recruited to the club was Paul Bowman. Raised in Proserpine, Bowman had been playing rugby union while attending university in Brisbane when the Cowboys arrived on the scene. In time, he would play 203 matches for the Cowboys, progress to the Queensland State of Origin side, and after retirement work for the club as a strength and conditioning coach.

Without the Cowboys, Bowman later admitted, his life would have turned out very different. 'I just wanted to have a career,' he said. 'I was very lucky. When I signed in '95, I didn't think I was capable of playing any first grade. I didn't set out to try and become a one-club person, or to play so many games. But by the time I was three or four years into my career I didn't want to go anywhere else. I had family close; Mum and Dad were season ticket holders from '95, so they were up here every home game.'

The opening match in Townsville was one of ten games being played across four time zones, as the Cowboys, the Auckland Warriors, the South Queensland Crushers, and the Western Reds were welcomed into the competition. Rugby league, for so long confined to two states on the eastern seaboard, had finally become a national sport.

But the battle for control was already underway. On one side was the establishment: the ARL and its Winfield Cup competition, on the other were the insurgents: News Limited and a vision called Super League. Even before the season began, News Limited executives had met with club representatives to sell them their idea for a new competition. Also at the meeting was Kerry Packer, who owned the free-to-air and pay television rights for the Winfield Cup via Channel 9 and Optus Vision. When he threatened to sue for breach of contract, the clubs rejected News Limited and signed on with the ARL.

The war had only just begun. On Wednesday 29 March, several players from Canterbury-Bankstown signed rebel contracts with News Limited – the first of many to join the breakaway movement. Next day, News Limited took the NSWRL and the ARL to Federal Court, alleging breaches of the Trades Practices Act. The battle, as journalist Mike Colman observed, 'would be fought on two fronts – a legal challenge to the validity of the ARL's Loyalty Agreements, and a lightning-swift sign-up of the clubs, players, coaches and officials'.[12]

The football itself soon became a secondary concern as ridiculous sums of money were offered to players to defect to Super League, or stay 'loyal' to the ARL. In Round 4, North Queensland lost to the Canberra Raiders, and then both clubs aligned with News Limited and Super League.

And so the Cowboys were now willing to turn their back on the competition they had only just joined. It broke Kerry Boustead's heart. By the time the Cowboys won their first game in April, he had resigned from his role as chief executive, moved to Brisbane, and stopped following the club altogether. 'I had just put so much leverage on the bosses of the New South Wales Rugby League – Arthurson and Quayle – to get us into that competition,' Boustead remembered. 'I'd call them every week and ask, "What do we need to do now? ... What do we need to do now?" They were instrumental in getting us in the competition, and what do we do? Stab 'em in the back!

'I just think it was wrong. Number one: you sign a document, put your hand on your heart, and pledge something. And then five days later you say, "Oh, sorry about that, we decided to go the other way!?" In fact, the way it worked out at the end, Rupert Murdoch's money went a long way to help the Cowboys. But I couldn't be there, because I could not go against my word.'

Firm friends and old loyalties were breaking up. Down south, the chief executive of Canterbury-Bankstown, Peter 'Bullfrog' Moore, resigned from his directorship of the ARL – a huge personal and professional loss for chairman Ken Arthurson. Journalists who worked for News Limited-owned newspapers, such as the *Courier-Mail* league reporter Steve Ricketts, were caught uncomfortably between their employer and their affection for the ARL. Queensland was split in half as the Gold Coast Seagulls and the South Queensland Crushers stayed loyal to the ARL, while the Cowboys and the Broncos defected to Super League.

'We went through a lot of pain,' recalled Greg Adermann, a QRL History Committee member who was employed by Foxtel at the time. 'I'm a traditionalist in everything, but I quickly became a Super League supporter because it was my bread and butter, and it was in my interest and my employer's interest that it worked.'

Not even the State of Origin series was immune from the crisis. When it became clear that only players aligned to the ARL would be considered for selection, Queensland coach Wayne Bennett, also coach of the Super League-aligned Broncos, resigned.

And yet, as crisis engulfed the game, a ragtag group of footballers would come together to produce one of the greatest underdog stories in Australian sport, reaffirm the value of State of Origin, and prove forever that Queenslanders are a different breed.

★

In late March 1995, as news of Super League tore through the game, the Queensland Bulls cricket team won the Sheffield Shield for the first time in 68 years. Many people likened the breakthrough win to a State of Origin atmosphere, as thousands of happy Queenslanders packed into King George Square to celebrate.

Throughout his childhood, Trevor Gillmeister played cricket and rode surf-boats in summer, and enjoyed soccer, rugby union, basketball, and Australian Rules. But when people would ask him what he wanted to be when he grew up, he told them he was going to play rugby league. His father, Ron, had taught him how to tackle. 'You can drag someone off the street and pass them a footy, and they can catch it and run with it,' Gillmeister recalled his father telling him, 'but not everyone can stop someone when they've got the ball.'

The Gillmeisters were old-school, no-nonsense Labor: they worked hard in blue-collar trades and valued loyalty above everything else. Queenslanders recognised those qualities in Trevor and responded in kind. When the Broncos cut him loose in 1993, forcing his move to Penrith, people were outraged. His teammates almost refused to play without him. 'I know I must accept it, for I cannot change the facts,' said Rupert McCall in a farewell poem to Gillmeister which was broadcast on *The Footy Show*. 'But why, for sake of money, did they have to sack the Axe?'

Expansion to 20 teams gave Gillmeister the opportunity to return to Brisbane. He joined the South Queensland Crushers in 1995 and skippered the team to its first Winfield Cup victory. And as the Broncos stars dropped out of the 1995 State of Origin series, he proved to be the perfect leader. 'I think Queenslanders are pretty remarkable at backing each other up,' he later explained. 'You have drought, you have cyclones, floods, and you'd have hundreds and hundreds of people helping people they didn't even know. When our backs are against the wall, we're at our best.'

For the first time in more than a decade, the Maroons were genuine underdogs. In fact, nobody gave them a chance. New South Wales had selected 11 Kangaroos representatives and were coached by Phil Gould, who had not yet lost a series, while Queensland selected nine players who had never played Origin before and were coached by *The Footy Show* host, Paul 'Fatty' Vautin. Vautin's halfback, Adrian Lam, had previously represented Papua New Guinea and needed special dispensation to be eligible for Queensland. His lock forward, Billy Moore, had represented New South Wales as a junior, while prop Tony Hearn was born in Canberra, fullback Robbie O'Davis was born in Sydney, and the hooker, Wayne Bartrim, was born and raised on the mid-north coast of New South Wales.[13]

For more than a decade, Queensland's success in State of Origin had been built on stability and familiarity. Those who laid the foundation – guys like Wally Lewis, Paul Vautin, Chris Close, and Mal Meninga – had come through the grades together as teenagers and played in the Brisbane competition. And while New South Wales had trawled through countless captains and player combinations, Queensland selectors fostered a tight-knit culture by selecting a similar group of guys year after year.

Yet as the game faced an uncertain future, many Queenslanders worried that the old spirit was dying. The Maroons had not won a series since Lewis's retirement in 1991, and Meninga, the last of the originals, had retired in 1994 and publicly backed Super League.

Moreover, the children of State of Origin had none of the chip-on-the-shoulder attitude that had previously given Queensland an identity. Not only had the younger generation grown up watching Queensland dominate the series, they now played for and supported professional clubs in Brisbane, the Gold Coast, and North Queensland, which competed every weekend against New South Wales opposition. 'I don't think the players have been as hungry as the old Queensland teams,' said Vautin in 1994, before he was appointed coach.[14] It was his job, alongside team manager Chris Close, to create a competitive side out of a disparate group of rookies and journeymen – many of whom had never played together before.

Ben Ikin, an 18-year-old with a face full of acne and a crook ankle, was the youngest. When he arrived at the team hotel, Vautin thought he was a starry-eyed kid hunting for autographs. Ikin's father, Alan, had migrated to Queensland from Victoria, and as a teenager Ben had played Australian Rules and hockey as well as rugby league. 'When I got selected in 1995, I had no frame of reference,' Ikin later recalled. 'I had been told the stories, but I had no personal experience with them. I remember not long after I took up league, I got a video cassette of all the highlights of Origin from 1980 through to 1985, which was a period of time which Queensland largely dominated. So by the time I ended up playing Origin, I had no hate for New South Wales and what had happened before 1980.'

Still, the youngsters knew they were entering a vitally important Queensland institution. Alan Ikin told Ben that his body now belonged to the state of Queensland, and the family would accept whatever they got back. '[My dad] was an adopted Queenslander,' explained Ben Ikin. 'Like most people who migrate to Queensland, they get inducted into the whole Maroon fairytale. It had become important to him as a fan, so I think in his own way he was trying to tell me how important it was for the people of Queensland.'

During a boozy team bonding session on the Gold Coast, Ikin relayed his father's instructions to Chris Close. 'Ben's the youngest player to be picked, and that's the message his dad sends him into camp with!' remembered Close. 'You can't get any stronger than that.'

Since retiring from football, Close had moved to Gladstone, taken over as coach at one of the local sides, and started work at the Moura mines. It was Dick 'Tosser' Turner, the Maroons' long-serving team manager, who brought him back into the camp.

'I didn't support the ARL and I didn't support Super League, I just wasn't smart enough to understand where it was all going to finish,' Close later said. 'It was like two parents fighting in a divorce. A lot of rugby league supporters walked away then. I was in the mines, and I can tell you people stopped talking about it in the crib-room.

You'd go out to work on your four-day shift with guys that are similar age, that played rugby league in regional areas, and rugby league was their game, and you'd sit down at crib and rugby league wouldn't be mentioned. Nobody wanted to talk about the shit-fight and all the money everyone was getting.'

But Close knew that all those disillusioned Queenslanders would still tune in for State of Origin. At the first team meeting, as he tried to explain how much it meant to him to play for Queensland, he was hit by a wave of emotion. His top lip began to quiver and the words dried up, but the message was not lost on the players. 'As he started losing his shit and started crying, I lost my shit,' remembered Robbie O'Davis. 'I just stood up and said, "Give me that fucking jersey, we'll play the cunts now!"'

By half-time in Game I, Queensland held a slender two-point lead. The New South Wales players were the first to return to the field. The Maroons soon followed: Trevor Gillmeister leading the way, Mark Coyne next, then Gavin Allen. And then came Billy Moore, the boy from the border, studs clattering on concrete, his eyes rolling around like a man possessed. As Moore marched down the tunnel of the Sydney Football Stadium, he began to chant: 'QUEEENSLANDAAH! QUEEENSLANDAAH! QUEEENSLANDAAH!'

Here was the voice of the past, reaching out to the players of the present, to guide them through troubled times. The Queenslander call had been introduced by Paul Vautin and Gary Belcher in 1987 as a way of revving up their teammates as they defended their line. In 1992, when Moore made his Origin debut, Peter Jackson had explained its significance. 'Jacko told me the three things that meant being a Queenslander to him,' Moore once told journalist Mike Colman. 'One, help your mates; two, find an answer; and three, no excuses.'[15]

Spurred on, for the next 40 minutes the Maroons defended as a unit to hold onto their lead. The 2–0 victory was the first time New

South Wales had ever been held scoreless, and the first try-less State of Origin match. 'Blokes I hadn't known a week before were mates for life,' Queensland centre Mark Coyne later recalled.'[16]

While the Queenslander call pumped up the Maroons, it drove New South Welshmen crazy. As the teams prepared for Game II at the Melbourne Cricket Ground, word got around that the Blues players were ready to belt the first player who yelled out 'Queenslander'. Within three minutes, the call went up and the punches started flying. 'They've come from everywhere like it was almost a rehearsal,' yelled match commentator Ray Warren excitedly, as all 26 players got involved in the scrap.

New South Wales were awarded the penalty but Queensland were the first to readjust, scoring the first try and going into the half-time break with a six-point lead. By full-time, the score was Queensland 20, New South Wales 12.

Yet Gillmeister, who was battling an infected stud gash, wanted a 3–0 series whitewash, and not even the threat of septicaemia could distract him from the task at hand. Hours before Game III in Brisbane, as he lay in bed hooked up to an antibiotic drip, he was joined by the team doctor, Roy Saunders, as well as Fatty Vautin, Tosser Turner, and Choppy Close. Saunders delivered the grave news: if Gillmeister's blood infection worsened while he was on the field, the consequences could be disastrous.

'Are you saying he could die?' asked Vautin.

'The doctor said yeah,' remembered Close. 'Gilly's not saying anything. And I looked at Gilly and said, "Fuck me, mate, what a place to die – captaining Queensland in the middle of fucken Lang Park. How good would that be?"'

Gillmeister made his decision: he would play.

Inspired by their captain, every Maroon stepped up a gear. Gary Larson, man of the match from Game I, threw himself tirelessly at the opposition. Robbie O'Davis, Brett Dallas, and Matt Sing buzzed around the backline. The Lang Park crowd worked itself into a frenzy as Ben Ikin dashed over for the final try. As Queensland celebrated an eight-point victory, Gillmeister was chaired from the field and taken to hospital to recover.

It would go down as one of the greatest Origin series yet. 'Origin needed us to win,' recalled Vautin years later. 'The game, in the middle of all the Super League war, needed something to remind us what makes the game so great. It is never about who has the best players. It's about who can get the best out of themselves.'[17]

By the end of the season, the North Queensland Cowboys would finish dead last, the South Queensland Crushers and the Gold Coast Chargers would finish in the bottom five, and the Brisbane Broncos would bow out in the first round of the finals. Yet Queenslanders would always look to 1995 as proof that State of Origin was more important than money, celebrity, or sectional interests. 'These guys,' said an ecstatic Peter Jackson, 'have brought a bit of faith back into rugby league at a time when it was desperately needed.'[18]

Eight months later, in February 1996, Super League staged the inaugural World Nines tournament in Fiji. In part, the nine-a-side competition was a show of News Limited's much-vaunted 'global vision' for rugby league. Present were representative sides from Australia, New Zealand, Papua New Guinea, Fiji, Western Samoa, Tonga, the Cook Islands, Japan, the USA, Morocco, Italy, France, Scotland, Ireland, Wales, and England.

The coach of the Australian team was Mal Meninga, one of Super League's star recruits and a vocal advocate for expanding rugby league to new markets. 'That's one of the reasons I joined with Super League,' he told a gathering of journalists at the National Press Club in September 1995. 'The league has been up and running for about 100 years now, but it's never been expanded internationally at all. It's still only played in five nations around the world.'[19]

In the days leading up to the tournament, the sun shone brightly. On the opening day, however, a monsoon hit the capital and torrential rain drenched Suva's International Stadium. Day two was called off.

Meanwhile, thousands of kilometres away in Sydney, more than 100 people crammed into the Federal Court of Australia to hear Justice James Burchett's verdict on the future of rugby league. In presenting their case, News Limited had attacked the ARL's Loyalty and Commitment Contracts, arguing that clubs had been forced to sign under duress. The ARL accused the rebel clubs of breaching their contractual and fiduciary obligations to the competition.

On every count, Justice Burchett found in favour of the ARL. He ruled that the organisation's loyalty agreements were valid and binding for both clubs and players, and criticised News Limited for 'intentional inducement of breach of contract'.[20] He also condemned the actions of the Brisbane Broncos directors, and former Broncos chief executive John Ribot, now the face of Super League. 'I am satisfied,' Burchett told the court, 'that the representatives of the Broncos knew very well what was "going on", and were intimately involved in a way that could properly be called clandestine.'[21]

Trust between the parties had by now completely evaporated. As Ribot, Ken Cowley, and Rupert Murdoch's son Lachlan vowed to fight on, the ARL worried that News Limited might entice their players to move overseas and broadcast the resulting competition back to Australia through pay television.

Initially, the rebels stood their ground. The Western Reds took out an advertisement in support of Super League in the *West Australian*. From the resort in Fiji, Meninga and Laurie Daley faxed their support for Super League. There was even talk that Daley would switch to Australian Rules football rather than return to the ARL.

Yet after forfeiting Round 1 of the new season in protest, the clubs aligned to Super League – Brisbane, North Queensland, Canterbury-Bankstown, Cronulla-Sutherland, Penrith, Canberra, Western Reds, and Auckland – rejoined the Winfield Cup competition. All the players, except for a 22-year-old second-rower by the name of Gorden Tallis, returned to the football field.

Born in Townsville in 1973, Tallis had grown up in a sports-obsessed family. His father, Wally, had played in England and had been part of the first Indigenous side to tour New Zealand. Young Gorden grew up in awe of Queensland's State of Origin heroes, and hung posters of Gene Miles and Wally Lewis on his bedroom walls.

When he was a teenager, his older brother had signed for the Broncos. The story goes that Gorden approached Wayne Bennett at a trial match in Townsville in 1990. 'You've got my brother, Wally, down there,' he reportedly told Bennett. 'Well, you got the wrong one, didn't you? I'm the one that can play ... and I'm off to St George.'[22]

In 1993, Tallis came off the bench in St George's Winfield Cup grand final loss to the Broncos. In 1994, he made his debut for Queensland in State of Origin. In 1995, despite being contracted to St George, he signed with Super League. In 1996, he moved to Brisbane and began training with the Broncos. Yet with Super League seemingly defeated in court, St George demanded he return to Sydney to honour the final year of his ARL contract. Amid speculation he would move to England, or perhaps defect to rugby union, Tallis decided to sit out the season rather than play in the ARL.

Although ineligible to play for the Broncos, or even wear the club gear, Tallis trained hard and ended up winning clubman of the year in 1996 along with Chris Johns. 'I learnt what it was like being retired early,' he later remembered.[23] For the man they called the 'Raging Bull', his stand against the ARL was the first of many battles in a career defined by conflict. Tallis, once wrote journalist Adrian McGregor, was 'the most charismatic and controversial Queensland rugby league player since Wally Lewis'.[24]

Like Meninga, Tallis signed with Super League because he appreciated News Limited's global vision and promise to look after the players. For the ordinary fan, however, the defection of players such as Tallis and the resulting courtroom saga were terrible for the sport. For all the problems of the ARL, the working men and women saw Super League as a corporate takeover of the game they loved.

'What I hated about the Super League war was the amount of average people turned off the game,' recalled league writer Steve Ricketts. 'It was the way it was done. I think I wrote in one of my columns: "if a raffle seller at the Prince of Wales Hotel in Nundah has now torn up his association with the game as a result of the greed of Super League, it hasn't been worthwhile."

'Because, you know, all of a sudden there were blokes who were barely reserve graders getting paid $200,000, and junior rugby league clubs were struggling to survive. I suppose it's a compliment to rugby league that there was this fight over it.'

In Queensland, attendances at Broncos and Cowboys matches dropped as much as 30 per cent from the year prior. The South Queensland Crushers faced financial collapse. The Maroons lost the 1996 State of Origin series 3–0, after failing to reintegrate the star Broncos players into Paul Vautin's no-frills squad. For the first time since 1948, there was no Foley Shield in the north.

By October, a full bench of the Federal Court overturned all 37 of Justice Burchett's orders, clearing the path for the first Super League season to begin in 1997. In the next 12 months the game would split into two separate competitions, old friendships would be tested, ordinary fans would give up on the sport forever, and rugby league would lose one of its favourite sons.

7

I'LL MISS THAT FEELING

1997

Australian rugby league entered 1997 a house divided. Super League, with its futuristic jerseys and ten teams spread across eight cities from Perth to Auckland, began with a loud fireworks and entertainment display in Brisbane. The ARL competition, with eight of its 12 clubs based in Sydney, stuck to old-school jumpers and traditional footy.

Peter Jackson – who was writing a regular column for the *Super League* magazine, employed as reporter for Foxtel, and working as a skills coach for Canterbury-Bankstown – was itching to get back on the field. 'The biggest thing about Super League, for Peter, was that he missed out,' recalled his wife, Siobhan. 'Peter loved a buck. All his mates were getting million-dollar contracts. He was devastated by that. I remember watching him trying to train and his ankle was so damaged; he couldn't get back.'

In his quest for one last payday, Jackson was, in many ways, a typical rugby league man. After all, the game in Australia had been formed after a group of working-class footballers, funded by local businessmen, split with rugby union due to issues of compensation and professionalism.

The circumstances of the 1997 split might have been different, but the root cause was eerily familiar. The players knew their careers were short, and that the injuries sustained would likely affect their ability to return to regular work. At essence, News Limited's promise to commercialise the game and look after the players was not so different to the inducements offered by the founding fathers.

In May, Jackson picked up another job as the assistant to Queensland coach Wayne Bennett. With both competitions battling for hearts and minds, Super League decided to try something different with State of Origin. While the ARL persisted with Queensland versus New South Wales, Super League introduced New Zealand to the mix, called it the 'Tri-Series', and marketed it aggressively to the public. 'While others may be content to cloak themselves in manufactured tradition and appeal to the "good old days",' read one piece of Super League propaganda, 'progression in any sport demands innovation.'[1]

Among other things, innovation allowed players to choose their own numbers, rather than be constrained by the traditional one to 13. New rules, designed to speed up the game and reward adventurous play, were introduced. And for the first time there was the presence of a video referee. It frustrated many onlookers, even those nominally within the News Limited camp. 'When Super League started, it was my job – I had to call the games,' remembered John McCoy, one part of the Foxtel commentary team. 'I must say, I didn't enjoy a lot of the Super League games because some of the rule changes they brought in didn't sit well with me.'

After lacklustre opening games to the Tri-Series, the fourth and final match was spectacular. New South Wales and Queensland each scored four tries in regular time, before a frenetic period of extra-time saw the Blues' halfback, Noel Goldthorpe, pot a field goal to secure victory after 104 minutes. It was, as one reporter wrote, 'a game to capture at last the very best of Rugby League'.[2]

And yet, for all the hype, the Tri-Series lacked intensity and raw feeling. 'It didn't feel the same as Origin, certainly not,' recalled Kevin Walters, Queensland's starting five-eighth. 'We were just doing what we thought was right with Super League, but I guess there was only one real Origin series.'

As the season progressed the crowds stayed away from the rebel competition. In Round 11, the first to be played following the Tri-Series, Brisbane hosted North Queensland at ANZ Stadium. Less than 15,000 people showed up for the all-Queensland derby.

Meanwhile, across town at Lang Park, the Brisbane Strikers won Queensland's first National Soccer League title in front of more than 40,000 spectators. The Strikers' assistant coach, Peter Tokesi, was a Brisbane boy who'd grown up playing rugby league. He loved the State of Origin concept, and could feel some of that atmosphere radiating around the ground as the Strikers beat a Sydney opponent. Lang Park, he later remembered, 'is hallowed turf for rugby league players, and here we were, having to shut the gates for soccer'.[3]

As a spectator sport soccer had never before threatened rugby league in Queensland, but the participation statistics showed a worrying trend: many more children were playing soccer than league, with the former growing at a faster rate. That, coupled with the existential threat of Australian Rules football, which had successfully managed its expansion from Victoria, not to mention rugby union's new Super 12 competition, provided serious grounds for concern.

Even though rugby league had entered the decade on a high following the expansion to 20 teams and the famous advertising campaign featuring Tina Turner, the Super League war had halted the game's momentum. 1997 would forever go down as a lost year.

Before the season was out, Peter Jackson sat down in his seat for a long-haul flight from Perth to Sydney and wrote an impassioned plea for the game to be reunited as one. Losing tradition was difficult, but the thought of losing the game altogether was too much to bear. The crisis, he wrote, 'is piggy-backing the Sydney Swans, the Brisbane Lions, the Super 12s and even David Hill's soccer mob' to unimaginable heights. 'Enough is enough,' he concluded. 'It's time for everyone to stop thinking about their wallet or their reputation, it's time to show true loyalty to the bloody game.'[4]

In that regrettable year of football, the established Super League sides – Brisbane, Cronulla-Sutherland, Penrith, Canberra, and Canterbury-Bankstown – all made the finals, while the new franchises in Perth and Adelaide struggled both on and off the field. The Broncos won the minor premiership after losing just three games all season. It all seemed very predictable, especially when compared to the fairytale story of Newcastle Knights winning its first grand final in the rival ARL competition.

But for Gorden Tallis, who had sat out the 1996 season due to the Super League war, it was good to simply be back playing footy. He began the year in scintillating fashion, scoring a try with his first touch of the ball for Australia in its win over the USA in Super League's World Nines tournament. In June, during the Broncos' win over Wigan in the World Club Challenge, he lived up to his 'Raging Bull' nickname after being sin-binned for punching Terry O'Connor repeatedly in the head. And on the first weekend of September he returned to his hometown, Townsville, to help the Broncos beat Cronulla-Sutherland in the major semifinal. 'I lost a whole year of football for this, that's how important it is to me,' he told reporters in the lead-up to the grand final. 'It's the one I've been dreaming about.'[5]

The first and only Super League final was contested by Brisbane and Cronulla-Sutherland – the best attacking team in the competition against the team with the best defence. The game had a distinct Queensland feel – in part because it was played at the Broncos' home ground, ANZ Stadium, and also due to the fact that the Sharks had four Queenslanders in its squad and was coached by a Maroons legend, John Lang. The Broncos scored four tries to win comfortably by 18 points and after full-time tears streamed down big Gordie's face. He had played through the pain of rib cartilage damage – suffered a fortnight earlier in Townsville – and produced a brave defensive effort. Even if the victory felt somewhat empty without the presence of the ARL teams, those interminable months he had spent on the sidelines were now well and truly behind him.

Many Queenslanders swelled with pride. Not only had the Broncos won the inaugural Super League grand final, they had done so in Brisbane in front of a record crowd of nearly 60,000 people. More than any other time in history, Australian rugby league's centre of gravity had shifted away from Sydney. After all, the idea for Super League had been hatched in the Broncos' headquarters, while several famous Queensland identities – such as John Ribot, Paul Morgan, and Mal Meninga – had been crucial in taking it from concept to reality.

Many New South Welshmen were convinced that Queenslanders were responsible for the mess. The *Sydney Morning Herald* reporter Roy Masters declared that Super League appealed to Queenslanders because it was 'part politics, part prejudice and part phobia'. Sydney rugby league historian Andrew Moore traced its roots to what he called 'Queensland populist nationalism':

> For it was the Brisbane sporting entrepreneur, Paul 'Porky' Morgan and his fellow New Right colleagues in the Brisbane Broncos club who inspired the schism. On the one hand they invoked the nostrums of economic rationalism, citing the stupidity of an organisation – the ARL – that was not consumed by the profit motive. On the other hand the Bronco separatists exploited, a la Bjelke Petersen, an aggrieved Queensland siege mentality staving off the southern socialist centralists, the Sydney-dominated ARL.[6]

Yet for all the hubris of Super League – the plans to take the game to China, the promises of a global television audience, Ribot's declaration that 'sport is business' – the grassroots game was struggling.[7] Chris Close, who at the time was living and working in Central Queensland, noticed his son's friends losing interest in rugby league. 'Even in the local junior competitions they were giving the game away,' he recalled.

For many people, the money being tossed around at the professional level was grotesque – particularly when compared to the trying financial state of their own community clubs. 'I hope that when the superstars of Rugby League sit down each night to count their fortunes, they will spare a thought for the tens of thousands of men and women who, over the years, have served the game for the love of sport and not for what they could get out of it,' wrote Ken McElligot, the state member for the seat of Thuringowa, in a letter to *Rugby League Week*.[8]

Although both the Broncos and the Cowboys had defected to Super League, there were as many Queenslanders who opposed News Limited as those who supported it. For country Queenslanders like Close and McElligot, rugby league was primarily about community integration, not power or money. Around the state, loyal rugby league people continued to volunteer their time to keep the game alive.

During the winter of 1996, at the height of the Super League war, a Broncos fan by the name of Steve McEvoy had set up a new competition to reignite rugby league in Stanthorpe and the surrounding border towns of the southeast. Following the exclusion of Stanthorpe from the Toowoomba Rugby League, McEvoy had signed up five neighbouring towns from either side of the 29th parallel. Together, they christened the new competition the 'Border League'.

For some towns it was a significant achievement just to get a team onto the park. When McEvoy asked Hector Hancock – the brother of former Australian international Rohan – about the possibility of entering a side from Killarney, he was told that there hadn't been a league team in Killarney for decades. But when Hancock called a town meeting, more than 100 people showed up in support of the idea.

In the end, six sides played in that inaugural season of the Border League in 1997: Stanthorpe Gremlins, Texas Terriers, Tenterfield Tigers, Wallangarra Rams, Inglewood Roosters, and the Killarney Cutters. The representative team, the Border Bushrangers, wore Queensland maroon and the sky blue of New South Wales in the spirit of cross-border cooperation.

The new competition reactivated a sense of civic pride. The queue of cars for the opening game in Wallangarra stretched out of the ground. 'I think the township had 500 people, and they reckon there was about 800 there on the day,' remembered McEvoy. Despite all the doubters and the critics, to him this was proof that the competition had a future. 'I wanted the *league* to survive,' he said. 'I didn't want to be known as the last president of the Stanthorpe Rugby League. The game had done so much for me in that five or six years I played, and I could see what it was doing for the community. I'd go to soccer games here and sure, we'd get 100 or so people watching, but I'd go to rugby league and the whole town would be around the ground. Rugby league is such an important part of community. That's what drove me, more than anything.'

Although it was a humble six-team amateur competition, the Border League represented a counterpoint to the swagger and braggadocio of the Broncos and Super League. It was not about power, politics, or interstate rivalry. Rather, it was about local people putting aside their differences and working together for the good of the sport. The competition, said one ARL official, was a 'shining light' during those uncertain times.[9]

At the professional level, too, there were stalwarts of Queensland rugby league who refused to be swayed by News Limited. The long-serving manager of the Maroons and chairman of the South

ILL MISS THAT FEELING

Queensland Crushers, Dick 'Tosser' Turner, threw emotional and financial support behind the ARL. 'That was the thing that upset me and a tremendous number of Queenslanders,' he told Mike Colman, the author of *Super League: The Inside Story*. 'It was not the concept, which I think everyone agreed had some merit. It was that this clandestine operation had been perpetrated by Queenslanders.

'Now while a lot of Queenslanders might say screw NSW or screw the ARL or whatever, that is never to be at the risk of destroying the fabric of the game. This whole thing was not about control of the game, it was about owning the game. There is a fundamental difference and in my mind it was simply not acceptable.'[10]

Tosser's stand against News Limited, which had tried in vain to recruit the Crushers to Super League, had been crucial to the survival of the ARL competition. It also influenced Trevor Gillmeister, who skippered both the Crushers and Queensland during the Super League war, to remain loyal to the ARL. 'I sat down with Tosser and had a yarn to him about the whole thing,' he remembered. 'It was all about TV. And Tosser being Tosser – a handshake man, he'd worked with the wharfies – he said, "Mate, I've given my word to John Quayle and Ken Arthurson, and I won't go back on my word." Well, that was good enough for me. I still admire him ... he was the last of the handshake men.'

Turner himself put up a significant amount of his own money to guarantee the viability of the South Queensland Crushers. Initially, attendances at Lang Park had hovered around 20,000 people. But for the next two seasons, as the Crushers managed just seven wins in 43 games and the Super League war created an atmosphere of disillusionment, the average home crowd fell below 10,000 people. In other words, the average attendance dropped more than 50 per cent in three seasons – a rate of attrition no club could withstand.

'You had players that were going from a $40-, 50-, 60,000 a year player, to a $240-, 250,000 a year player, simply because people were scrambling over each other trying to sign enough players to field a team,' recalled Alan Graham, who worked as both a general manager and CEO of the Crushers. 'So while your player payments skyrocketed, because of the fragmentation of the game the support died. That was reflected both in crowds and in fragmenting commercial support as well. That put the Crushers in a poor financial position.'

Outside of Broncoland, it was an unhappy period for rugby league in Queensland. The clubs of the old Brisbane Rugby League competition had shrunk almost beyond recognition; the Broncos were miles ahead of the Crushers; and even the Gold Coast Chargers struggled to find a space of its own in Southeast Queensland against the Broncos behemoth.

The Broncos were notorious for forming short-lived partnerships with some of the old clubs in the city in order to farm out its reserve-grade players. In 1997, lifelong Brothers supporter Tom Cranitch watched on forlornly as his historic club effectively became a feeder side for the Broncos, while the Crushers moved into the premises that Brothers had built and rebranded it the Crushers Leagues Club. 'I tried to feel some attachment to the Crushers, maybe because they were at the old clubhouse, but I was probably trying to buy myself back into it,' Cranitch later recalled. Yet nothing could replace his feeling for the old Brisbane competition.

The Gold Coast Chargers, meanwhile, had lurched from one crisis to another. The club faced constant financial problems, ownership issues, and a lingering identity crisis. It was never recognised as a truly Queensland institution in the way that the Broncos or the Cowboys were, but nor was it a team for Northern New South Wales, either. In ten seasons, the club had been known as the Giants, the Seagulls, the Gladiators, and the Chargers; changed the colour combination on its jersey several times; played at two home grounds on either side of the border; and burned through too many chief executives and coaches to name.

Season 1997 had actually finished with Gold Coast making its first finals appearance, but by then the club was already on death row. A rumoured merger between the Crushers and the Chargers never eventuated. Instead the Crushers went into administration and were culled, and the Chargers would limp on for one more season before being expelled as well.

In Queensland, the clubs loyal to the ARL were the biggest losers, while the Broncos was the only club to emerge stronger from the Super League fiasco. Brisbane, with its army of State of Origin stars and big corporate backers, were like an enormous Moreton Bay fig tree under which nothing could grow. And yet, in that divisive, destructive year, a brand new rugby league institution began to take shape.

*

Of all the numerous successes of the State of Origin concept, perhaps the series' greatest gift to Australian rugby league was its ability to transcend the turmoil that surrounded it in the regular season. Particularly in Queensland, Origin was *the* calendar event and the most treasured rugby league tradition.

Every year since the inaugural series in 1980, Alf Abdullah, the secretary of the Sarina Crocodiles, would purchase a stack of tickets from the Queensland Rugby League, organise a crew of his mates from the Mackay region, and enjoy the trip to Brisbane. 'What I liked about Origin,' he later recalled, 'was it felt like the country meeting the city.'

Many of the former players, though, felt as if they had more to give. They had put their bodies on the line to build a commercial and cultural juggernaut for rugby league, but once they retired from football they were effectively out on their own, with sore joints and fading memories their only link to that breakthrough decade of the 1980s. 'It was hard yards,' explained Gene Miles, who retired from the Queensland side in 1988. 'Back in the day, once you had finished State of Origin footy, nobody wanted to know about you. We couldn't get a ticket to the game. Meninga couldn't get a ticket, Lewis couldn't get a ticket. It was as simple as that.'

That was not good enough for Tosser Turner. He treasured the time he had spent with the players and looked after them wherever he could. In return, the players loved him for his big-hearted approach to team camps and his stirring motivational speeches. 'They call him the Godfather of Origin, and that's what he was,' Mal Meninga once said. 'It wasn't about the footy, either, it was about the person. It was all about looking after his boys. That's what I learned from Tosser: footy teams are mateships and relationships. It's about caring for people, looking after them, making sure their families are looked after really well. Tosser started those traditions out of his own pocket.'

Although he served as chairman of the Redcliffe Dolphins and the South Queensland Crushers, Tosser remained above petty club politics. He appreciated every player who pulled on a Maroon jersey, no matter who they played for week-to-week. Once, when asked by a reporter to name his favourite State of Origin player, Tosser responded: 'As far as Queensland is concerned, you are talking about a family environment. There are no favourites.'[11]

During 1997, as the Origin series split in two, Turner and fellow South Queensland Crushers board member Alan Graham decided to call a reunion for all the former Queensland State of Origin representatives at the Caxton Hotel in Brisbane. Some of the men hadn't seen one another for years, and the goodwill that the catch-up created inspired Turner and Graham to formalise it into something permanent and official. From that simple reunion the Former Origin Greats – or FOGs, as it came to be known – was born.

The Former Origin Greats was created to serve two interrelated purposes. First, it was a means of recognising and connecting those men who had worn the Maroon jersey – whether for one game or 30.

'It was about trying to remember each other,' recalled Mike McLean, who played five games for Queensland in 1991 and 1992. Second, it was an opportunity to raise money for various causes, such as Origin camps, junior competitions, charities, rural programs, and Indigenous education initiatives.

In the years to come FOGs would develop a business model that allowed Gene Miles to become the organisation's first full-time employee and create a valuable link to state and federal governments. In some ways, FOGs was not unlike an RSL club in the sense that it channelled the community standing of veterans for wider social purposes. It also adopted a number system for the players – Arthur Beetson was given the No. 1, Wally Lewis No. 9, Allan Langer No. 50, and so on.

The fact that guys like John Ribot, who should have theoretically been Tosser's enemy during the Super League war, were appointed to the board of directors was illustrative of the magnanimous spirit of the organisation. 'During that period, I'd see Tosser and I'd say hello,' recalled Ribot. 'We weren't going out for dinner but he understood what I was about and I understood what he was about. There was a bigger calling with Tosser – he was such a proud Queenslander.'

The players treated Tosser as another member of the team. When Peter Jackson retired from Origin, he wrote an article for *Rugby League Week* about all the things he would miss from the team camp. 'I'll miss that feeling of running onto Lang Park when 30,000 people make the noise of 100,000,' he wrote. 'But if I could say that I'll miss something the most, it would be the look on Tosser Turner's face at fulltime when we've won the game.'[12]

Jackson, member No. 44, was one of the best-loved and most passionate Queenslanders. Tragically, however, he would not take part in the various activities of FOGs. He had been struggling with his own private demons.

Most people within rugby league knew that Jackson was a wild child. He had partied as hard as anyone during the 1980s, and during the '90s entertained fans as a radio and television personality. Once, during an appearance on *The Footy Show*, he celebrated the birth of his youngest son, Ned, by cradling a fake baby and pretending to feed it a bottle of beer.

'He was a unique individual,' recalled Mike McLean, who played alongside Jacko for Queensland. 'He could lift a room. There's not a lot of people that can do that. He just had that aura. He had a lot of close mates, but we were reasonably close. I didn't pick the end as well as I thought I could, but … how do you?'

Not many people, except for his wife Siobhan, knew that beneath the fun-loving exterior was a childhood trauma that had quietly affected him for years. As a child, Jackson went to The Southport School, an Anglican boarding school for boys. There, he was sexually abused by Hugh 'Ossie' McNamara, who worked as a house master and coach of the rugby union side. McNamara was convicted of child sex offences in 1995, but still hardly anyone was aware that he had assaulted Jackson, too.

By 1997, a royal commission into police corruption and protection of paedophile rings in New South Wales was nearing its conclusion. Jackson, a former Queensland police officer, wrote that the inquiry 'triggered memories of what happened to me and I fell into a deep state of depression. I was admitted to a psychiatric hospital and went on anti-depressant drugs, from then until now I have only existed, not lived.'[13]

Friends and colleagues had already begun to notice Jacko's erratic behaviour. He confessed to his friend Lex Marinos that he had started using heroin. 'It was hard, because I tried to have a rational talk about what a wonderful guy he was, what a great future he had, what a fantastic family he had,' recalled Marinos. 'Ned was just a baby, and Siobhan is just such a dynamic, wonderful woman. And it was like, *Pete, how could you threaten this? You have so much to live for.*

But that's the terrible thing that drug-takers have: at one level they know all of that, but the pull of the other is just too strong. He was clearly looking into the abyss.'

By the beginning of November, Jackson had come out of the rehabilitation clinic and was preparing to move into a new family home in Stanwell Park, a beachside town between Sydney and Wollongong. But on the day they were set to move in, he was found passed out on the side of the road and taken to Liverpool Hospital. He checked himself out and returned home. 'I'm not staying in that fucking hospital,' he told Siobhan. His mind altered by a cocktail of prescription and non-prescription drugs, he got in the car and drove off. The removals van came that afternoon and the family moved into the new home without him.

Next day, Siobhan received the news from the police: Jackson had overdosed on heroin in a motel room. He was 33 years old. 'I don't think he knew what he was doing,' recalled Siobhan. 'He was using rohypnol by then … it was just … he was in a really bad place.'

It was a tragic end to the darkest year in Australian rugby league. Despite his issues, Jackson had mates all over the country. After all, he had played football in Brisbane, in Canberra, and in Sydney. Nobody had a bad word to say about him. Even during the divisive period of the Super League war, one reporter remembered, Jackson was 'one of the few who genuinely remained everybody's mate'.[14]

'The thing I liked about Jacko was his intelligence, his communication skills, his laugh, how he brings people together,' recalled Mal Meninga, who had played alongside him for Southern Suburbs, Canberra, Queensland, and Australia. 'He's a team-first player. He's a mate; he wouldn't let you down. On a rugby league field you need people you can trust, and you could trust him enormously.'

In time, the FOGs would honour him by creating the Peter Jackson Medal for the greatest contribution to the Maroons camp. Winners would include Chris Close, Tosser Turner, and Kevin

Walters. 'I loved everything about Jacko,' recalled Walters. 'I loved his competitiveness, I loved the way he gave himself to the team. He's just one of those guys you wanted to be around. I considered myself a good friend of his – a close friend – and I didn't have any idea. It's very sad when you think he had so many friends, yet none of us could reach out and help him.'

Walters and Mike McLean were responsible for spreading part of Jacko's ashes at the beach at Stanwell Park. First, the two men took a tinny out into deeper water and shared a cigarette. To honour Jacko, who never seemed to have his own packet of smokes, Walters bummed one from McLean.

Then, as part of his official duties, McLean began to spread the ashes. Despite his experience as a sailor, he inexplicably threw them into the wind. Watching on from the shoreline, Wally Lewis noticed McLean put his head in his hands, and figured he must be wiping away tears. *The poor bastard*, thought Lewis, *imagine having to do that*. In fact, the ashes had caught the wind and blown back in McLean's face. McLean decided to think of it as one last bear hug from Jacko. 'For fuck's sake, Kevvie,' he said to Walters, brushing the ashes from his face. 'You can never get rid of this bloke – he's all over us still!'

And that was that. Siobhan and their three young children soon moved to North Queensland, where she eventually took a job working at the Lockhart State School in Cape York. The remainder of her husband's ashes were scattered at Lang Park, but for a while she stopped watching rugby league altogether.

The game carried on. Truce talks between the ARL and Super League were already being held, and reunification of the two competitions was not far away. But Peter Jackson, a loyal league man right to the end, would not be there to see it happen.

8

MY OLD LANG PARK

1998–2001

Robbie O'Davis laid his head on the pillow and stared up at the ceiling. He had earned the right to call himself the best fullback in rugby league yet lacked the self-confidence to truly own the title. His understudy was a quiet, blond-haired 21-year-old from Queensland.

O'Davis had seen this young man play for the Brisbane Broncos in Super League, and although he had looked sharp, international footy was a different proposition altogether. *Am I good enough to be the best fullback in the world?* O'Davis wondered. Sleep came before he could come up with an answer.

Next morning, O'Davis pulled on the green-and-gold No. 1 jersey and lined up to play New Zealand at Auckland's North Harbour Stadium. It was late April 1998. The Australian Rugby League premiership he had won with the Newcastle Knights – and his Clive Churchill Medal for best-on-ground in the grand final – was now in the past. A new season in a reunified competition, rebranded as the National Rugby League, lay ahead.

Within minutes, O'Davis went down with a knee injury. His understudy from Queensland came on to replace him while he was sent to hospital for treatment.

'Sitting there watching the replay of the match, I see this kid lose the game for Australia by himself; he dropped the ball three times,' O'Davis remembered. 'That weekend was the last trial match before Origin sides got picked. I missed out on the game and the young blond-headed kid goes back to the Broncos. Gets man of the match. Gets selected in the first Origin side. Now there's a fucking highway built from Brisbane to my hometown in Toowoomba with his name on it!'

The young blond-haired kid's name was Darren Lockyer. He was the brightest prospect to emerge from the Super League war.

In Game I of the 1998 State of Origin series, played just one month after his forgettable debut for Australia, Lockyer was picked for Queensland ahead of O'Davis at fullback. He converted four from four – including one from after the full-time siren – to help the Maroons to a thrilling one-point victory over New South Wales.

In Game III, O'Davis was shifted to the wing, Lockyer held the fullback position, and Queensland won the series. As O'Davis's career began to unravel following a positive test for performance-enhancing drugs, his peers rated Lockyer the best fullback in the country.

During the 1998 season, Lockyer played more games than any other fullback in the competition, scored 272 points and helped the Brisbane Broncos win the minor premiership and the grand final. In one of the greatest Broncos sides ever, among a group of players who were determined to win rugby league's first reunified season, he was the breakout star.

One of the most striking aspects of the Broncos' 1998 season was the quality of its young players, most of whom broke into first grade. In addition to Lockyer there was Wendell Sailor, a winger from Sarina in the north; Shane Webcke, from a Leyburn farm in the South Downs region; Phillip Lee, a rugby union junior from Nudgee College in Brisbane; Brad Thorn and Tonie Carroll, two New Zealand-born Brisbane boys; Lote Tuqiri and Petero Civoniceva, both sons of retired Fijian rugby union internationals; and the Walker brothers Ben, Shane, and Chris from Toowoomba. Despite their diverse upbringings, each of these young men arrived at the Broncos with one thing in common: they had been recruited by Cyril Connell Jnr.

Born in Rockhampton in 1928, Connell was an honest, kind-hearted old bloke with an exceptional eye for up-and-coming footballers. He had represented Queensland and Australia in the 1950s, and before he joined the Broncos in 1990 he was a well-respected, well-connected administrator in the Queensland education department. A love of meat pies and a fear of flying caused him to spend many hours behind the wheel, traversing Queensland by car to scout players.

He was the Broncos' backroom hero – 'a lovely, stately man', according to Civoniceva, who was identified by Connell at a junior carnival in 1993. 'He had a style about him. I remember he'd stand by himself at the end of a football field, rather than on the sideline, and he'd watch the play from there. Just his humility; you'd never have known he was a Kangaroo, you'd never have known he had great success and was held in such high regard in Queensland's education circles. If it wasn't for him, maybe the Broncos wouldn't have been the club they were.'

Like Dick 'Tosser' Turner, Connell made every one of his players feel important. But Lockyer was something special. The manner in which he was discovered in outback Queensland was typical of Connell's superb scouting network.

When Lockyer was a boy, the family had moved from Brisbane to Wandoan, a small farming town in the Western Downs, where they took over running a 24-hour service station. In Brisbane, Lockyer's father, David, had played soccer and Australian Rules football, and Darren also enjoyed a range of sports including Aussie Rules, cricket, and athletics. Yet after being selected for the Queensland under-12 side he never looked back. 'That was the first rep team

I played for,' he later remembered, 'and the reason I continued to play rugby league.'[1]

After a few years, the family moved further west along the Warrego Highway to Roma – the home of Artie Beetson, Willie Carne, and not much else. Lockyer had already become accustomed to the two fundamentals of sport in country Queensland: long-distance travel, and hard football played on rough, weather-beaten grounds. According to his mother, Sharon, 'they played on bindii patches, dust and, when it rained, mud'.[2]

Although Roma was out in the sticks, Connell had contacts everywhere. He had known Ray Bruton, a local schoolteacher and sporting administrator, from his days in the education department. Bruton gave him the tip, Connell travelled to Ipswich with Wayne Bennett to watch Lockyer play in a junior carnival, and before long he was on a scholarship, working behind the bar at the Broncos Leagues Club, and training with the first team. 'As soon as I saw him, I told Cyril Connell we had to have him,' recalled Bennett in 1997.[3]

By the beginning of 1999, Lockyer had already won two premierships, a State of Origin series, and established himself as the starting fullback for Australia. Queensland's production line of talent was now beyond question. Just as Allan Langer had emerged in the final years of Wally Lewis's career, Lockyer would soon take over from Langer as the chief playmaker for the Broncos and for Queensland.

★

The opening of Stadium Australia seemed to herald the dawn of a new era in rugby league. On Saturday 6 March 1999, the cavernous new facility, which had been purpose-built for the 2000 Olympic Games, played host to a double-header featuring three Sydney clubs and Newcastle. Seventeen tries, 89 points, a world record crowd of more than 100,000 people – it was, as one reporter put it, 'an occasion to regenerate a jaded game'.[4]

In truth, it was the beginning of an awkward season in which four clubs would be forced to merge and another would be cut altogether from the competition; a momentous year that marked the end of the millennium and the end of suburban football in Sydney.

Ninety years had passed since the establishment of the Sydney competition, and the city and its rugby league had changed almost beyond recognition. Sydney was now a café society, home to an increasingly middle-class, transient population, connected to the rest of the world by the internet, cable television, and cheap travel. Soccer was the booming participation sport; Australian Rules football, via the Sydney Swans, the most fashionable spectator sport.

Of the nine original rugby league clubs, four were struggling. Eastern Suburbs, now known as the Sydney City Roosters, survived thanks to its wealthy benefactors, but support for Balmain, North Sydney, South Sydney, and Western Suburbs had eroded. Despite the grandeur of the attendance record at Stadium Australia, in many respects the crowd of less than 5000 for the fixture between Norths and Wests, held a day later, was a truer reflection of the game's standing in Sydney.

There were simply too many teams in the city, and no foundation club would be immune to the impending restructure. Even the mighty St George – which had won 15 premierships since entering the competition in 1921 – had already partnered with the Illawarra Steelers. The National Rugby League, which was jointly owned by News Limited and the ARL, gave clubs until the end of July to discuss possible mergers, before an announcement on the 14 teams made at the conclusion of the season. The problem facing rugby league, wrote one reporter, 'is that the code is at the crossroads – it is still too much of a sport to be a business, yet too much of a business to be a sport'.[5]

The intrusion of corporate spivs and their boardroom jargon had worn down rugby league's true believers. Moreover, the symbiotic link between the player and the fan – once a key part of the game's tribal culture – had been put under severe strain during the Super League war as the players were seen to get rich at the expense of the clubs. Rugby league was now a game played by wealthy professionals and watched by working-class battlers.

'Years later, when we were still in the Origin camp, I was sitting with Wayne Bennett,' once recalled Chris Close. 'The Super League had come and gone, and the fallout was there, and I said to him, "Wayne … why? Why were you such a strong advocate? What did you see that I didn't see?" And he said, "They talked a good game, Chop …"'

In this stressful, uncertain period, even the Brisbane Broncos went through its worst form-slump in history. It took six rounds to register a victory. Then, in Round 8 against the North Queensland Cowboys, captain Allan Langer was subbed off 15 minutes before full-time. The match ended in a draw and Alfie tearfully announced his retirement three days later, citing a lack of motivation. By the time the Broncos got back to winning ways, the crowds had dipped to below 10,000 people at ANZ Stadium. Was it possible, some wondered, that Brisbane had already fallen out of the love with the Broncos?

The club had stopped giving away free tickets, and it could no longer harness the 'us against them' parochialism of the early 1990s. After winning four premierships in 11 seasons, it was hard to claim the underdog status Queenslanders traditionally thrived on.

As the crowds stayed away, ANZ Stadium began to feel soulless. Rows upon rows of empty seats had fans longing for a return to Lang Park. Management tried to divert media attention away from the problem, but Kevin Walters admitted that '90 per cent' of his teammates preferred to play at the club's former home ground. 'The facilities at ANZ are great, but the atmosphere just isn't the same,' he told *Rugby League Week*.[6]

Yet without Lang Park securing a major winter tenant, there were big questions looming over its future. Compared to Sydney's Stadium

Australia, which was booked to host a State of Origin fixture in June, the old lady of Queensland rugby league seemed like a throwback. 'Something had to be done,' recalled Brisbane commentator John McCoy. 'As much as I loved the old Lang Park, I just felt that it was flood-prone, and around there is all factories and residential areas. I really thought they should have redeveloped the Roma Street railway yards.'

McCoy wasn't the only one ready to say goodbye. The Brisbane City Council, with support from the *Courier-Mail*, wanted a new stadium built at the RNA Showgrounds in Bowen Hills, while the Liberal–National opposition published its plans for a riverfront sporting precinct in Hamilton.

But the state Labor government, with its long-standing ties to rugby league, decided to commit to the game's traditional home. The Lang Park where a heavily concussed Brisbane Rugby League player, Fonda Metassa, had once jumped out of the back of an ambulance to continue playing; where Queenslanders had watched the first ever State of Origin and the first Broncos victory; where Senator Ron McAuliffe had been farewelled and part of Peter Jackson's ashes had been spread, would soon be renovated to keep up with its new name – Suncorp Stadium.

Since the rebrand in 1994, many Queenslanders had flatly refused to accept the new title. 'I was in a conversation with a couple of blokes at Westfield Chermside, we were talking about football and this bloke had his son with him,' remembered Fonda Metassa's brother, John. 'I'm mentioning Lang Park, and he kept saying, "Where's Lang Park, Dad?" That's why they should never have lost the name – the history! You know, the next generation, and the generation after it, they'll just remember Suncorp Stadium. But what about all the prior shit that happened at Lang Park? The incidents that happened that are still folklore in people's minds? Lang Park has given Brisbane and Queensland an identity.'

Indeed, Lang Park was still home for the everyday rugby league fan. It had become completely synonymous with State of Origin, the only known reservoir of that famous Queensland spirit. In the 1999 Origin series, an under-strength Maroons were without Allan Langer, while Darren Lockyer was absent for the first two games and Kevin Walters for the last. Queensland won Game I in Brisbane, lost Game II in Sydney, but did enough to draw Game III at Lang Park to retain the Shield for another year.

As deadline day approached in the NRL, and talk of mergers and rationalisation dominated the headlines, the 1999 grand final, held on Sunday 26 September at Stadium Australia, was seen by many as a final victory for News Limited in the Super League war.

St George-Illawarra, the first joint-venture club since the truce talks of 1997, were defeated by the Melbourne Storm, a new franchise created by Super League mastermind John Ribot and stacked with refugees from the clubs sacrificed in the war – the Western Reds, Gold Coast Chargers, South Queensland Crushers, and Hunter Mariners.

News Limited now had a controlling interest in the game. The Brisbane Broncos, North Queensland Cowboys, Melbourne Storm, and Canberra Raiders were all part- or wholly-owned by Rupert Murdoch's media empire, while other clubs that had defected to Super League, such as Penrith and Cronulla-Sutherland, continued to receive News Limited subsidies.

In the end, five clubs that had shown loyalty to the Australian Rugby League – the North Sydney Bears, South Sydney Rabbitohs, Western Suburbs Magpies, Balmain Tigers, and Manly-Warringah Sea Eagles – were the most afflicted. Wests and Balmain merged to become the Wests Tigers, while Norths eventually joined forces with Manly-Warringah and moved to the Central Coast as the Northern Eagles. South Sydney was expelled from the competition.

The fallout was immediate. Souths fans and former players joined politicians, celebrities and even a few News Limited journalists in protest. Most wore Souths' famous emerald and red colours; others wore club jerseys from their team in Sydney. 'Rugby league is historically the working man's game, and a Sydney working man's game at that,' wrote one reporter who attended the rally.[7]

In these trying times, the insularity of the Sydney rugby league community became clear. Although they cloaked their self-interest in grand appeals to 'tradition', those very people had said nothing when Valleys – a club just as old and successful as the foundation clubs of Sydney – hit the wall. They said nothing when Brothers, or Wests, or Redcliffe, or any other club in Queensland lost their status and prestige.

At the time Marty Scanlan, a stalwart of the BRL competition, was asked by a radio station to comment on Souths' axing. 'I know how they must feel,' he later recalled saying, 'but you didn't ring me up when Valleys got kicked out of the competition. There was no support from anyone then […] South Sydney didn't worry about the BRL clubs up here.'[8]

Wayne Bennett had voiced similar concerns in 1998. 'This thought that the game starts and finishes in Sydney has to stop if we are to move forward,' he cautioned. 'There are clubs here in Brisbane who have been sacrificed because of the Broncos; there are also clubs in Townsville, and Newcastle, and Wollongong and Canberra who have done the same thing so a team representing their city can survive.'[9]

Nothing changed. There would soon be a second-coming for South Sydney, but not for Valleys. The survival of Queensland's rugby league institutions, no matter how rich their tradition, was not a high priority. Instead, many Sydneysiders continued to grumble about the Broncos and the Cowboys and their News Limited money, as if they were intruders into their competition. 'Plenty of league fans down south still can't accept that our competition is called the National

Rugby League, not the Sydney Rugby League,' once quipped Trevor Gillmeister.[10]

Although Queensland lost a great deal during those uncertain years of the 1990s, the administration of the game had managed to create new institutions that would continue to churn out talent. Queenslanders adapted to the new world far quicker than their southern counterparts. The Queensland Cup, for example, took over from the old BRL and Winfield State League. Beginning in 1996 with 16 teams from across the state, the league had a larger footprint than most national football competitions elsewhere in the world. 'It ended up being very inclusive,' recalled sportswriter Phil Lutton, who grew up in Gympie. 'I don't know how passionate people are about the Queensland Cup teams, but it's a very effective tool for producing kids. There's a very direct path. The junior rugby league feeds all the way to the top. It's an almost brutally effective second-tier.'

By the year 2000 there were signs of rebirth and renewal. The Brisbane Broncos played its 300th game and for a third time managed to win both the minor premiership and the grand final. Darren Lockyer took out the Clive Churchill Medal, and Michael Hancock, the last of the originals, retired a winner.

North Queensland had one of its worst seasons in history and finished last after winning just seven games, but the Foley Shield returned in the north for the first time since 1995. Matthew Bowen, a future Cowboys star, led Townsville to triumph over Mackay in the grand final.

In State of Origin Queensland suffered a series whitewash, with New South Wales registering the series' biggest winning margin in Game III. Still, the humiliation led to the return of Wayne Bennett as Maroons coach for the third time in his career. In the newly created position of director of coaching and planning, Bennett would totally reshape Queensland's approach, using the Queensland Academy of Sport to prepare underage and emerging Origin squads.

'The future of the game appears brighter than it has for many years,' declared the annual report of the QRL. 'The trials and tribulations the game endured in the 90s are fast disappearing beyond 2000.'[11]

★

From the postwar period to the beginning of the 1990s, Brisbane had struggled to reconcile two visions of the city. There was the 'big country town' Brisbane – the city of old timber Queenslander house on stilts, of subtropical plants and winding creeks – a comfortable but conservative collection of suburbs once described by novelist David Malouf as 'quite simply the most ordinary place in the world'.[12]

Then there was the Brisbane of the future – a city of brick veneer homes, air-conditioned shopping malls, and gleaming skyscrapers rising from the CBD. It was this vision, first put in motion by former premier Joh Bjelke-Petersen and his 'Minister for Everything', Russ Hinze, that favoured growth and enterprise over environmental and heritage concerns.

Since his election in 1991, the lord mayor of the Brisbane City Council, Jim Soorley, had worked to reshape Brisbane into Australia's most liveable city. As thousands of interstate migrants continued to pour over the border, liveability, he felt, would be Brisbane's comparative advantage to the hustle-and-bustle of Sydney and Melbourne.

The task for the council and for the state government was to resolve the tension between commerce and sustainability; to bring forth a city that was modern and progressive without losing those historic qualities that made it distinctive. The looming battle over the redevelopment of Lang Park was, in many ways, symbolic of these competing visions of Queensland's capital city.

For almost 100 years Lang Park had grown with Brisbane – from the suburban parkland of the 1900s, to Queensland's home ground following World War II, to a site of national significance in the 1980s and '90s. During that time it had provided the stage for Wally Lewis, a lead actor in Queensland's cultural renaissance. 'I can guarantee that I stepped onto Lang Park more than any other player – I'd go pretty close to saying in rugby league history,' Lewis later recalled. 'Both of my grandparents lived within 300 metres of the ground. We used to go over there, jump the fence – which was only about five-foot high in those days – and we'd run over there and have a good time kicking the footy around. It was a special place.'

And yet, as much as Lang Park's community feel and accessibility had been part of its charm, by the dawn of the new century Brisbane needed a larger stadium that could accommodate several sporting tenants, host large concerts, and attract international events.

For the Brisbane City Council it was a risk: why cram a super-stadium into a dense residential area, when it could be built elsewhere? And what was wrong with ANZ Stadium, which was in an out-of-the-way suburb on the southside of the river, and which they had already invested in heavily with the Broncos? On Tuesday 6 March 2001, after years of discord between Mayor Soorley and the state Labor government over stadium policy, the council finally approved the proposed redevelopment of Lang Park.

With Game I of the State of Origin series just two months away, the decision alerted people to the fact that this would be Lang Park's final big-time rugby league fixture. Already there was enormous pressure on Queensland to right the wrongs of the previous series' whitewash. Now, the players were saddled with the added responsibility of farewelling Lang Park with a victory.

By late afternoon on game day, the Caxton Hotel, located 500 metres up the road from Lang Park, was awash with Fourex beer, Bundaberg rum, and maroon jerseys. There were jeers for *The Footy Show* host Mario Fenech, who was dressed in the blue of New South Wales, and cheers for the premier of Queensland, Peter Beattie. The crowd were waiting, as usual, for a bus.

For two decades, it had become an annual tradition for drinkers to line Caxton Street and hurl beer cans and abuse at the New South Wales players as their bus drove past. Everyone loved it – this was rugby league at its most primal, a throwback to the old days of hard-scrabble tribalism. 'I'm not sure about the health and safety of everyone through Caxton Street in those days,' admitted Kevin Walters, 'but it was just amazing. The bus virtually had to slow to a crawl to get through, and the crowds would just bang on the side of the bus.'

As kick-off approached, however, there was still no bus. News filtered through to the restless crowd that police had diverted the convoy to avoid the mob. Tonight, it seemed, everyone would be saying goodbye to the running of the buses as well as Lang Park. Following years of turmoil in the game, this series felt to many like the end of an era.

Against a New South Wales squad stacked with representative talent, Wayne Bennett had selected ten rookies. Among them was Petero Civoniceva, a late-blooming 24-year-old prop forward from the Brisbane Broncos.

As a boy attending State of Origin during the 1980s, Civoniceva had sat on the Milton Street terraces and fell in love with the idea of representing Queensland. Now, as he ran out of the tunnel to make his debut, he cast an eye towards those terraces. 'It was one of those moments I'll never forget,' he said.

Civoniceva took the third hit-up of the game and crashed through a would-be tackler, setting the tone for a dominant display by the home side. Queensland scored three tries in either half to win by 18 points – their biggest winning margin in 12 years.

The drama and emotion of Game I illustrated why Lang Park needed to be preserved, and the immense task that lay ahead for the architects responsible for its redevelopment. As much as players and commentators spoke about its carnal atmosphere, Lang Park's deep emotional value was built on continuity.

A great stadium is, at essence, a storehouse of memories, and each of the ten rookies who ran through Lang Park's tunnel and out onto that sacred strip of Brisbane turf knew they were literally following in the footsteps of Artie, Wally, Mal, Choppy, Jacko, Alfie, and Gilly. That meant something. And it imbued those young men with a sense of great purpose and responsibility. 'It was the holy grail – the ultimate – to be at Lang Park,' remembered Civoniceva. 'So much of my history in falling in love with rugby league was all around that field, seeing the great games.'

While many Queenslanders looked forward to returning to a rebuilt stadium in a couple of years' time, a group of local residents were concerned that the transformation of Lang Park would totally colonise their suburb. Their fears were well-founded: Lang Park had historically been a walk-up ground with little surrounding space for traffic or carparks, and the trend in Sydney and Melbourne was to build new stadiums in designated precincts, far away from residential areas.

Fearing interminable delays and court battles, the minister for state development, Tom Barton, called in the project under the Integrated Planning Act – in effect blocking the right of residents to appeal in the Planning and Environment Court. Outrage ensued. The state opposition leader compared the decision to 'the dark old days of Russ Hinze and Joh Bjelke-Petersen', while the Petrie Terrace Residents Association called it a 'return to the Joh era of government arrogance'.[13]

Although the politics might have been reminiscent of the Bjelke-Petersen era, the results would be rather different. In the past Queenslanders had been appalled by the demolition of heritage buildings such as the Bellevue Hotel and the Cloudland Ballroom. But the redevelopment of Lang Park, under the guidance of architect Alastair Richardson, would be a resounding success. When the new stadium opened its doors to the public, journalist Bruce Wilson reflected on the changes visited upon his childhood football ground.

'When it was empty,' he wrote, 'I walked around my old Lang Park – or Suncorp Stadium as we now must call it – and knew that if a sporting stadium should speak for its city, this one will do fine.'[14]

Two weeks after guiding Queensland to victory in Game I of the 2001 State of Origin series, Gorden Tallis led the Broncos onto ANZ Stadium for its Round 12 fixture against the Northern Eagles. Midway through the first half, he copped a high shot from an Eagles player, stumbled, tried to play the ball, and collapsed to the ground. He was still feeling pins and needles a day after the game.

The trip to the doctors was worse than expected. They found that Tallis was suffering from a congenital narrowing of the spinal canal, which would require immediate surgery. Although he would eventually recover to play three more seasons, this was the beginning of the end of his career.

It also sidelined him for Game II of State of Origin in Sydney, which New South Wales won by a convincing margin to level the series. 'All of a sudden,' recalled Wayne Bennett, 'the Broncos had lost their captain and Queensland had lost their captain and spiritual leader.'[15] Faced with a severe lack of experience in the team, Bennett's mind soon turned to Allan Langer, the last remaining legend of Queensland's golden era in the 1980s.

Since 1987, when Bennett was still a rookie representative coach and Langer was a virtual unknown from Ipswich, their careers had blossomed in unison. They won the Origin series in their first year together. In 1988, the Broncos had entered the Sydney competition with Bennett as coach and Langer as halfback. By the end of the 1990s, each of the Broncos' four premiership victories had been achieved with Bennett in charge and Langer as his chief playmaker.

They may have been an unlikely pair – Langer, a ratbag and enthusiastic gambler; Bennett, a quiet, no-nonsense teetotaller – but theirs was a formidable partnership.

Bennett, in particular, had become one of the most intriguing characters in Australian sport. He never seemed to smile, not even when his team won, and he regularly treated the press with disdain. Reporters often found him difficult to work with, but hung on his every word nonetheless. He was the mystery man they all yearned to understand.

Yet even for Bennett, resuscitating Langer's Origin career seemed to be a stretch. Since his sudden, mid-season retirement from the NRL in 1999, Langer had changed his mind and jetted off to play with Warrington in the English Super League. In his absence no player had truly claimed his No. 7 jersey for themselves, leaving too much pressure on Lockyer, who had also just taken the responsibility of captain following Tallis's injury. Lockyer couldn't do it all from fullback.

Although comfortable in England, Langer had privately longed for a final game in Queensland to atone for his hasty exit. When the call came from Bennett, he responded, 'What took you so long, Coach?'[16]

In Ipswich, where Langer's parents still lived, various signs welcoming him home were plastered around town. The young players at Camp Maroon on the Gold Coast hinterland treated him with reverence. At training, diehard Queensland supporters lined up for his autograph and the chance to wish him luck. 'It was a bit like the prodigal son returning,' later recalled Wendell Sailor.[17]

But there were doubters, too, particularly south of the border. After all, no Origin player had ever been selected from England, and Langer was nearly 35 years old. Some wondered whether his recall was a marketing strategy to help sell tickets. League writer Ray Chesterton, from Sydney's *Daily Telegraph*, mockingly suggested the Maroons pick Joh Bjelke-Petersen on the wing to join Langer at halfback. 'Typical Brisbane,' he sneered. 'Modern city one day. 1987 the next.'[18]

None of it worried Alf, who had been doubted all throughout his career. 'A lot of the things said this week have taken me back to when I was first picked for Queensland in 1987,' he wrote in a column for the *Courier-Mail*.[19]

For the opening 25 minutes, the game was a whirlwind of big hits, line breaks, and handling errors. Queensland led New South Wales by two points. Langer was clearly enjoying himself, kicking with the cheeky abandon of old and throwing himself into tackles. As the half-hour mark approached, he collected the ball 20 metres out from the try-line, perfectly positioned to send in a little grubber kick or a high bomb. Instead, as Craig Gower rushed off his line to close him down, Langer stepped off his right foot and left Gower clutching at thin air.

Two more defenders closed in from either side as he approached the ten-metre line. Before they could sandwich him in a tackle, Langer got the ball away to his five-eighth, Daniel Wagon, who laid on the try for Dane Carlaw.

For Langer to have come up with *that* play, at that particular moment in the first half, was undoubtedly the turning point for the Maroons. After the half-time break, Langer scored a try that put Queensland 24 points ahead. Again at first receiver, he shaped to pass to his right, ducked left under one tackler and was taken around the legs by another. Landing on his back, he reached both arms above his head and placed the ball over the try-line.

Paul Kent, a journalist for the *Daily Telegraph*, noticed Bennett leave his seat to watch the rest of the game as a spectator with his wife and children. The master-coach began to chant Alfie's name – 'something that was so unlike Wayne Bennett, the few that saw it had trouble believing it,' wrote Kent.

The chant became a dull anthem, picked up by 50,000 people at ANZ Stadium, heard at home through television microphones, and the anonymous man who started it all was the Queensland coach, sitting with his family and enjoying the game.[20]

By full-time the score was Queensland 40, New South Wales 14. Queensland had won the series two games to one. 'BLOODY ALF' screamed one front-page headline in the Sydney press.[21]

Yet for all the focus on Langer's heroics, the young Maroons deserved high praise for their efforts. Lote Tuqiri was unstoppable on the wing; Petero Civoniceva, John Buttigieg, and Dane Carlaw worked tirelessly through the middle. The North Queensland centre, Paul Bowman, crossed over for two tries in the decider, while Brad Meyers, Brisbane's red-headed second-rower, was arguably the best player on the park. Incredibly, Chris Walker scored four tries in three games.

For Queensland it was a deeply symbolic end to yet another thrilling Origin series. A sensational farewell to the old, represented by Lang Park and Alfie, was fused with a rising anticipation for the new, represented by the promise of a redeveloped home ground, 12 new Maroons, and a fresh captain in Darren Lockyer.

In the years to come, Lockyer – Queensland's first star of the post-Super League era – would lead a generation of Maroons to success at Suncorp Stadium, affirming beyond all doubt that the famous Queensland spirit could be adapted to the modern age.

PART III

HOW RUGBY LEAGUE EXPLAINS ...
RACE AND RECONCILIATION

SUNCORP STADIUM IN 2005
'... IF A SPORTING STADIUM SHOULD SPEAK FOR ITS CITY, THIS ONE WILL DO FINE.'
(PHOTOGRAPH COURTESY OF THE NRL)

9

BLACK AND WHITE BROTHERS

2002–2005

Take a drive north along the Bruce Highway – beyond the white-sand beaches of the Sunshine Coast, past those old goldfields around Gympie, away from the iconic Bundaberg Rum distillery, and through the cattle farms of Capricorn. The countryside here will be sparse, the speech a little slower, the timber houses hoisted high on stilts. 'There is a saying in Queensland,' once wrote the novelist Thea Astley, 'that the real Australia doesn't begin until you are north of Rockhampton.'[1]

Mackay and the Whitsundays are next, and then on to Townsville. Everything looms larger in Queensland's northern metropolis. There's the sprawling army barracks, which is a major economic driver of the region, and Castle Hill, a dry, rocky mountain overlooking the city. And that tall 70s-style hotel on Flinders Street, which locals refer to as 'the Sugar Shaker'.

Press on through Ingham, the home of Slim Dusty's famous pub with no beer. The scenery up here is so lush, so alive with promise, that it alone will provide new momentum. Up ahead are plumes of smoke from the sugar mill in Tully. The tourist attractions and bright lights of Cairns begin to play on the imagination – so close now after what feels like an eternity on the road.

Resist their lure and stop in Innisfail, a town featuring art-deco buildings, old-school Italian delicatessens, and surrounded by down-at-heel country pubs. There's the Mena Creek, a traditional Queenslander-style hotel next to the highway. The Criterion, in South Johnstone, where cane trains rattle by so close that the building shakes and yarning drinkers need to pause their conversation. And the historic Garradunga Hotel, which comes alive during State of Origin.

This is the town that raised Billy Slater. He lived, for a time, at the crook of Goondi Bend, beside green fields of banana trees and endless rows of sugarcane and a great big racetrack.

When Slater was little, he followed the Brisbane Broncos and idolised Allan Langer. In 1995, when he was 11 years old, the North Queensland Cowboys entered the Winfield Cup. He soon began supporting the Cowboys and imitating the club's fullback, Reggie Cressbrook, in his backyard.

Slater was exactly the type of young footballer that the Cowboys were built for. Here was a North Queensland native – the son of a Foley Shield veteran, a country kid who loved horses, who wasn't much good at school but had a big heart and plenty of character. Slater was exactly the right age, too: among the first generation of North Queensland kids to dream of playing for the Cowboys as an adult. And he came not from any old town but from *Innisfail* – the home of the Cowboys' founding father, Kerry Boustead.

As a teenager, Slater spent six months in Sydney as a trackwork jockey for the famous horse trainer Gai Waterhouse. Homesickness soon got the better of him, however, and before long he was back in the tropical far north. He joined the Innisfail Leprechauns, one of the great survivors of Queensland rugby league.

Leprechauns was the next evolution of the Brothers club that had played for decades in the local competition. During the golden years of Innisfail rugby league, Brothers had three other rivals in town:

Uniteds, Babinda, and Southern Suburbs. Yet according to Vince O'Brien, who played for Brothers and Suburbs, 'it was inevitable that Innisfail would become a one-team town'. Brothers had poker machines, the others didn't. As there was already a Brothers club in the Cairns competition, the merged entity adopted a new set of colours and the Leprechauns moniker, and based itself at the Innisfail Brothers Leagues Club on the banks of the North Johnstone River.

O'Brien, a life member of the Leprechauns, witnessed the emergence of both Kerry Boustead in the late 1970s and Billy Slater in the early 2000s. Kerry had more talent, but Billy, O'Brien recalled, 'was a pest'. 'He was on the go all the time, he had so much energy. He was a typical Slater. He wasn't blessed with the most natural ability, but by God he had the heart. That's a Slater trait.'

In late 2000, Slater had played well for a local representative side in a friendly match against the Cowboys' Young Guns, but there was no further offer for him to trial or join the National Rugby League club. He held them no ill will: he was a little man in an era of power and brute force, and was used to being overlooked. 'I didn't make the North Queensland representative side as a kid and I didn't play in any of the big school carnivals, either,' Slater remembered.[2]

Faced with two options – stay in Innisfail and work towards becoming the starting halfback for the Leprechauns' senior team, or try his luck elsewhere – Slater hopped in his car and drove south along the Bruce Highway. He travelled past Townsville, past his beloved North Queensland Cowboys, and continued on to Brisbane. It took 20 hours in total, but it ended with him being picked up by Norths Devils, Melbourne Storm's feeder side in the Queensland Cup.

In time, Slater would play more than 350 games for Melbourne, Queensland, and Australia, and redefine the role of the rugby league fullback. At the beginning of 2002, however, he was still an unknown quantity, working part-time jobs around Brisbane and waiting for his chance to break into Norths Devils' first-grade side.

That February, the Cowboys football manager, Peter Parr, spoke at a breakfast function held at the Innisfail Brothers Leagues Club. One attendee asked why the Cowboys had overlooked Slater. Parr, only a few months into the job, could not provide an answer. 'I'd never heard of Billy Slater when I arrived here,' he later admitted.

Around that time, the Cowboys travelled to Ingham for a team photo at Laurie Spina's farm. Spina, the club's inaugural captain, had carefully positioned a white ute and a harvester in front of a field of sun-bleached sugarcane. The props had to be just right. The players posed for the photographer, thanked Spina for the use of his property, and made for the team bus. 'Where are you going?' asked Spina. 'We've been cooking for days ...'

Inside waiting for them was a spread of antipasto, salads, and barbecued steaks. Spina hadn't just prepared the backdrop for his favourite team – he wanted to provide something substantial as well. It was a moment of old-school country hospitality; a timely reminder that the Cowboys were, at essence, a team that belonged to the community of North Queensland.

There was a perception, following the turmoil of the Super League war and the departure of local hero Kerry Boustead, that the Cowboys lacked direction and purpose. 'There were some struggles for the Cowboys through the late '90s,' recalled foundation player Paul Bowman. 'I think the club just got away, to a certain extent, from the original mission of bringing North Queenslanders through. Of course you need experienced players from outside of the region to supplement good young players, but the focus was on a lot of older players who were brought in. It showed that it didn't work.'

Many of the imports who had cycled through the Cowboys had been underwhelming. The first big signing, Jonathan Davies, had left after just a few months, criticising the city and its football club on his way out. Other high-profile players, such as Julian O'Neill and Tim Brasher, were more successful but still arrived at the end of their careers, not at their peak. In that context, missing local youngsters like Billy Slater only reinforced the view that the Cowboys valued profile over personality, bulk over brains, and short-term outcomes over long-term strategy.

As Slater made his first Queensland Cup appearances in Brisbane, back in North Queensland the Cowboys lost its first four matches and conceded 180 points. It was the club's worst-ever start to a season. 'Same old Cowboys, same old result,' read one headline following the Round 1 loss to the Broncos.[3] The coach, Murray Hurst, was sacked after just three games and replaced by Graham Murray.

The recruitment of Murray, who was a well-respected figure in the NRL, complemented a bigger backroom shift already underway at the Cowboys. Having barely survived a dire period in which the club was almost disbanded, News Limited had taken control in 2001 and appointed Frank Stanton, a former coach of the Kangaroos, as the interim chief executive. Stanton had subsequently brought in Peter Parr as football manager and Billy Johnstone, a former boxer and first-grade player, as fitness coach. Stanton also recruited Denis Keeffe, the former boss of the Townsville Crocodiles basketball side, to replace him as CEO.

In the short term, News Limited simply wanted the Cowboys to start winning football matches. Developing players, recalled Parr, was a secondary concern until the club had stabilised its finances off the field and started producing better performances on it.

Yet many people also believed that meaningful success would only come if the club returned to the parochial, developmental ethos it had been founded upon. 'The underlying fault,' wrote outgoing coach Murray Hurst in an article for the *Courier-Mail*, was that the Cowboys had 'consistently sold its north Queensland heritage short'.[4] The constant churn of 'outside players and coaches', he concluded, 'makes it hard for north Queenslanders to accept them as their team'.[5]

Even so, that club photo from the Spina family farm was testament to the growing contingent of locals in the squad – many of whom had been brought back to the region from other clubs in the NRL. More than half the first-grade players had roots north of Capricornia, while the Cowboys Young Guns were filled with players from the region. 'Of the 34 players running around in both our A and reserve-grade teams, about 25 of them are born-and-bred locals,' boasted CEO Denis Keeffe in an interview with *Rugby League Week*.[6]

Evidence of this commitment came in the form of a quicksilver Indigenous fullback named Matthew Bowen. Born in Cairns, raised in the Aboriginal Shire of Hope Vale, schooled at Abergowrie Agricultural College, and a Foley Shield winner with Townsville by the age of 20, Bowen was a true child of North Queensland.

The Cowboys media man, Tim Nugent, first saw a teenage Bowen carve up his opponents during a Confraternity Shield match in Townsville. 'In one of the games he scored some ridiculous number of tries single-handedly,' remembered Nugent. 'It was pointed out to me that this gentleman was coming to our club. And then I got the details – he was Indigenous, he was from a little place called Hope Vale outside Cooktown – and I couldn't help but think immediately of Kerry Boustead, because of the localism. At the time, the people of North Queensland wanted a North Queensland superstar ... Matthew was the one.'

In Bowen's breakthrough season in 2002, the Cowboys supporters warmed to him in the same way that a previous generation of Broncos fans had adopted Allan Langer. Like Langer, he let his football do the talking. 'At a club that's crying out for big hearts and not big mouths,' wrote one reporter, 'those who are softly spoken often make the best impression.'[7]

While Billy Slater might have been the one that got away, the Cowboys were now nurturing Bowen's development in a manner that would have been unimaginable at any other NRL club. Indeed, Bowen was living proof of the importance of the Cowboys' survival.

Rather than needing to move to Brisbane or Sydney, where he surely would have become homesick, he was able to stay close to family and his community while still pursuing a professional career.

Bowen's emergence in the No. 1 jersey, along with the recruitment of good football men like Peter Parr, Graham Murray, and Billy Johnstone – not to mention the establishment of the new leagues club in the centre of Townsville – meant that 2002 was a turning point in the history of the North Queensland Cowboys. The club's tendency to overlook its own backyard would soon be consigned to the past.

★

Down south, thousands of kilometres away from Townsville, expatriate North Queenslanders were spread right across the competition. Many of them – Gorden Tallis and Scott Prince in Brisbane, Brent Webb in Auckland, Rod Jensen in Canberra, and Shannon Hegarty, Justin Hodges, and Rhys Wesser in Sydney – were of Aboriginal or Torres Strait Islander heritage.

By 2002, no other state in Australia had a higher proportion of Indigenous people than Queensland, and roughly half of those Indigenous Queenslanders lived north of Rockhampton.[8] Accordingly, the Cowboys fielded a significant number of Indigenous first-grade players. In Round 8, North Queensland started with front-rower John Buttigieg as captain, Matthew Bowen, Ty Williams, and Matt Sing in the backline, while John Doyle came off the bench to score a try.

The increasing number of Indigenous North Queenslanders in the NRL was, in many ways, reflective of a growing confidence in the community.

Cathy Freeman, an Indigenous woman born into a rugby league family in Mackay, made headlines around the world after raising the Aboriginal flag following her victory in the 400-metre final at the

2000 Sydney Olympic Games. Pop duo Shakaya, consisting of two young Indigenous women from Cairns, were releasing hit singles. And for two decades, North Queensland activists and academics such as Eddie Mabo, a Torres Strait Islander who lived in Townsville, and Noel Pearson, an Aboriginal lawyer from Hope Vale, had been at the forefront of a national fight for land rights and self-determination.

Between 1992 and 1996, the Mabo and Wik decisions had been handed down by the High Court of Australia, granting Indigenous people Native Title to their traditional lands and ending the myth that Australia had been uninhabited at the time of European settlement. Queensland, and in particular the vast plots of land in the north, became 'the proving ground' in the fight over Native Title, according to historian Raymond Evans.[9]

It had been a bruising decade for Queensland's Indigenous population, with moments of deep, heartbreaking division. In 1992, Eddie Mabo's grave in Townsville had been ransacked and daubed with racist slogans. In 1996 and 1998, the electoral backlash to the High Court decisions had been led by an Ipswich fish-and-chip shop owner, Pauline Hanson. Her party, One Nation, was anti-immigration, anti-multiculturalism, and highly critical of what she called 'the Aboriginal industry'.[10] It always received greatest support in Queensland.

By the beginning of the new century, the major fault line in Queensland was between Indigenous and non-Indigenous people – just as it had been since the white settlers first arrived. And yet, through it all, rugby league remained the bridge between black and white.

'For blackfellas – even with all the bullshit and racism around you – that's the place where we could be the best,' once explained Dr Chris Sarra, who grew up in Bundaberg. 'Even as a school kid, we'd have all this racism – Joh Bjelke-Petersen was the premier, you've got a guy over the road calling us "black boongs" and my mum a "black gin" – yet when you're on the football field, if you're going to be racist, you want to be good because there's no place to hide. You could smash somebody and take your frustrations out, but also you could be the best.'

Rugby league also enabled Indigenous Queenslanders to identify – however briefly – with the sons of police officers and white landholders. And for whitefella Queenslanders to rejoice, even if only for 80 minutes, in the success of blackfellas: in the legend of Artie Beetson, in Steve Renouf's dazzling footwork, and in Gorden Tallis's uncontrollable passion for the Maroon jersey.

Years after the death of Peter Jackson, his wife, Siobhan, visited Eddie Mabo's island in the Torres Strait in her role as an educator. 'We were on an island called Mer – a beautiful island – and someone came up and said, "You have to meet this man, he's a fanatical Raiders supporter",' Jackson recalled. 'Even his house was painted in the Raiders colours! We went up in the bus and I knocked on the door. I said hello, and that I was married to Peter Jackson. And the man showed me photos of Peter he had in the house. He was crying, and I was crying, and we were hugging each other.'

Perhaps it was the simplicity of rugby league that brought black and white Queenslanders together. Or maybe it was the game's raw, equal-opportunity brutality. Whatever the case, in pubs around the state people could sit together, wear the same colours, yell obscenities at the same referee and cheer at the same moments. It didn't fix anything, of course, but rugby league offered the divided state of Queensland a unity of activity, and a unity of purpose, like no other cultural phenomenon.

The fact that there was a common enemy in New South Wales also helped. State of Origin 2002 would provide several moments that were starkly illustrative of the opportunities granted to Indigenous players on both sides of the border.

The squad speculation had already begun at the beginning of May, three weeks before Game I. One of the game's shrewdest tacticians, Phil Gould, was in charge of New South Wales, and the absence of Jamie Ainscough and Adam MacDougall meant that he needed to find two fresh wingers.

For three consecutive seasons, Nathan Blacklock, an Indigenous winger from St George-Illawarra, had been the leading try-scorer in the NRL. Yet despite playing for Australia in 2001, he had all but given up on being selected by New South Wales. 'Even if I was playing good and scoring two tries a game I still wouldn't be there,' Blacklock told the *Daily Telegraph*.[11]

Blacklock was expressing a view shared widely among many Indigenous people from New South Wales. For two decades, the Blues hierarchy had rarely elevated Indigenous talent. Laurie Daley, who played 23 games for New South Wales between 1989 and 1999, had been the only Indigenous player to be picked on a consistent basis, and even he admitted that most people thought he was Greek or Italian during his playing days.[12] In the year 2000, David Peachey, a gun Indigenous fullback from Cronulla-Sutherland, had been handed the Blues No. 1 jersey for Game I of the series. He had scored the deciding try in a New South Wales victory, but was the only player to be dropped for Game II. He was never selected again. In 2001, despite having the largest Indigenous population in the country, New South Wales did not have a single Koori in the squad.

In Queensland it was a very different story. Arthur Beetson, a proud Indigenous man, had been the Maroons' inaugural State of Origin captain and also a successful coach. Colin Scott had been Queensland's first Origin fullback. Mal Meninga, who is of South Sea Islander descent but often thought to be Aboriginal, had scored more points than anybody else. Tony Currie had been a reliable utility option from the bench. Sam Backo, Joe Kilroy, Steve Renouf, Wendell Sailor, and Carl Webb had been crowd favourites, while Gorden Tallis was the incumbent captain.

Some Blues supporters began to notice the discrepancy. 'I was always aware that Queensland had a strong Indigenous representation in their team,' recalled Lex Marinos, an actor, director, and playwright from New South Wales. 'Right from the first game Indigenous people had leadership positions in their team. They were clearly at least as equal as the other players. Whereas with New South Wales, I always felt it was an almost tokenistic representation.'

By 2002, Timana Tahu, from Newcastle, was the Blues' sole Indigenous representative. Nathan Blacklock soon defected to rugby union to play for the New South Wales Waratahs. 'I thought I was wasting my time with rugby league,' Blacklock later explained. 'All I wanted to do was play for New South Wales. Personally, it really hurt me, and I tried to hide it … I had to play for New South Wales somehow, so I played for the Waratahs.' He could never figure out why he was deemed good enough to play for his country but not his state. 'I think I would have had a better chance playing for Queensland in State of Origin,' he said.

It may never be known exactly why Indigenous New South Welshmen were used so sparingly in State of Origin. What had become clear by the turn of the century, though, was that the Blues were losing the support of its Indigenous population. Thousands of Kooris, including Blacklock, began to cheer for Queensland.

Brad Cooke, a Bidjigal man from Sydney and a commentator for NITV, always backed the Blues but couldn't help but notice how many people in his community were supporting the Maroons. 'Regardless of New South Wales or Queensland,' Cooke once explained, 'we have to remember that those borders are not Aboriginal borders. They are white, state borders of colonial history. When you look at New South Wales versus Queensland, that's not what blackfellas ultimately see. We're many nations in a big place along the east coast: saltwater country mixed with freshwater country.

'I noticed there were so many Aboriginal players that had played one game, two games, but very few that had played a lot of games for New South Wales. But whenever a Queensland Aboriginal player played Origin, invariably they didn't just play one or two games – they played five, ten, or 15! That's the thing which frustrated a lot of Kooris in New South Wales: we saw that in Queensland, Murris were getting more game time and becoming heroes of their community.'

After New South Wales won the opening game of the 2002 series, Queensland returned in Game II with several new players. One of them was Justin Hodges, a rookie Indigenous winger from Cairns, who had already developed something of a bad-boy image after leaving the Brisbane Broncos for Sydney.

Hodges began the game full of nerves. He fumbled a regulation kick from Andrew Johns, dropped a high bomb, and then knocked-on to give away possession in Queensland's half. But the worst was still to come. In the 27th minute, with Queensland leading by four points, he collected the ball in-goal, threw a wild pass in the direction of Darren Lockyer, and watched in horror as Blues five-eighth Braith Anasta dived on the loose ball to score. And then, in the second half, he compounded his error by throwing yet another speculative pass across his own in-goal area. Luke Ricketson pounced on the error to bring New South Wales to within six points.

Shellshocked, Hodges was promptly substituted while Queensland held on to win the game. It was, without doubt, the worst Origin debut of all time. 'Hodges replays the hazards of Duke,' read one headline in the *Australian* newspaper, recalling the calamitous in-goal error made by New South Wales's Indigenous winger Phil Duke in the 1982 Origin decider.[13]

The similarities between Duke's mistake in 1982 and Hodges' errors in 2002 were remarkable, not least because both players were on debut, and both were Indigenous. Yet while Duke was never again picked for New South Wales, Hodges would go on to make another 23 appearances for the Maroons and join the coaching staff in retirement.

There were many contributing factors in the differing fortunes of both men. For one thing, Hodges was a genuine star – he won a premiership with the Sydney Roosters later that season – while Duke was a virtual unknown who had been plucked from the obscurity of country football. Also, Hodges' mistake didn't cost Queensland the game, as Duke's had in 1982.

Above all, Hodges would become a vindication of the 'pick and stick' culture of the Queensland Origin camp. Between 1980 and 2002, Queensland selected 134 players to New South Wales's 179.

Part of the reason for this was because there were more professional clubs from New South Wales, there were simply more New South Welshmen to choose from. But Queensland was also home to 'the Origin player' – the otherwise unremarkable club footballer who grew in stature once he pulled on the Maroon shirt. And the creation of the FOGs, in 1997, had helped engender a culture of reverence and loyalty to those who had played for Queensland.

According to Gene Miles, the chairman of the Former Origin Greats, 'pick and stick' was a necessity because of the limited player pool Queensland had to draw from. 'That's been our policy from day one – right back to 1982,' explained Miles, who became a Queensland selector in 2001. The Maroons stayed loyal to its players, he added, because Queensland 'never had the depth that New South Wales had'.

The focus on Hodges was quickly diverted to another Indigenous Queenslander, Gorden Tallis, who in Game III made a tackle that came to define his career. In the 15th minute, with New South Wales leading by two points, Blues winger Brett Hodgson dashed towards a gap in Queensland's defence. As he stepped over the 30-metre line, Tallis grabbed him by the collar and swung him round and round along the turf and into touch. It sent the Sydney crowd wild with indignation.

Later, as Queensland scored a last-gasp try to secure an 18–18 draw and retain the series, Tallis would deliver the opposition fans a controversial two-fingered salute. Unbecoming though the gesture may have been, this was Gorden Tallis – the 'Raging Bull' – at his finest. The two-fingered salute, he later explained, was a response to a perceived slight on his mother from the crowd. But the cruel lasso tackle was pure Gordie, reminiscent of an outback farmer wrestling a helpless sheep. It was spectacular – 'a defining moment in Origin history', according to team manager Chris Close.[14]

The 2002 series, which would forever be remembered for the performances of two Indigenous Queenslanders, was a prelude of things to come. For the next decade and a half, Indigenous players would dominate the Queensland State of Origin side in a way that few other Australian representative teams had ever managed before.

*

When Cameron Smith was little – before his 400-plus first-grade games, before he captained his state and nation – he wore out the grass in the backyard of his family home. The Smiths lived in Logan, a downtrodden city between Brisbane and the Gold Coast, among the factories, housing estates, and endless shopping centres of Southeast Queensland.

Like Billy Slater, Smith was born into a rugby league family and played junior football for a Brothers club. Founded in 1976 by one of the nuns from St Paul's Catholic School, Logan Brothers wore green and gold, not the traditional blue-and-white butchers stripes, and became an institution of the region.

Yet as was the case for many players of his generation, a significant part of Smith's football education came from watching televised matches. He grew up admiring Queenslanders – the attacking, free-flowing football instigated by Wally Lewis and Allan Langer, and the legendary work-rate of hard-men like Gary Larson.

The Smith family observed State of Origin like a religious ritual, with Lang Park as Mecca. Cameron would wear his Maroon jersey to school and turn his backyard into a field of dreams. 'We had a two-storey house,' he later recalled, 'and I'd come walking out from the bottom storey – it was like I was walking out onto Lang Park.'[15]

By 2003, as Smith began to play regularly for Melbourne, the Lang Park of his youth had been totally transformed into the ultra-modern all-seater Suncorp Stadium. Its re-opening, though, was a somewhat muted affair. On the final weekend of May, the Brisbane Broncos lost to the Newcastle Knights at their new home ground, and then in early June New South Wales defeated Queensland in Game I of State of Origin.

Game II in Sydney was an even more emphatic victory for New South Wales, as the Newcastle connection of Andrew Johns, Danny Buderus, Timana Tahu, Ben Kennedy, and Matthew Gidley tore apart a lame Queensland defence. No matter what happened in Game III the series was decided, and New South Wales would be the first team to lift the Shield at Suncorp Stadium.

One of the key problem areas for Queensland was in the ruck. The Maroons' hooker from Game I, P.J. Marsh, was out injured, while Mick Crocker, the makeshift No. 9 from Game II, was always more comfortable in the second row or coming off the bench. In the third and final game, Cameron Smith was drafted in despite only having played a handful of first-grade games at hooker. 'There are not a great deal of options open to us,' admitted Queensland selector Gene Miles.[16]

Yet the 20-year-old from Logan rose to the occasion, delivering good, clean ball out of dummy half, holding his own in defence, and even crossing over for a try ten minutes from full-time. The game finished Queensland 36, New South Wales six. Smith's debut, said New South Wales prop Robbie Kearns, was 'right up there with the very best', and he was voted best on ground by his fellow players.[17]

It was the perfect introduction to State of Origin. 'I can't believe I've actually done that, in a real Origin game,' Smith told one reporter. 'After I scored, my family and girlfriend were the only people in the whole stadium I could hear. My dream has come true.'[18]

Ten months and ten days later, in Game I of the 2004 series, Smith's housemate, Billy Slater, joined him in the Queensland starting lineup. In a squad drawn primarily from the Brisbane Broncos, North Queensland Cowboys, and several Sydney clubs, they were the only players from the Melbourne Storm.

Born on the same day in 1983, Smith and Slater had first met in 2001 at Bishop Park in Brisbane's northern suburbs. After a season with Norths Devils in the Queensland Cup, both men had settled into the Storm's starting lineup in 2003. Smith made 24 appearances that year, Slater 26. 'I didn't realise it at the time, but this was the period when my life began to run parallel with Billy's,' Smith later recalled.[19]

In 2004, Queensland narrowly lost Game I in Sydney but levelled the series by winning Game II in Brisbane. The turning point in the match came after an hour of football, with New South Wales ahead by two points. The play began with Darren Lockyer, who received the ball out of dummy half from Smith. Seventy metres out, with one tackle remaining, Lockyer spotted Billy Slater rushing headlong towards a gap in the Blues' defence. He rolled a well-weighted kick into Slater's path.

Collecting the ball on the fly, Slater now had 50 metres to run and a few more New South Wales players to evade. At first he stepped off his left foot and surged forward on a diagonal run towards the goalposts. Then, noticing that two opponents were closing in, he lofted a chip-kick over Anthony Minichiello's head and veered left. The kick was delivered at full speed but it could not have been more perfect. The ball bounced twice, hovered tantalisingly over the try-line, and was collected once again by a diving Slater.

From there Queensland never lost the lead. And although New South Wales would end up taking out the series two games to one, Slater's wonder try was the most memorable moment of the year. It was a play of incredible dexterity, summoning the deft footwork and the youthful creativity of Allan Langer's famous zigzag dribble-try in 1988. 'I remember when I was growing up, I always used to pretend I was Alfie Langer,' Slater later explained. 'I'd be running around in the backyard at home, chipping and chasing and diving in puddles.'[20]

Five days after Game II, Smith and Slater both returned to Queensland to celebrate their 21st birthdays – the latter with what seemed like the entire town of Innisfail. Thousands of locals lined the streets to welcome Slater, who grinned and waved from an open-topped BMW. The mayor of the Johnstone Shire Council declared 18 June 'Billy Slater Day', while Bob Katter, the federal member for Kennedy, handed Billy an Australia flag and his mother a bouquet of flowers. A school band played 'Happy Birthday', and a convoy of well-wishers followed the Slaters to the Garradunga Hotel to continue the biggest party of the year.

It was the first of many tributes to a young man who would always be known as 'Billy the Kid'. Later, Callender Park – the field where he had played barefoot rugby league as a child – would be renamed the 'Billy Slater Oval' and Innisfail's welcome sign would proudly advertise that motorists were entering Slater's hometown.

Even though Queensland had not won an Origin series outright since the retirement of Allan Langer, 2004 would prove to be a pivotal year. Modern rugby league was won and lost in four key positions known as 'the spine': fullback, five-eighth, halfback, and hooker. Lockyer, who had played his first 16 Origin matches at fullback, had successfully transitioned to five-eighth. Cameron Smith, a former halfback, was now a reliable option at hooker. And Billy Slater, who had grown up as a halfback, was primed to take Lockyer's place at fullback. All Queensland needed now was a halfback to step into the shoes vacated by Langer.

Shaun Berrigan, a versatile 25-year-old from Brisbane, was the logical heir at both the Broncos and Queensland. Others felt that Scott Prince – a 24-year-old playmaker from the Wests Tigers – had the potential to make the Maroon No. 7 jersey his own. Both men had an encouraging balance of youth and Origin experience on their side.

But in that decisive, transitional moment, Johnathan Thurston – a big-eared 21-year-old reserve-grade five-eighth from the Canterbury-Bankstown Bulldogs – agreed to join the North Queensland Cowboys in 2005. It would prove to be the signing of the decade.

*

Go west from Brisbane along the Warrego Highway. The 750-kilometre stretch of road, which connects the city to the outback, passes through several towns steeped in rugby league. There's Ipswich, home of the Jets, the Walters brothers, and Allan Langer. Toowoomba, the breeding ground for a 'golden generation' of Queensland footballers during the 1920s. And Roma, the place where they found Artie Beetson and Darren Lockyer.

For Johnathan Thurston, the Warrego represents family, history, and opportunity. He was born in Brisbane, just three weeks before Billy Slater and Cameron Smith, to a Kiwi father and an Aboriginal mother. His mother's family are from Mitchell, a small town located an hour's drive from Roma. It's rough country out west, haunted by the tremendous violence of the frontier days. Between 1840 and 1860, Aboriginal tribes had been massacred or deliberately poisoned in places like Marburg, Grantham, the Darling Downs, and on the brown plains of the Maranoa district. One explorer, William Stamer, travelled through the region in the 1860s and was horrified by the violence. 'It was enough to make one's blood run cold to listen to the stories that were told of the diabolical manner in which whole tribes had been "rubbed out" by unscrupulous squatters,' he wrote. 'No device by which the race could be exterminated had been left untried.'[21]

Thurston was a descendant of that dispossession. As a youngster, however, he didn't know much about that side of the family history. 'I didn't even know what an Aboriginal was until I went to school,' he wrote later in his autobiography.[22]

Growing up in Sunnybank, a working-class suburb on the southside of the Brisbane River, Thurston spent his childhood playing barefoot rugby league. As a teenager he ran into trouble, so his family decided to move him west to attend St Mary's College, a prestigious football school in Toowoomba.

Toowoomba, on the crest of the Great Dividing Range, is the focal point of the western region. Thurston – like Slater in Innisfail and Smith in Logan – played for the local Brothers club. He worked part-time as a butcher's assistant and waited for an opportunity. A few NRL clubs sized him up and decided he wasn't the right fit. Eventually, after much uncertainty about his future, Canterbury-Bankstown signed him to its under-20 Jersey Flegg side.

Moving from Brisbane to Toowoomba was one thing; shifting from Toowoomba to Sydney in 2001 was another entirely. There were doubts – 'like with a lot of smaller Indigenous players', recalled Bulldogs recruitment officer Mark Hughes – about Thurston's ability to match the big bodies in first grade.[23] Before long he became desperately homesick. One of the coaches at the Bulldogs, Ricky Stuart, had to convince him to stick it out. In tears, Thurston went home for the weekend but returned to Sydney with renewed sense of purpose. That season, he helped Canterbury-Bankstown's under-20 side claim the Jersey Flegg Cup.

In 2002 and 2003 Thurston played a few games in first grade but could not displace the established halves pairing. Then he broke his leg in early 2004, which sidelined him for three months. He had also been drawn into the gang rape scandal that engulfed the Bulldogs that year. Later, Thurston denied having anything to do with the woman who had made the allegations. 'The press absolutely hammered us,' he wrote, 'and it felt like the public thought we were all guilty even though a charge had not been laid.'[24]

His decision to join the North Queensland Cowboys, confirmed in the winter of 2004, was made out of desperation rather than grand design – he wanted to play first grade; the Cowboys had an opening in the halves. Importantly for North Queensland, Thurston was an up-and-comer rather than someone at the tail-end of his career. That, above all else, was what made the Cowboys' signing of Thurston different. His decision to join the club was, in many ways, a validation of the changes put in place by the football department since 2002. 'We actually had a *team* to sell him,' remembered Cowboys football manager Peter Parr. 'There's no doubt that remuneration is the biggest thing in a contract, but if you get the remuneration right, they're still going to look at the roster and how competitive the team is going to be. We probably had a bit more to sell to him than the Cowboys had previously to younger players.'

Not long after Thurston agreed to terms, he watched from Sydney as the Cowboys overcame years of mediocrity to qualify for the finals series. It was a historic moment for rugby league in North Queensland. Led by forwards Travis Norton, Luke O'Donnell, Shane Tronc, Paul Rauhihi, and an explosive contingent of local boys, the Cowboys' success precipitated an immense wave of confidence and expectation in a historically neglected region. The crowds at Dairy Farmers Stadium were big and raucous. Locals started to feel pride in their team again. And when the Cowboys beat Canterbury-Bankstown in the first qualifying final, the rest of the competition began to take them seriously for the first time. North Queensland was no longer there just to make up the numbers.

The challenge that lay ahead in the semifinal against the Brisbane

Broncos, though, was incredibly daunting. In 16 outings the Cowboys had never once beaten their southern rivals. This match, however, would be about more than just football: the Queensland derby was rich versus poor, big brother versus little brother, city versus country.

Many in North Queensland still held deep affection for the Broncos, in part due to the fact that the club had a seven-year head-start on the Cowboys. The goodwill was reciprocated down south. The Broncos even forfeited the neutral ground in Sydney and allowed for the game to be shifted to Townsville. Was it simply mind games from Brisbane? Not according to Wayne Bennett. The Cowboys deserved to host the final, he told his readers in the *Courier-Mail*, and besides, 'it was much more important for the game in the north of the state than it was for us'.[25]

In the days leading up to the semifinal, people travelled from all over North Queensland to join fellow Cowboys fans in Townsville. The Sydney-based rugby league media travelled north, including the cast of *The Footy Show*. Some supporters camped overnight to line up for tickets, and in the end all 25,000 sold out within an hour.

By half-time the home side led by eight points thanks to the boot of Josh Hannay and a try created by a Matthew Bowen chip-kick. However it was the Cowboys' defence that made the difference. Every player tackled and scrapped and chased as if their lives depended on it.

Trailing by ten points with eight minutes remaining, the Broncos worked themselves into a perfect position – 20 metres out from the try-line with three tackles remaining. Shane Webcke, perhaps the toughest prop in Queensland, charged towards the Cowboys defence, urging his team back into the contest the only way he knew how. Previously, it was in moments like these that games had turned in favour of the Broncos, as depth and big-game experience came to the fore. Yet on this occasion the Cowboys found another level. Webcke was hit with a jarring two-man tackle which dislodged the ball, halted the Broncos momentum, and set in motion yet another Cowboys attack. The match finished 10–0 to North Queensland – not only had the Cowboys beaten the Broncos for the first time, they had held them scoreless, too.

For Gorden Tallis, who had played the final match of his career, his disappointment at losing was tempered by the fact that his hometown was now on the up.

North Queensland would never be the same again. Local support for the Cowboys, which had been steadily gathering momentum since the club's overhaul in 2002, now reached unprecedented heights. 'I remember the early games of the mid- to late-90s and the crowd would probably be 70 per cent going for Brisbane and 30 per cent going for us,' said Cowboys centre Paul Bowman. 'That game in '04, I distinctly recall running out and the noise for us was deafening. And on the flip side, when they were running out, the boos. That night flipped the support; you could feel it.'

The Cowboys soon became one of the most intensely loved sporting sides in the land. More and more people – not just from the north, but throughout country Queensland – began to invest their hopes and aspirations in the fate of this giant-killing football team. It was a club that battling regional communities could identify with. 'The average cowboy had gelded a lot of broncos in his day,' remarked Bob Katter, the federal member for Kennedy, in the days following. 'North Queensland is walking with its tail so high in the air today we may just have to consider statehood.'[26]

The following night, on the other side of the semifinal draw, Canterbury-Bankstown met the Melbourne Storm in Sydney. Johnathan Thurston, the North Queensland Cowboys' playmaker-in-waiting, came off the bench for the Bulldogs to score two tries and create another.

Yet his performance was still not enough to secure a starting spot in the preliminary final. Canterbury-Bankstown's incumbent five-eighth, Braith Anasta, returned, Reni Maitua shifted to the bench, and Thurston was left out of the squad entirely. But as the Bulldogs beat Penrith and North Queensland lost to the Sydney Roosters in the preliminary finals, Thurston was recalled to the grand final squad following an injury to club captain Steve Price.

Price, a tough 30-year-old prop raised in Toowoomba, had gone out of his way to mentor Thurston through bouts of homesickness and self-doubt. Like Thurston, he was leaving the Bulldogs at the end of the season. The 2004 grand final was supposed to be Price's final game for the club after more than a decade of service.

But Canterbury-Bankstown won it even without him. After the trophy presentation, Thurston collected his premiership ring, walked straight over to Price, and said, 'I want you to have this. It's your ring, you deserve it.' Later, during the victory lap, Thurston was asked by a sideline reporter about the gesture. 'I gave him my ring,' shouted an emotional Thurston, 'because he's the best bloke on this earth!'

And on that selfless note, Thurston left Sydney and headed north to Townsville.

In many ways, moving from a premiership club to the Cowboys was a risky move. Up north he lived life 'at a hundred miles per hour', recalled the Cowboys football manager, Peter Parr. He was a great-looking, fun-loving young man with a wayward streak that would twice see him arrested in Brisbane and Townsville. 'We called him Ratboy,' remembered Matthew Bowen. 'He'd get around with his cap on backwards and the seat in his car was so far back you could hardly see him.'[27] Still, when it came to football, he trained and played as hard as anyone in the competition. 'It's one of the reasons I backed him at different times when he was in trouble,' said Parr. 'He always struck me as someone who wanted to be better.'

With the ball in hand Thurston could be mesmerising. Steve Ricketts, a league writer for the *Courier-Mail*, first saw him at an Emerging Origin camp in Brisbane. 'I remember saying to the photographer, "Get a photo of him",' said Ricketts. 'He had this charisma. Watching him go through his skills, I just thought, *This kid has something.*'

Although Thurston had previously played for Queensland's under-19 side, he had not yet been selected for a proper State of Origin series. Yet after a bright start to the 2005 season in Townsville, he was called up alongside Cowboys teammates Matthew Bowen, Ty Williams, Carl Webb, Matt Sing, and Paul Bowman. The combination of Thurston and Bowen, in particular, was flourishing. They played football like two young kids in the park, constantly searching for gaps in the line, always ready to try something new or outlandish. Most of all, they played for each other. Had it not been for that nippy Aboriginal fullback, Thurston may never have ended up at the Cowboys at all. The opportunity to play alongside Bowen, he later explained, was one of the 'big drawcards of coming to Townsville'.[28]

In Game I of the 2005 State of Origin series, held at Suncorp Stadium in Brisbane, both men produced match-winning performances for the Maroons. In the 78th minute, Thurston kicked a field goal to level the scores. Six minutes later, during a nervous period of golden-point extra time, Bowen came up with a stunning interception on the right flank and raced away to score the winning try. For many Indigenous Queenslanders it was a moment of pure elation – two Murri brothers had come up with the decisive plays in a cliffhanger game.

Wayne Smith, a reporter for the *Australian* newspaper, was watching the match with Noel Pearson, an Indigenous leader who hailed from Bowen's hometown in Hope Vale. 'Even before Matt Bowen's team-mates could rush to embrace him, Pearson's fellow Queensland activists were thumping him on the back,' observed Smith.

'You know,' boomed one, 'Matty Bowen's just done more for reconciliation in the past 30 seconds than we will do in 10 years of political struggle.' And Pearson, ruefully reflecting on how even he had been guilty of judging people by appearances, heartily agreed. 'You're bloody right!' he said.[29]

Queensland went on to lose the following two games and New South Wales retained the Shield for another year. Incredibly, after 25 years and 74 games of State of Origin, the Maroons and the Blues were level at 36 wins each, with two drawn matches. It was a sporting contest unlike any other in Australia for sheer competitiveness.

Yet on the field that year was a brand new Queensland spine: Billy Slater at fullback, Johnathan Thurston at halfback, Darren Lockyer at five-eighth, and Cameron Smith at hooker. It was a combination that would soon prove unbeatable.

The 2005 Origin series also marked the beginning of the Thurston ascendency. At the beginning of September he became the first Cowboys player to win a Dally M award for player of the year. By the end of the month, he guided North Queensland to its first ever NRL grand final. He was the pivot for one of the competition's most explosive attacking sides.

It was also one of the most representative. More than half of the squad were locally produced and one-third of the players were of Indigenous heritage. In other words, the Cowboys now looked and sounded like North Queensland. That sense of localism was not lost on the supporters. In an interview with the *Townsville Bulletin*, the mayor of Thuringowa, Les Tyrell, said that reaching the grand final was 'a great result for the whole region, particularly the smaller areas where some of the players come from'.[30]

Professor Gracelyn Smallwood, an Indigenous health worker from Townsville, felt that the Cowboys 'played a major role in positive reconciliation' in North Queensland. For her, there was nothing quite like the experience of going to the football, sitting in a black and white crowd, with everyone supporting a multi-racial team. 'Seeing the black and white brothers coming together as one family through the Cowboys – win or lose – gave us so much empowerment,' she remembered.

In the final days of September, thousands of supporters travelled south to attend North Queensland's first NRL grand final. The lucky ones flew straight to Sydney from Townsville or Rockhampton. Others took the Tilt Train to Brisbane, before switching to a New South Wales Country Link train bound for Sydney.

Professor Smallwood, along with a group of friends, piled into a minibus and drove 24 hours down the east coast. She carried a special banner with the 'Cowboys' name fashioned into an acrostic poem. The letter C was for *Courageous*, O for *Our mob*, W for *Winners*, B for *Boys from the bush*, O for *Outrageous*, Y for *Young guns*, S for *So, so deadly*.[31]

Down south many more people found themselves caught up in the hype. 'Supporters have joined the Cowboys stampede,' wrote the mayor of Townsville, Tony Mooney, 'because of the way the team plays the game – fast, hard and exciting.'[32]

The first try of the match set the tone for an exhilarating grand final. It began with a hit-up by Paul Rauhihi, who stood in the tackle and offloaded to Thurston. Thurston veered left and spread the ball to Bowen. Bowen drew three men and flicked the ball inside to an onrushing Justin Smith. Smith threw a Hail Mary pass back over his head back to Thurston, who delivered one final ball for Bowen to score. But Wests Tigers were the better side over 80 minutes. Benji Marshall's flick pass put the Tigers in front, while Mount Isa-born Scott Prince – a former Cowboy – was awarded man of the match as the Tigers won 30 points to 16.

After the final siren, Thurston sat hunched on the turf, tears in his eyes, devastated by the result. 'You lose a grand final,' he later explained, 'and it haunts you for the rest of your life.'[33] More than he knew, though, his decision to join the Cowboys had fundamentally changed the trajectory of his own career and the dynamic of Queensland rugby league in general. He was the first player to prove that you could move to Townsville and still make it as a footballer. The voyage north would no longer be the road less travelled.

10

A SENSE OF BELONGING

2006–2010

The 2005 State of Origin series was Chris Close's last as team manager. His passion for Queensland had not wavered, but he now had a pub to run in Rockhampton and found that he could no longer commit to the workload.

A veteran of 17 Origin campaigns, Close was the kind of bloke who made others feel proud to be a Queenslander. A knucklehead on the field and a gentle giant off it, he had caused controversy during Game I of the series for giving the finger to Phil Gould and the New South Wales bench in the celebrations that followed Matthew Bowen's famous intercept try. He could not have cared less that it made him unpopular down south. After all, this was the same old Choppy Close who had slapped, punched, and wrestled Queensland to victory in the early 1980s.

At his farewell function, held at the Castlemaine Perkins Brewery and attended by state premier Peter Beattie, Close had stressed the importance of maintaining the foundations of the Origin concept. He was concerned, in particular, about the constant speculation that Queensland's next coach would be Melbourne Storm boss Craig Bellamy. Bellamy had played first grade for Canberra and completed his coaching apprenticeship under Wayne Bennett in Brisbane, but was born and raised in New South Wales. 'That was never going to sit well with all us old guys,' recalled Gene Miles, the chief executive of the Former Origin Greats.

During his farewell speech Close had openly raised the possibility of the FOGs withdrawing its services should Bellamy be given the job. 'They need people with expertise and most importantly they need Queenslanders leading the way,' he told the audience. 'I want nothing to do with the appointment of a foreigner.'[1] And so, led by Tosser Turner, the FOGs played a decisive role in turning the tide for one of their own – Mal Meninga.

By his own admission, Mal's coaching career at the Canberra Raiders had been unspectacular. Yet he was the ideal candidate for the job. He still held the record for most appearances and most points scored in State of Origin. He was the only man to be selected for four Kangaroos tours, was a valued member of the FOGs family, and held in high esteem among his peers. By October 2005, he was ushered into the head coaching job promising to bring back the pride and passion of an earlier time.

However things did not begin as planned. Queensland lost Game I and were facing the prospect of becoming the first side to lose four series in a row. The Maroons senior players – guys like Darren Lockyer, Steve Price, and Petero Civoniceva – were all under as much pressure as their new coach.

There were also doubts about whether that old Queensland spirit still resonated among the new generation set to replace them. So much had changed since the 1980s: the national competition was now well established and the game was increasingly dominated by Polynesians. Some even wondered if it was time to allow foreign players to participate in Origin. Others simply felt the series had served its purpose but was now past its use-by date.

And then there was the controversy around Queensland picking

Greg Inglis, a 19-year-old Aboriginal winger from the Melbourne Storm. In Game I of the 2006 State of Origin series, Inglis – born and raised in Northern New South Wales – crossed over for two tries in a Maroon jumper. Queensland lost the game by a single point but even so, Inglis's selection seemed to make a mockery of the eligibility criteria. He had played all his junior football south of the border and only one season at Norths Devils in Brisbane.

Yet Inglis was not an impostor nor was he a mercenary. In fact, he had grown up supporting Queensland and his connection to the state had been forged while spending a year living with Adrian Coolwell, a former Brisbane Rugby League player, while playing for Norths in 2004. The Coolwells were like a second family to Inglis. Adrian, who worked in the police watch house, took him there for a visit and told him if he made the wrong choices he could end up inside as well. Coolwell also took him to the North Plaza at Suncorp Stadium, to show him all the Indigenous names etched on plaques along the players walk. 'He did support Queensland as a kid – Arthur Beetson was his idol,' recalled Coolwell. 'I'd say at that time as well, he probably would have seen a lot of Indigenous guys were getting the opportunity here in Queensland. Indigenous guys who were absolute certainties in New South Wales weren't getting a run. I pointed it out to him that the guys aren't getting a go there.'

Inglis's decision to play for Queensland was vindication, perhaps, of the Indigenous community's deep frustration with the New South Wales selectors. He had elected to play for Queensland at a time when the Maroons were at their lowest ebb. While playing in the Queensland Cup, he later recalled, he was handed a registration form. 'It said, tick a box: Queensland or New South Wales,' said Inglis. 'I picked Queensland. People forget that I came in with six debutantes in 2006, on the back of a three-year losing streak. You know, I came to Queensland for a reason – because I felt a sense of belonging; I felt a sense of family.'[2]

It should have sent shockwaves through the administration of the New South Wales Rugby League. Instead, the New South Wales hierarchy treated the whole affair with a mixture of disbelief and disdain. They appeared to be more concerned with loopholes in the eligibility rules than the fact that one of their own had turned his back on the Blue jersey.

In Game II, Inglis was sidelined with a hamstring injury, but his replacement, Adam Mogg, scored two tries to help Queensland to a 24-point victory. With the series level and the final match scheduled for Melbourne, Game III would be the first time a decider was held on neutral ground.

The timing could not have been more perfect for Maroons fan Tom Cranitch, who was living in Melbourne with his young family. State of Origin was his last remaining link to rugby league. 'I can't remember not being passionate about it,' he recalled. 'Origin is so much bigger than everything else that's going on. This is where the cliché is a reality – it actually does mean something to a whole lot of people. There are kids sitting in hospital beds who'll be looking forward to Wednesday night; there's people in shitty jobs who will look at it as the highlight of their year if we can win a series. It means a whole lot of things to different people. To me it means a connection.'

Cranitch had witnessed the decline of many important institutions in his life. His own club, Brisbane Brothers, and the old Brisbane competition had effectively ceased to exist. The Catholic Church had lost its moral authority and was steadily losing parishioners. The Labor Party had been transformed from a working-class movement to a cabal of professional bureaucrats. Even the newspaper which he edited, *Eureka Street*, had given up on print and switched to online publishing. The world had fundamentally changed around him. And now, as rugby league continued to shed its old culture of tribalism, he was preparing to say farewell to State of Origin, too.

For Cranitch, the cumulative effects of the Super League war, the formation of a national competition, the increasing commercialisation of the game, the changing demographic of the players, and the Greg Inglis selection saga all pointed to an end of tribalism and therefore an end to Origin. Ten days before the decider, he wrote a column for *Eureka Street* detailing his concerns. 'In spite of the cracks,' he wrote, 'I will be there in the throng of supporters with my eight year-old son, cheering fervently for a Queensland victory and trying mightily to instil in his young mind the passion I felt three decades earlier. However, unless tribalism is revitalised in rugby league, I can't see how his generation will persist with the concept.'[3]

By half-time the scores were level at 4–4. In the second half the referee did Queensland no favours, disallowing what seemed like a certain try before gifting New South Wales the lead after a questionable knock-on call. Then the video referee awarded New South Wales a try despite the fact that Brett Hodgson had clearly knocked the ball forward in the build-up. The three dodgy calls, all of which occurred in a frenetic ten-minute period, seemed to spell the end for Queensland. The Maroons were now trailing by ten points when they arguably should have been ahead by six.

A nervous 20 minutes passed and still the score remained 14–4 to New South Wales. High up in the stands, Cranitch sat with his son among jubilant opposition supporters. 'We were surrounded by Blues people who were giving it to us,' he recalled. 'You could see Dan starting to look downhearted. I said to him, "Dan, we're Queenslanders … we never give up."'

Almost on cue, Johnathan Thurston received the ball 25 metres out from his own line, stepped off his right foot through a gap in the Blues defence and passed to an onrushing Brent Tate, whose runaway try brought Queensland to within four points.

There was a spring in the Queenslanders' step as that old feeling of Maroon momentum began to sweep around the ground. A wayward pass from dummy half gave them the opening they were looking for. The Queensland captain, Darren Lockyer, stepped forward to claim the loose ball. In a flash he was over the try-line, and Clinton Schifcofske's resultant conversion secured Queensland a famous two-point victory.

On the sideline Ben Ikin, FOG No. 89, had completely lost his composure, screaming excitedly into his Channel 9 microphone. At his pub in Rockhampton, Chris Close cheered with a bar full of Queenslanders. 'The roof nearly went off the pub when we won,' he recalled. And as Maroons fans in Melbourne entered a state of total delirium, Cranitch nearly crushed his son in the wild celebrations. 'I think I actually bruised him,' he remembered.

It was, for many people, the defining Origin moment of the new millennium – proof that Queenslanders could still perform those last-minute miracles.

And so began the era of Mal Meninga: a golden decade that spanned ten consecutive series from 2006 to 2015. Under his watch, State of Origin would never be the same again. He would bring history into the camp, first by delegating coaching and motivational duties to select members of the FOGs, second by schooling the players on the achievements of long-forgotten men old enough to be their grandfathers. He would take professional players, most of whom resided in Sydney, Melbourne, and Brisbane, on ambassadorial trips to struggling country towns to connect with supporters. And he would create a dressing room culture that valued discipline and teamwork, while also allowing individuality to flourish.

During those years it felt almost as if Meninga had wrapped his enormous arms around the entire state of Queensland, drawing everyone into one great big bear hug. 'Through storytelling,' he later recalled, 'we created a sense of who we were – what the Maroon jersey represents, and what the expectations are upon every player given the honour of wearing it.'[4]

Blessed with a rich seam of young talent drawn from every part of the state, Meninga would write a story of Queensland in all its complexity and diversity. That squad in 2006, for example, included men born in Cairns and Townsville, Longreach and Rockhampton, Toowoomba and Brisbane, Fiji and New Zealand and even New South Wales. 'I think Queensland's a state of mind, not a place,' Chris Close once explained. 'If you want to be a Queenslander, you've got to be there in your state of mind. There's no more shining example than Greg Inglis. We've stretched the fucken border a long way! But you know, in all fairness, in his mind he's a Queenslander.'

In the end, rather than cheapening the series, the emergence of Inglis became an affirmation of the enduring power of the Maroon jersey. In the next 15 matches, ten Indigenous Queenslanders were selected, and not a single game was played without a Murri in the starting lineup. In the decade that followed the 2006 series, Queenslanders black and white would combine to create one of the most inspirational sporting sides Australia had ever seen – an elegant yet unstoppable combination of flair, grit, soul, and maturity. 'You're not playing for yourself,' Johnathan Thurston told one reporter after the 2006 decider in Melbourne. 'You're playing for family, your teammates – you're playing for the whole of Queensland.'[5]

★

On the first day of August 2007, three weeks after Queensland won another State of Origin series, residents on Palm Island gathered for a funeral. They mourned Eric Doomadgee, an 18-year-old local who had committed suicide. The Indigenous people on Palm Island, which lies just off the coast of Townsville, wear rugby league jerseys everywhere. On this day, wrote journalist Chloe Hooper, 'Eric's friends, Palm Island's young men, had dressed in long sleeved maroon shirts and black trousers. Others wore maroon, yellow or white: the colours of his favourite football team, the Brisbane Broncos.'[6]

Eric's suicide followed the death of his father, Cameron, also known as Mulrunji, who in 2004 had died in the Palm Island police watch house. Mulrunji's body had been broken – ruptured spleen, fractured ribs, and a liver almost cleaved in half. They were injuries more often associated with high speed motor vehicle crashes. 'I believe the same as everybody else on this island – that he was bashed to death in the cell,' Eric Doomadgee had told a reporter in 2004.[7]

Yet in the days leading up to Eric's death in 2007, Senior Sergeant Chris Hurley – the policeman charged with manslaughter and assault – had been acquitted by an all-white jury at the Townsville Supreme Court. Sergeant Hurley maintained that he had not bashed Mulrunji, and that his death was a result of a fall in the cell.

Taken together, the deaths of Mulrunji Doomadgee, in 2004, and his son Eric, in 2007, brought into sharp focus two major issues in Queensland: Indigenous people were more likely to die in police custody, and much more likely to commit suicide, than non-Indigenous people.

The tragedies made headlines around the country, but there was no show of support from the rugby league community. Rather, the Broncos Leagues Club in Brisbane had hosted a rally of around 2000 police officers in support of Sergeant Hurley. Blue wristbands printed with '6747' – Hurley's badge number – had also been distributed for police officers to wear.

That rugby league brought black and white together had become almost an article of faith in Queensland. Professor Gracelyn Smallwood, who acted as a spokesperson for the Doomadgee family during that time, was one of many believers in the healing power of the sport. 'I was a crazy, angry activist, and my balance was football,' she once recalled. Yet here was a young Indigenous man being lowered into the ground surrounded by Broncos colours, while the Broncos Leagues Club had all but backed the white police officer charged with killing his father. 'There was no connection, absolutely no connection at all,' explained Professor Smallwood. 'Football, even though it brings people together ... the death in custody on Palm Island was too sensitive for any football club to deal with.'

In 2007, apart from a few protest marches, there wasn't a lot of public support for the Doomadgee family. 'Doctors are a conservative mob, but we were out there,' recalled Dr Mark Wenitong. 'I was in Townsville at the time, working for James Cook University, and I put out a press release from our perspective. I'm a doctor and I can tell you now: a simple fall off three steps does not cleave your liver in half and bust your spleen.'

However Dr Wenitong, a rugby league tragic, noticed the lack of advocacy from other prominent Queenslanders. At the time the Queensland State of Origin side was filled with Indigenous players. And yet, as always, the footballers stayed away from political matters. Their role was simply to turn up for training, take part in community and sponsor events, and perform on the weekend – not to publicly voice their opinions on the issues of the day.

They performed their duties well. Greg Inglis scored the most tries in the 2007 Origin series and was awarded the Clive Churchill Medal for best-on-ground in the grand final, Johnathan Thurston won his second Dally M award for player of the year, Matthew Bowen won fullback of the year, and Justin Hodges centre of the year.

Queenslanders were in the ascendancy in both football and politics. By the beginning of 2008, after the famous Kevin '07 campaign, Kevin Rudd assumed office as prime minister – becoming the first Queenslander to lead the nation in more than 50 years. He appointed Quentin Bryce, a former governor of Queensland, as the governor-general, and Wayne Swan, a Queensland rugby league fanatic, as treasurer.

One of the new Labor government's first orders of business was to say sorry, on behalf of the nation, to the Stolen Generations of Indigenous people. The national apology, delivered on 13 February 2008, was a landmark moment watched by millions around the world. 'The time has now come,' said Rudd in an address in Parliament House, 'for the nation to turn a new page in Australia's history by righting the wrongs of the past and so moving forward with confidence to the future.'

The apology brought forth a wave of Indigenous consciousness within sport, and in particular rugby league. Later that year, an Indigenous Dreamtime team was assembled for the first time to play a curtain-raiser at the Rugby League World Cup, and the Australian Rugby League became the first sporting organisation to commit to a Reconciliation Action Plan.

The Barefoot Rugby League Show, the first Indigenous television program of its kind, began showcasing the cultural side of the game, telling stories of bush footy from an Indigenous perspective. Hosted by Tony Currie, from Queensland, and Brad Cooke, from New South Wales, the program put many black faces on screen – from Sam Backo to Chris Sandow, David Peachey to Vern Daisy, George Rose to Carl Webb.

Although it reached a relatively small audience on NITV, *The Barefoot Rugby League Show* had a profound effect. For the first time rugby league players began talking openly about their connection to First Nations. If they weren't sure about their family and cultural history, they were encouraged to find out.

Before long, mouth guards and headgear and boots with Indigenous colours and designs started to feature throughout the competition. And in Round 4 of the 2008 season, for the first time in history, all three Queensland NRL clubs were captained by Indigenous men. Justin Hodges led out the Brisbane Broncos, Scott Prince the Gold Coast Titans, and Johnathan Thurston the North Queensland Cowboys. In other words, in the National Rugby League there was an observable shift from merely recognising the presence of Indigenous culture to actively celebrating it.

Yet at the lower levels old battles remained. In New South Wales, the Moree Boomerangs – a fearsome all-Aboriginal side that had been banned from their local Group 19 competition in 1998 – were still without a league to play in. And in Queensland, a long battle over the name of a grandstand came to an uncomfortable end.

For nearly a decade Stephen Hagan, an Aboriginal man from Cunnamulla, had been campaigning to have the E.S. 'Nigger' Brown Stand at the Toowoomba Sports Ground renamed. Edward Stanley Brown, who died in 1972, was a legendary former player, manager and president of the Toowoomba Rugby League. A much-loved local identity, Brown had been given the nickname due to his fair skin and snowy blond hair. The grandstand, which had been named after him in the 1960s, had included the word 'Nigger' on the sign for as long as anyone could remember.

'I played on that field,' recalled Dr Chris Sarra, an Indigenous educator and the 2004 Queenslander of the Year. 'I remember running out and looking at the stand and thinking, *Does that say "Nigger" up there?* It was strange. It gets into your psyche a little bit. It doesn't make you devastated or anything like that, but you start to think, *That's the kind of society and community we live in.*'

Hagan, who was new to Toowoomba, was not asking for the stand to be completely renamed. Rather, he simply wanted the word 'Nigger' removed from the sign. 'I wish to make it very clear to your committee that I have the greatest respect for the sporting achievements of Edward Stanley Brown and also wish to not offend his family,' Hagan had written in a letter to the Toowoomba Sports Ground Trust.[8]

That sentiment was soon forgotten, though, amid the furore over the word 'Nigger'. When Hagan first raised the issue, he was met with a backlash of epic proportions. Seemingly everyone – John

McDonald from the Toowoomba Sports Ground Trust, the state premier Peter Beattie, the *Toowoomba Chronicle*, even the local Aboriginal community – went against Hagan.[9] Arthur Beetson, the first Indigenous footballer to captain Australia, supported retaining the name. 'I don't have a problem with it and when I read about it I found it quite laughable,' Beetson told one reporter.[10] His comments were subsequently published on page one of the *Toowoomba Chronicle* under the headline: 'Big Artie backs "Nigger"'.[11]

The newspaper also published many letters from the general public attacking Hagan's motives, his credentials and even his identity. 'If you are so offended by the position of the Toowoomba Sports Ground Trust,' read one letter, 'I suggest you relocate to another town.'[12] Feral abuse and death threats soon followed.[13]

Both the Federal Court and High Court dismissed Hagan's attempts to have the sign changed, but in 2003 the United Nations Committee on the Elimination of Racial Discrimination ordered its removal. Unperturbed, the Toowoomba Sports Ground Trust simply ignored the UN directive and slowly the issue disappeared from the headlines. The sign remained. Finally, on 29 September 2008, the grandstand was demolished completely, and although the offending sign did not return, the discord around the word 'Nigger' was left totally unresolved.

All told, the deaths on Palm Island, Kevin Rudd's apology to the Stolen Generations, and the controversy around the E.S. 'Nigger' Brown Stand showed that Queensland was still the major battleground in Australian race relations. And that rugby league, Queensland's most culturally important game, was never far away from those moments of unity and division.

By 2009 Queensland had effectively become the black team of State of Origin. From Mal Meninga to Justin Hodges, Sam Thaiday to Karmichael Hunt, Petero Civoniceva to Neville Costigan, around half of the Maroons squad were either of South Sea, Aboriginal, Torres Strait Islander, Maori, Fijian, or New Guinean descent. The freakishly talented, all-Aboriginal combination of Johnathan Thurston and Greg Inglis – affectionately known as 'JT' and 'GI' – was a decisive factor in Queensland's winning run. JT scored the most points and GI crossed over for the most tries.

Despite being born in New South Wales, Preston Campbell – an Indigenous half from the Gold Coast Titans – loved watching Thurston and Inglis and the rise of this unbeatable Queensland side. Campbell was never selected by New South Wales, but for him it was never about state-versus-state – he just loved watching good footballers go around. He enjoyed living on the Gold Coast and felt that he had been adopted as a Queenslander. 'People treat me as if I'm from Queensland,' he recalled. 'They ask me all the time – because I started on the Gold Coast – "Why didn't you play for Queensland?"'

Campbell had captained the Indigenous Dreamtime side that played against New Zealand Maori in 2008. After the game was over, he recalled, an official came up to him and said, 'I'm glad you enjoyed it, because it'll never happen again.' The comment got under his skin.

For as long as there had been Indigenous rugby league teams there had been opposition from sensitive whitefellas. The Koori Knockout, an annual Aboriginal-only football carnival, had long struggled with the administration of the NSWRL. And the Moree Boomerangs, an Aboriginal club in northeast New South Wales, were widely disliked by opponents. 'I'd rather trust a black snake than a Moree Boomerang,' a local official once told the *Sydney Morning Herald*.[14]

In Queensland, though, there had been a tradition of all-black sides playing in a small country town 500 kilometres west of Rockhampton. Every year from 1963 to around 1984, teams would form along racial lines and play in Barcaldine – the spiritual home of the Australian Labor Party and the home of the black-and-white rugby league carnival.

Many famous footballers had been involved. Cathy Freeman's father, Norm, was said to have played in an all-blacks side one year. Importantly, those black-and-white games were a force for reconciliation, not tension. When Martin Flanagan, a journalist for the Melbourne *Age*, visited Barcaldine in 2007 he was amazed by the story for two reasons:

> The first is that, having been involved in reconciliation initiatives, I know how hard they are to get off the ground and then sustain. The second is that I've been writing on sport and black-white relations for a couple of decades and I knew nothing about what happened in Barcaldine, which, to my knowledge, is the most successful venture of its kind in Australian sporting history.[15]

And yet, as Flanagan acknowledged in his essay, much of that history had already been forgotten. When Queensland's Indigenous players grouped together to take a photo with the State of Origin Shield in 2009, for example, a minor controversy ensued and they were forced to deny that the squad had split along racial lines.[16] In other words, the rugby league community generally preferred Indigenous players to assimilate into predominantly white teams rather than create their own.

Still, Campbell wanted to do more with the Dreamtime idea. With the assistance of Michael Searle, a former first-grade player and the founder of the Gold Coast Titans, together they launched the Indigenous All Stars concept.

By the end of the 2009 season, thousands of fans had voted on the players they wanted to see in the inaugural side. And on 13 February 2010, the Indigenous All Stars beat the NRL All Stars in front of a capacity crowd on the Gold Coast. Indigenous fans came from everywhere to be there for that emotional evening. They went wild when Wendell Sailor scored the first try, picked up a corner post, and played it like a didgeridoo. Around him was a crew of Indigenous teammates, including Preston Campbell and Johnathan Thurston, performing an impromptu shake-a-leg dance.

Many people, including NRL All Stars coach Wayne Bennett, likened it to the first State of Origin match in 1980. But according to 73-year-old Alf Abdullah, who had travelled 1000 kilometres from Sarina, 'it reminded me of the black-and-white games out at Barcaldine'.

Abdullah loved the Indigenous All Stars. He had grown up in an orphanage and although he wasn't certain of his heritage, he suspected that his father might have been Aboriginal. Whatever the case, the colour of his skin meant that he recognised racism when he saw it. And he could see the pride and joy that the All Stars had brought to a community of people who had always been relegated to the bottom of the social order.

The Indigenous All Stars came from Queensland and New South Wales, from saltwater country and freshwater country. They were big and small, light-skinned and dark-skinned, with nappy black hair, dreadlocks, and straight red hair. Some of them were deeply immersed in their culture; others had only recently found out about their bloodline.

During a training camp before the game, Dr Chris Sarra had asked the players to separate into three groups – one group for those who didn't know anything about their heritage, one for those who knew a little bit, and one for those who knew a lot. 'JT stood in the middle,' remembered Preston Campbell. 'He just mentioned that he didn't know too much about where he comes from, and who his people were.'

At the time Thurston was being chased by cashed-up rugby union clubs in Japan and France. His future in Queensland was far from certain. But the experience in camp with the Indigenous All Stars prompted him to go on a journey of self-discovery. 'He knew there was some connection,' explained Campbell, 'but through that first camp it gave him drive to want to find out more.'

★

Three months after the All Stars match, in Game I of the 2010 State of Origin series, Queensland edged out New South Wales in a thrilling 52-point contest. Thurston won man of the match while Inglis, the adopted Queenslander, scored the decisive try of the night. It was GI's ninth try in ten games.

In the lead-up to Game II, during a boozy New South Wales team bonding session, Blues assistant coach Andrew Johns called Inglis a 'black cunt'. In the days that followed, Timana Tahu, a 12-game New South Wales veteran, sensationally walked out of the team camp.

Tahu, born to a Maori father and an Aboriginal mother, was a former teammate of Johns's at both club and Origin level. But he had seen and heard enough. His decision to remove himself from the team was a line-in-the-sand moment for rugby league. Here was a man standing up for an opposition player – not just in any game but in State of Origin, one of the fiercest rivalries in Australian sport.

The controversy also brought attention to the ongoing lack of Aboriginal players in the New South Wales team. The All Stars game earlier that year had shown the huge disparity between Queensland and New South Wales. While eight of the 11 Murris selected in the Indigenous All Stars had already played Origin for the Maroons, only two of the 13 Kooris selected had played for the Blues.

'Take a look at the topline Indigenous players that scooped big awards but for some reason couldn't be put in a sky blue jersey,' a frustrated David Peachey told *Rugby League Week*. 'Nathan

Blacklock was top try-scorer three years in a row and a specialist winger – couldn't get picked. Preston Campbell was Dally M player of the year in 2001 – couldn't get picked. Nathan Merritt was top try-scorer in 2006 – couldn't get picked.'[17]

As more and more Indigenous supporters began to look north to Queensland, Tahu's career went on a downhill spiral. He was never again selected for New South Wales or Australia. Yet he remained a part of the Indigenous All Stars, and in the years to come would lead the pre-game war cry.

Meanwhile, Andrew Johns apologised for his comments, resigned from his job with New South Wales and continued his media and coaching career elsewhere. To many Indigenous people the lack of consequence for Johns's slur was typical of how racial issues are handled in sport. 'It's a regular occurrence,' said Brad Cooke, a commentator for NITV. 'And that's what Aboriginal players and people in community feel. It's like, *Oh well, you can get away with it*. Whereas Timana Tahu sacrificed his entire career based on that fact that he wasn't going to hear it about another Aboriginal player – regardless of whether they played for another state.'

Unsurprisingly, Queensland smashed New South Wales in Game II to secure a fifth consecutive series win, and then won Game III to complete its first 3–0 whitewash since 1995. The Blues were in such a bad state that the NSWRL hired Brian Canavan, a leading NRL official, to conduct a review into its operations.

It was a striking admission of defeat, not least because Canavan was born, raised and began his football career in Queensland. During the late 1980s and early '90s he had also worked as a strength and conditioning coach in the Queensland State of Origin camp and as a trainer for the Brisbane Broncos.

After interviewing 96 people, including Wayne Bennett and Phil Gould, Canavan identified 'two major differences' between the Origin set-up of New South Wales and Queensland. 'One was at a program level,' Canavan later remembered. 'Wayne Bennett had implemented these Emerging Origin squads, so he'd already started the enculturation process; it was well down the track. The other one was just from a motivational point of view – and a lot of Origin is motivation. It was that underdog status and that sense of "oneness" … *we're in this together.*'

Some compared Queensland to the national rugby union team of New Zealand. There was remarkable similarities in the way that the Maroon jersey and the All Blacks jersey seemed to effortlessly unify people of different ethnic, racial, and socio-economic backgrounds, and drive everyone to a higher place. Both team cultures had been built on a foundation of respect, humility, and tradition. 'I'd read articles on the All Blacks as part of the New South Wales State of Origin review,' said Canavan. 'Having been through the Queensland era as a strength and conditioning coach, I was able to feel this deeper emotion – a deeper pride – in the jersey. Every Queenslander wanted to play Origin.'

In any winning culture, the health and cohesiveness of the team always takes precedence over personal desires or individual ambition. In Queensland, those who did not fit in to the team culture did not last long. To be accepted Murris had learned to assimilate into rugby league's rigid Anglo-Celtic culture, and by fitting in off the field, found space to express themselves on it. Every Indigenous rugby league player who had excelled for Queensland remained uncontroversial and apolitical – from Lionel Morgan in the 1960s through to guys like Arthur Beetson, Steve Renouf, Matt Sing, Gorden Tallis, and the Indigenous stars of Meninga's record-breaking side.

Indeed, it was the Kooris from New South Wales – guys like Anthony Mundine, Preston Campbell, Dean Widders, and Timana Tahu – who were the most vocal about the issues facing their community.

Dr Mark Wenitong, who was born in Queensland but lived for a time in New South Wales, believed there was no distinction between sport and politics. 'Having said that,' he once explained, 'at the elite level, if you're Indigenous you probably can start living in a bit of a dream world. You don't forget about your communities and your culture, but you're in an environment with the boys and you forget there are sensitivities around these things with your mob back home. I think you can lose yourself.'

The case of Greg Inglis was proof that many Indigenous people saw Queensland as a place of opportunity. As a result, the rugby league field was treated as a space for integration, not political activism. Yet something was already changing within Johnathan Thurston.

By the end of 2010, his career was at a crossroads. The North Queensland Cowboys had finished the season in last place after winning just five games and there were also rumours that he would be stripped of the captaincy following his arrest for public nuisance in Brisbane.

At the same time, he had surpassed 150 NRL games, been named in the Indigenous team of the century, and was now being touted as Queensland's greatest ever halfback. And his curiosity about his Gunggari heritage would culminate in an emotional family trip to his mother's hometown of Mitchell in Queensland's west. It set him on a path to find out more about his family history and, eventually, to speak about issues such as Indigenous health and education, stolen land, the Stolen Generations, and even call for a conversation around changing the date of Australia Day.[18]

Over the next five years, as the North Queensland Cowboys qualified for the finals every season, Thurston would grow as a leader for his club, his state, and his country. Participating in that inaugural Indigenous All Stars camp wasn't the only contributing factor to his development, but it was an important piece of the jigsaw puzzle. 'I like to think that was a pivotal moment for him that enabled him to speak more confidently about his culture and his people,' Dr Chris Sarra once explained. 'I think he became a better man. If you're going to be solid on the field, you have to be solid in your skin as a blackfella.'

11

HEARTLAND

2011–2014

A new year came but the rain, which had been falling since the beginning of summer, did not stop. From Burketown to Bowen to Brisbane, Queensland had splashed through a wet season of almost biblical proportions. In Banana Shire, inland of Gladstone, one town had already been completely evacuated due to flooding. The Port of Bundaberg was closed, delaying the export of thousands of tonnes of sugar. The terrifying rush of murky-brown water through Toowoomba was described as an 'inland tsunami', while in the Lockyer Valley, the entire town of Grantham would eventually need to be rebuilt on higher ground. In Ipswich thousands of buildings, including Allan Langer's junior rugby league club, were completely submerged.

By mid-afternoon on Tuesday 11 January 2011, the banks of the Brisbane River broke. The 300-metre, 1000-tonne floating riverwalk became dislodged and hurtled down the river. At the Rocklea Markets, hundreds of thousands of dollars of produce was destroyed. A sculpture in New Farm designed to commemorate the 1974 floods went under. Residents paddled canoes and makeshift rafts around inner suburbs to survey the chaos.

Next day, Premier Anna Bligh fronted the press. It was the worst natural disaster in the state's history, she said, acknowledging its enormous human, financial, and emotional toll. But, the premier continued, her voice shaking, 'We are Queenslanders; we're the people that they breed tough north of the border. We're the ones that they knock down and we get up again.'[1]

As she spoke, the water kept rising at Suncorp Stadium. The famous bronze statue of Wally Lewis was dressed with floaties and goggles, while the real Wally picked up a bucket and helped local residents bail out their waterlogged home.

In 1974, the old Lang Park had been just one damaged site among many. In 2011, Suncorp Stadium became a symbol of the tragedy as local, national, and international media narrowed their attention on the shocking image of a modern football arena swamped in dirty-brown water. The flood wiped out the dressing rooms, clogged the drainage system, and even caused a small fire in the building. 'We weren't the only ones suffering, but we became the iconic image, if you like,' later admitted Greg Adermann, the stadium's spokesperson during the disaster.

Considering more than 30 people lost their lives, some Queenslanders objected to the reverential coverage of Suncorp Stadium. 'I cannot understand how Channel 10 news can liken a bit of water covering some plastic, steel and concrete as tragic,' read one letter from a resident of Gympie, published by the *Sunshine Coast Daily*.[2]

Alan Graham, the stadium's general manager, saw it differently. To him Suncorp Stadium was more than just its material essentials. 'Our view was that Suncorp Stadium is so symbolic of Queensland, and if they could see that the stadium had recovered, that would send a message out that there is hope, and things would improve,' he later explained.

And then came Cyclone Yasi, thrashing North Queensland just as the floods had torn through central and southeast parts of the state.

The Category 5 tropical cyclone crossed the coastline at Mission Beach, a small town in between Townsville and Cairns, on Thursday 3 February – just weeks after the worst of the floods. Yasi tore the roof off a post office on Palm Island, smashed boats into marinas in Cardwell, and felled banana trees in Innisfail. In Tully, entire fields of sugarcane were destroyed along with the home ground of the local rugby league club. 'The goalposts look like spaghetti,' said Tully Tigers president Peter Lucy.[3]

Dairy Farmers Stadium, the home of the North Queensland Cowboys, suffered damage and the wild weather followed the team to Darwin, where they were hit by Cyclone Carlos just two weeks after enduring the chaos of Yasi. 'To go through one cyclone in the pre-season is rare – I don't think any team would have ever gone through two,' football manager Peter Parr told the *Courier-Mail*.[4]

Bunkered down in Brisbane was Mal Meninga, leader of the all-conquering Maroons. During the floods he lost a trove of precious newspaper clippings, photos, and other items he had collected during his footy career. Rather than dwell on the losses, however, it focused Meninga and his players' attention on the task at hand. Victory in State of Origin, they knew, would put a smile on tens of thousands of Queensland faces. 'Reminders of who and what we are playing for should not be necessary,' Darren Lockyer told the *Courier-Mail*, 'but we only have to think of who we are representing, in this of all years, in which Queenslanders have lost so much in floods and cyclones.'[5]

Although the images from Brisbane had been more spectacular, it was in little towns like Emerald, 300 kilometres west of Rockhampton, where the crisis really hit home. Everyone and everything seemed to be affected: shops, homes, parklands, major roads, carparks, the railway line, schools, the botanic gardens, the racecourse, the showgrounds, and the golf course. Alan McIndoe Park, named after a local boy who played State of Origin, was drowned in a metre of muddy water.

At the time, Emerald was home to around 12,500 people. On Wednesday 8 June, with Queensland leading the State of Origin series 1–0, Meninga took his players to meet those who had been affected by the floods. Locals ditched school and work to welcome their rugby league heroes. 'A visit from one player would have been enough to have the town draped in Maroon,' reported Phil Lutton for the *Sydney Morning Herald*. 'When the entire team rolled up, Emerald almost had a collective heart attack.'[6]

As the players shuffled along Edgerton Street to the town hall, some clearly overwhelmed by the turnout, they posed for photos, signed autographs, and smiled along with 4000 jubilant residents. A crowd of around 1000 continued on to Alan McIndoe Park to watch the team train. No one from Emerald could ever recall seeing crowds that big.

The fan day made as much of an impression on the players as it did on the town. In the years to come, the Maroons would attend similar fan days in country towns such as Roma, Bundaberg, Longreach, and Proserpine. Those country trips 'were as valuable as any training session', recalled Billy Slater in his autobiography.[7]

After Queensland lost Game II in Sydney, the series was set for a decider in Brisbane. In the lead-up to Game III, the sports editor for Sydney's *Daily Telegraph*, Phil Rothfield, wrote that Meninga's assistants, Neil Henry and Michael Hagan, 'have called most of the shots during Queensland's five-year reign as Origin champions'. In a column clearly designed to unsettle the Queensland camp, Rothfield cast doubt on Meninga's ability and labelled his methods 'the most bizarre coaching set-up I've ever seen at club or representative level'.[8]

Rothfield was correct in one sense – Meninga had surrounded himself with specialist coaches, many drawn from the Former Origin Greats. Yet Rothfield failed to appreciate the extent to which Meninga was redrawing the role of the State of Origin coach. In fact, Meninga's methods worked wonders on the playing group and the wider Queensland camp. 'He makes everyone accountable,' said Trevor Gillmeister, who worked under Meninga as a defensive coach. 'He's very good at delegating; he gives everyone responsibility. To me, that's smart. Players get sick of the same bloke spruiking all the time.'

Whatever the case, the emotion of the floods and cyclones, Rothfield's column, and the impending retirement of Darren Lockyer created an incredibly intense build-up to the Game III decider. And it was at moments like these when Queensland usually found an extra level.

By half-time the Maroons had raced to a 14-point lead. The first try, after 15 minutes, went through the hands of Lockyer, Slater, Matthew Scott, and Thurston, before Inglis touched down in the corner. Early on in the second half, however, Thurston – who had created one try and kicked four from four conversions – was stretchered off with a serious knee injury. His early departure set the stage for Lockyer, playing in his 36th and final Origin match, to guide Queensland to a ten-point victory.

Quiet and dependable, Lockyer had been the bridge between two eras. As a blond-haired, exuberant young fullback or a bald-headed, wizened five-eighth, he had been there during the Super League war, stood tall through the troubles of the early 2000s, and led Queensland into its famous unbeaten streak. It was Lockyer who had picked up that loose ball in Game III in 2006 and scored the try that began the Maroons' decade of dominance. By 2011, with Lockyer now 34 years of age, it was the right time for him to say goodbye.

At full-time, as the players milled around to congratulate Lockyer, a wheelchair-bound Thurston was rolled back into the arena to rapturous applause. He and Lockyer shook hands, embraced, and Lockyer lifted the Shield one last time. For the next six years, as Thurston shifted from halfback to fill Lockyer's vacant five-eighth role, Queensland would continue its winning ways.

In the days that followed Queensland's victory, Meninga celebrated his 51st birthday in Brisbane. Still seething at Rothfield's provocative article, he wrote his own version of events in a column published by the *Sunday Mail*. 'Looking across the river to the gleaming buildings of the CBD, it was easy to forget that not so long ago this was a city with a broken heart,' he wrote.

> Back in January, that same picturesque river did its best to bring Brisbane to its knees, delivering devastating floods that swamped parts of the city and that added to the agony of Queenslanders across the state in a summer of disaster. But on Friday, I saw a city and a state that have emerged from their darkest hours to once again stand proud and successful [...] Like the city of Brisbane, the Queensland team have managed to restore their glory despite the almost irresistible surge of forces beyond their control, through the commitment and pride of their people.

Queensland's triumph, he continued, 'was a victory against the very rats and filth that tried to poison a monumental team with lies, personal attacks, arrogance and disrespect'.[9]

It was vintage Meninga. Here was a man who could remember what it was like to be treated as a second-class citizen, when New South Wales ruled the game and Queensland was an afterthought. Even in 2011, at the height of Queensland's unbeaten streak, he found a way to draw upon natural disasters and the state's keen sense of injustice to create a feeling that Queenslanders were being hard done by. It was, if nothing else, a neat psychological ploy. After six consecutive series wins, Queensland somehow managed to hold onto the underdog narrative.

★

Gene Miles stood at the entrance to Dreamworld and glanced at his watch. It was 10 am. He was waiting, along with a crowd of Indigenous children and several FOGs, for the arrival of Arthur Beetson. They were there as part of the ARTIE program, a new Indigenous education initiative run by the FOGs. 'It's all about getting the Indigenous kids to school – closing the gap – and we use rugby league as the vehicle,' Miles once explained. ARTIE – an acronym for Achieving Results Through Indigenous Education – was named in honour of Beetson.

On the first day of December 2011, the program, participated in by several schools around Southeast Queensland, was ready to celebrate a successful first year. Miles's phone rang. *This'll be Artie*, he thought. It wasn't. Instead, he was informed that Beetson had just passed away. 'Slowly we had to tell the players, and then the kids,' Miles recalled.

Beetson had been riding his bicycle that morning in Paradise Point, not far from Dreamworld on the Gold Coast, when he suffered a heart attack. Paramedics had tried to revive him but were unsuccessful. Big Artie was 66 years old.

Within an hour, Premier Anna Bligh interrupted question time in Parliament to honour the 'knockabout bloke from country Queensland'.[10] The ARTIE fun day at Dreamworld continued in a sombre mood, and rugby league went into a period of mourning. Tributes flowed from former teammates, sportswriters, and politicians of every ideological persuasion. The Labor senator and minister for sport, Mark Arbib, said Beetson was his childhood hero. Lee Rhiannon, a Greens senator from New South Wales, thanked him 'for making rugby league such a great game'.[11] Bob Katter, the federal member for Kennedy, recalled meeting Beetson in his electorate and being 'surprised to find out' that he was Indigenous.

Men like Beetson had come of age during the era of assimilation, when state and federal governments – and much of the population – hoped that Aboriginality could simply be bred out to create a single white Australian culture. Big Artie was known to say that he was 'an Australian first, a Queenslander second, and a part-Aboriginal third' – although according to Roy Masters, later in life he reversed the order. In his final years he had grown ever closer to his community. As well as fronting the ARTIE program, he became the face of many government programs, supported several outback and Indigenous rugby league carnivals, and was a regular on *The Barefoot Rugby League Show* on NITV.

At the inaugural Murri Carnival, held on the Gold Coast just two months before his death, he had sat beside the field and beamed as he watched the new tournament take shape. 'He was so happy,' recalled Paula Maling, the producer of *The Barefoot Rugby League Show* and one of the founders of the carnival. 'He sat there and watched every game. I'm running around stupid, because we're broadcasting every game, and he pulled me up. This is the last thing he ever said to me. He goes, "Come here, kiddo." I said, "You right? You need anything?" He goes, "I just want you to know how proud I am of you." But he wasn't proud of me – he was proud of seeing this.'

More than simply a legend of Queensland, Beetson was a hero to rugby league devotees around the world. The British Parliament even paused to recognise his contribution. In his own country, meanwhile, Beetson-worship transcended state borders and racial differences. 'Arthur was one of the smartest human beings I've struck, footy and beyond,' recalled Brian Canavan, who worked with him in the Queensland camp as well as for the Sydney Roosters.

Beetson's funeral was held at Dolphin Oval in Redcliffe and attended by hundreds of people. He was the second Redcliffe man to be farewelled in three years. In 2008, Dick 'Tosser' Turner, the Maroons' legendary team manager and founder of FOGs, had died aged 76. The passing of Artie and Tosser meant Queensland was now without two of its elder statesmen.

But in Mal Meninga, Queensland had a coach who recognised something eternal about the contribution of both men, about how they had set a platform for Origin so it would outlive themselves. At Beetson's funeral Meninga spoke about how Artie had inspired him to learn more about his own South Sea Islander heritage, while his eulogy at Tosser's memorial service in 2008 had included a poem by George Bernard Shaw. 'Life is no brief candle to me,' Meninga read aloud. 'It is a sort of splendid torch which I have got a hold of for the moment, and I want to make it burn as brightly as possible before handing it on to future generations.'[12]

The dramatic build-up to the 2012 State of Origin series showed that the flame still burned in Queensland. Even before the series began, Justin Hodges told reporters that he and his teammates would win it for Beetson, just as they had done for the victims of the natural disasters in 2011.[13]

Before Game I, Ewen Jones, the federal member for Herbert, reminded his fellow parliamentary members of Beetson's legacy. 'When the mighty maroons run out in Melbourne on Wednesday night, they will carry Arthur Beetson with them,' said Jones. 'He is our heritage. He is Queensland. He is rugby league north, south, east, and west of the border.'[14]

And on the eve of the decider in Game III, a bronze statue of Beetson was unveiled outside Suncorp Stadium alongside bronze Wally, the State of Origin memorial walk, and Tosser Turner's plaque in the North Plaza. 'He is there above us, him and Dick "Tosser" Turner,' said Meninga as he unveiled Beetson's statue. 'They're all around, all the time. We're fully aware of the contribution they have made to Queensland rugby league and State of Origin football in particular. They're part of the reason why we don't want to let Queensland down.'[15]

The Maroons' opponents, though, were better prepared than in previous years and desperate to win a series. And with Darren Lockyer now retired, Queensland had seemingly lost its unbeatable spine. Johnathan Thurston shifted to five-eighth and Cooper Cronk, a diminutive halfback, took on Thurston's No. 7 jumper.

Alongside Smith and Slater, Cronk had graduated from Norths

Devils in the Queensland Cup to first grade for the Melbourne Storm. He was not as creative as Smith, Slater, or Thurston, but he had a perfectionist streak that complemented their genius. In 2010 and 2011, Cronk had been an unremarkable bench player for Queensland. In Game III of 2012, however, he would announce his entrance to the Origin arena in stunning fashion.

With scores tied up and just six minutes left on the clock, he called for the ball from dummy half. The eyes of 52,000 spectators and millions more television viewers widened as his drop-kick soared more than 50 metres, high and straight between the uprights.

As Cronk later explained to the *Herald Sun*, it was a moment of either madness or invention. 'I was in a state of grace at that particular moment – within those few split seconds of time between actually receiving the ball and landing it at its intended destination, there was no noise in my head whatsoever,' he said. 'Every sinew in my body came together in one perfect whole. But those who have ever experienced that feeling – and it doesn't happen very often – will tell you it's in a whole other place of experience from the usual ego or vanity that drives my game. So I'm not afraid to own it for what it was. I didn't feel good or bad about myself afterwards. I began to realise when we are being completely free of our own expectation, the body extends into its natural form, without impediment. And things happen.'[16]

Perhaps there had been better field goals than Cronk's, but never before had a rugby league footballer articulated his actions so beautifully. The game finished Queensland 21, New South Wales 20. Incredibly, the Maroons had extended their winning streak to seven consecutive series.

The man in charge, Mal Meninga, had done what many thought was impossible: he had pushed Queensland's state parochialism to even greater heights. Deliberately harnessing the twin forces of history and geography, Meninga had turned the 'Queensland spirit' from an unspoken bond into a highly effective program of action that could be reproduced again and again.

What had changed since Meninga's playing days, however, was the intense focus on beating those southerners from New South Wales. By the 2000s it had become much more about upholding a legacy, about affirming the passion for that special Maroon jumper, and about making their fellow Queenslanders proud.

'I travel to many parts of Queensland,' once said former National Rugby League player Preston Campbell, an ambassador for the Deadly Choices health program. 'They're passionate in New South Wales about rugby league, but I think there for a while New South Wales wanted to knock Queensland off the perch. But Queensland wanted to win *for Queensland*. That was a big difference. And that's part of the reason why they were dominant, the reason why it gets them over the line year after year.'

State of Origin, which had begun as an experimental exhibition game, was now an unstoppable sporting and commercial phenomenon. The 2012 series decider was watched by a record television audience of 4 million people nationally – a remarkable outcome for a sport that was still played seriously in only two states.[17]

'State of Origin has now become such a marketing colossus, but it works because it's real,' once recalled sportswriter Phil Lutton. 'And that's the trick. If you go with Queensland to any of these country towns, the whole town shuts down. They live and breathe it. I remember as a kid, if Queensland lost an Origin I would be so upset that I wouldn't even want to go to school the next day. That's how much it meant. When you strip it all back, at the heart of Origin – and why it's so successful up here – is that it's real. That's the secret to it.'

Origin was so strong that many fans and pundits now built their season around that intense six-week period. From March through May, all the talk would be about who was getting picked for Queensland and New South Wales. From May to July, the three games would take precedence over everything else.

For the players, Origin was the biggest stage, the most competitive football, and the richest payday. Greg Veivers, a lionhearted former captain of Queensland, loved the concept. He had missed out, in part, due to a blood clot which forced him into an early retirement in 1979 – just before the advent of State of Origin. 'The only thing I'm disappointed about,' Veivers later recalled, 'is that Origin wasn't there in 1920, '30, '40, '50, '60, or '70. It seems to me that the only focus on rugby league players seemed to have occurred from the Origin period. The others never got recognition.'

That was not good enough for Mal Meninga. To him, men like Veivers were to be idolised, not forgotten. 'Growing up, for me, was all about the BRL. It wasn't about Sydney footy,' he once said. 'I didn't know the Reg Gasniers or the Johnny Rapers; I was more following Marty Scanlan, Hughie O'Doherty, Greg Veivers, Johnny Grant.'

So on Monday 27 May 2013, at a big gala dinner to announce the Queensland squad, Meninga introduced members from the 1959 Queensland team – the last Maroons side to win an interstate series prior to Origin. Joining the current crop of players on stage were guys like Noel Kelly, a hard-man hooker; Frank Drake, a fullback once known as the Elvis Presley of rugby league; and Barry Muir, that fiery halfback who had coined the term 'cockroaches' for New South Wales all those years ago.

Meninga, said Muir, was the first person in the Origin era to properly recognise him and his fellow Queenslanders who had toiled away in the interstate series. 'He was tremendous,' Muir recalled. 'He didn't overlook the fact that there was football before State of Origin. He made sure everybody knew. He got the '59 side together and had a big dinner and presented us jerseys. He had all the present State of Origin players at the do, to let them know there was football before 1980.'

It was not just a token gesture. On the wall of the team room, Meninga hung a scoreboard of the old interstate series to remind the players that Queensland's seven consecutive series victories paled in comparison to New South Wales's dominance during the 1960s and '70s. 'As Mal has said to us, we have some catching up to do,' Cooper Cronk told one reporter.[18]

Meninga was typical of the generation of Queenslanders who created the legend of State of Origin. Anyone over the age of 40 knew that success would always be measured against the memories of being beaten every year by New South Wales. 'That's the part that I think New South Wales people just don't get,' once explained Dr Chris Sarra. 'I still remember what it feels like to be broken-hearted. Even if I'm on the rugby league commission, and we've won 25 years in a row, I won't care – I still know what it felt like.'

Meninga's great legacy was to breathe new life into that old story, and re-purpose it as motivation for yet another series victory in 2013. 'When you're having success,' he later explained, 'you gotta find a why … you gotta find a purpose.'

In the end, though, 2013 would be the final year of Queensland's eight-year unbeaten streak. It had been a wild ride for the players and their ever-growing army of supporters. Ray Warren, the legendary Channel 9 commentator, had called 75 State of Origin games and was convinced that he was watching one of the greatest sporting teams in Australia. 'These past eight years have been among my fondest memories,' he wrote in the *Men of League* magazine. 'With Wally and Alfie we had two genuine superstars; Wally was the best, but this current Queensland side offered us five who could be called by the same: Smith, Cronk, Thurston, Inglis, and Slater.'[19]

The rise of these five men was made all the more remarkable by the sequence in which they made their mark on Origin – Smith in 2003, Slater in 2004, Thurston in 2005, Inglis in 2006, and Cronk in 2012. Backed by a supporting cast of Justin Hodges, Nate Myles, Darius

Boyd, Brent Tate, Matthew Scott, Corey Parker, and Sam Thaiday, this was the greatest parade of talent Queensland had ever known. More than just a team of footballers, they had become figureheads for the state of Queensland. The regional fan days in country towns had become highlights of the calendar, while their success in State of Origin projected a sense of Queenslander-ness to the nation and the world.

On the eve of the 2014 State of Origin series, the chief executive of the NRL, Dave Smith, even claimed that Queensland was the 'heartland' of rugby league. For many Sydneysiders, Smith's admission was sacrilegious. But there was a lot of truth to his statement. Suncorp Stadium was clearly the best rugby league ground in the country, the Maroons were the best side, Meninga was the most successful coach, and Thurston the best player.

At 31 years of age, JT was the face of Queensland's unbeaten streak. He had played 27 consecutive games and scored 158 points – just three shy of Meninga's all-time Origin record. In many ways, Thurston embodied the traits that Queenslanders had loved about Wally Lewis and Allan Langer, and then added to them to create his own legend. His larrikin streak, outstanding passing game, and ability to take control at crucial moments had echoes of Lewis. He matched Langer's creative short-kicking game, little-guy toughness, and youthful appeal. He started his Queensland career as a halfback before switching to five-eighth. And he could kick for goal, too.

In 2011, one Sydney reporter had dubbed him 'the most misunderstood man in the game'.[20] By 2014, he had settled down with his partner, Samantha, become a father, and grown into a leader on the field. Maturity led to success, and Thurston had won virtually every available accolade. More than anything else, however, he wanted to win a title with the North Queensland Cowboys. That 'unfinished business', as he called it, kept him in Townsville despite strong offers from clubs down south.[21]

On the first day of September, Thurston scored a try, converted three goals from three attempts, and potted two field goals in the Cowboys' one-point victory over Cronulla-Sutherland. A week later, he scored a further ten points as the Cowboys beat Manly-Warringah to secure a spot in the top eight. Next, in an all-Queensland qualifying final against the Brisbane Broncos, he converted all six attempts on goal in a 12-point victory to the Cowboys.

North Queensland bowed out in the semifinal against the Sydney Roosters the following weekend, but the measly crowd at the Sydney Football Stadium illustrated a bigger cultural shift taking place. The Roosters had money, more than 100 years of history, and a city of nearly 5 million people to draw upon, yet could only pull 18,000 people to a home semifinal.

The Cowboys, meanwhile, were a 20-year-old club in a sparsely populated, economically depressed catchment area. Yet every time North Queensland had hosted a finals match, the stadium in Townsville would swell with crowds in excess of 20,000 people. For many observers it pointed to a changing rugby league landscape: for the first time in history, the game's centre of gravity was shifting north of Brisbane. The only thing left for the Cowboys to do now was win a premiership.

12

GOD IS A QUEENSLANDER

2015

Johnathan Thurston had been kicking a football since he was a four-year-old ball boy for his father's pub team in Brisbane. Learning to manipulate the Steeden – to shape its flight or make it bounce a certain way – had been a lifelong preoccupation.

Thanks to a combination of dependable technique and unshakeable nerve, Thurston was often the difference between a win and a loss in both club and representative football. Who could forget that crucial field goal during his Origin debut in 2005? Or that remarkable stretch of seven games in 2010 when he slotted 24 conversions on the trot for the Cowboys? It seemed, for a time, as if he would never miss again.

Immediately after each kick conversion, regardless of whether it was successful, he would collect the tee and hand it gently to a starstruck ball boy. It was gestures like these that helped to create a bond between footballer and fan that few other players in the modern era could match.

Thurston was no angel but he typified the recuperative quality of rugby league. Rough, honest, emotional – it was clear just how much effort he put into everything he did, whether it be tackling a bigger opponent, darting through a gap in the defensive line, or talking to the media. He was not blessed with the effortless grace of Darren Lockyer, but his determination and focus were unmatched.

The arc of Thurston's career told a story that league people could identify with: here was a man who had grown up in a housing commission suburb, who had to work for a contract after being overlooked by several scouts, and who always seemed a chance of falling off the rails entirely were it not for the support of his family, a bit of luck, and his intense love of the game.

While Thurston could never be defined by a single attribute, it was his kicking – those small moments of individual brilliance – which so often created the impression that he could win football matches single-handedly. In any given match, he might smash an opponent in defence, orchestrate the attacks, create the try – or score it himself – and then turn four points into six with the conversion. If his team needed a late field goal, JT was the man. Most of all, Thurston's kicking highlighted his tremendous ability to step up at just the right moment. Those big swinging conversions and clutch field goals created the aura of a legend.

By 2015 he was being mentioned in the same breath as Darren Lockyer, Wally Lewis, Allan Langer, and Andrew Johns. Johns's brother, Matthew, predicted that Thurston would become the greatest halfback of all time while Bob Fulton, the first player to become an Immortal, said it would not be long before JT joined the exclusive club. 'To me, he is the complete package,' said Fulton. 'In fact, six years ago I was asked to name one player who you could build a club around and I nominated JT.'[1]

Yet the new season did not begin well for Thurston. The Cowboys lost to the Sydney Roosters in Round 1, Newcastle in Round 2, Brisbane in Round 3 and, with ten minutes to play in the Round 4 clash against Melbourne, were facing the prospect of a fourth defeat in a row. The sun had set in Townsville and Cooper Cronk, Thurston's opposite number, had just converted a field goal to put Melbourne seven points in front.

It was Thurston who changed the game. With three minutes left on the clock, the Cowboys crossed over in the corner and JT was tasked with converting from the sideline. Hastily he went through his usual routine – the wiggle of the toes, the steps back and to the side, the visualisations – and struck it sweet and true. From the moment the ball left his boot it homed in on the target like a tracer missile, bringing the Cowboys to within one point.

In the final play of regulation time, with the Cowboys still trailing by one, the ball was shovelled to Thurston from dummy half. From 30 metres out, directly in front of goal and with several Melbourne players bearing down on him, he launched a textbook field goal to level the score.

Thurston waved his arms to the Townsville crowd, urging them to lift. There was still more to do. Five minutes of extra time passed, and once again JT was fed the ball from dummy half. From almost exactly the same spot as his first field goal, he fired another drop-kick over the black dot to win the game.

'As much as the players were under the pump for losing the first three games, it was just as much if not more pressure on us as staff,' explained Paul Bowman, the Cowboys' strength and conditioning coach. 'That's a trademark of some of the great players – and JT's right up there with the greatest – they just want the big occasion. They thrive on the pressure of the situation and being the hero, whereas most normal people probably crumble under that sort of pressure.'

The victory immediately changed the trajectory of the season. From there the Cowboys went on a club-record unbeaten streak, defeating Penrith, South Sydney, New Zealand, Newcastle, Canterbury-Bankstown, Brisbane, Wests Tigers, Manly-Warringah, Parramatta, and Canberra.

By May, as State of Origin rolled around once more, pundits and fans alike were ready to believe that North Queensland could finally win a premiership. For one thing, the Cowboys had built a squad to rival any other in the National Rugby League. Under the guidance of head coach Paul Green, there was brains, brawn, and balance to complement Thurston's brilliance.

In 2015, JT would once again be the star performer in the NRL and in State of Origin, becoming the first man to win four Dally M Awards for player of the year. And the North Queensland Cowboys, following a run of four consecutive finals appearances between 2011 and 2014, would finally go one better. Through it all, Thurston would land 93 conversions and a career-best six field goals. His right boot would determine one of the finest seasons in the history of Australian rugby league.

If Thurston was the most popular footballer in Queensland, Mal Meninga was the most respected. His career, more than any other individual, had been defined by State of Origin. On Tuesday 8 July 1980 – the night of his 20th birthday – he had kicked seven goals from seven attempts at Lang Park to help Queensland win the very first Origin match. Now, exactly 35 years later, he quietly marked his 55th birthday in camp with the Maroons and prepared for the Game III decider at Suncorp Stadium later that evening.

The night before his birthday, Meninga had been treated to a lavish dinner at the Bacchus restaurant in South Bank, before retiring to the Rydges Hotel. It wasn't so long ago that this shiny cultural precinct was a down-and-out hovel of warehouses, carparks, and decrepit boarding houses. Brisbane and the southeast were now booming – thanks in large part to continued interstate migration from New South Wales and Victoria – and the place felt sophisticated and modern. The north, meanwhile, was more accessible than ever.

Still, many Australians felt that Queensland was somehow

'different' to the rest of the country. For urbane Sydneysiders and Melbournites, in particular, Queensland remained the 'Deep North': a redneck, freakshow state which had introduced the likes of Pauline Hanson, Bob Katter, George Christensen, Peter Dutton, and Clive Palmer to the nation. In fact, Queensland's most persistent difference to other states was its rural and regional character. Mining and agriculture remained a major part of the economy, while more than half of the population still lived outside the capital city, making Queensland the most decentralised state or territory in mainland Australia.

That fact, as well as the sheer size of the state, meant that many Queenslanders continued to live separated by enormous distances, often in vastly different places and circumstances. In 2015 alone, Queensland was hit by freak rainfall in Caboolture, snow in Stanthorpe, Cyclone Marcia in Rockhampton, and Cyclone Nathan in Cooktown. A coastal earthquake rattled homes from Bundaberg to Burleigh Heads, while 80 per cent of the state suffered through crippling drought. Observers often linked the extremity of the climate with the eccentricity of Queensland's people and politics. 'Queensland had settled in the tropics,' wrote historian Raymond Evans, 'and the tropics had settled in them.'[2]

Since the end of the Bjelke-Petersen era, Queenslanders had elected eight premiers in less than 30 years, making it one of the most politically unstable places in Australia. In Queensland, wrote political scientist John Wanna, 'the winds of electoral change can hit like a cyclone'.[3]

For more than a century there had been concerns that Queensland was simply too big and too unwieldy to remain as a single, united entity. Even despite the advances in infrastructure and telecommunications, many people believed Queensland should be split in half to become two separate states. At a meeting of the North Queensland Local Government Association in 2010, for instance, 98 of 100 mayors from Mackay to Mount Isa voted in favour of statehood for North Queensland. And in April 2015, Bob Katter, the federal member for Kennedy, put the issue of North Queensland separation on the agenda once more. As if to emphasise the point, the front page of the *Tully Times* led with the headline 'Let us go!', accompanied by a photo of Katter tipping a North Queensland Cowboys hat.

The developing rivalry between the Cowboys and the Brisbane Broncos always had the potential to divide Queensland, to further amplify the wider socio-political tensions that existed between the north and the southeast. In truth, though, rugby league was a symbol – perhaps even *the* symbol – of Queensland unity; something that even Katter himself admitted. 'When anyone calls me a Queenslander I always correct them and say, "I'm a North Queenslander",' Katter once explained. 'Having said that, let there be no doubt that I've had heart attacks trying to bring the Queensland side home.'

In every country pub worth drinking at, whether in Ipswich or Innisfail, there would be a framed Maroon jersey hanging on the wall – often beside a local club jumper or team photo. And while the other football codes and cricket tended to be Brisbane-centric, rugby league had established three NRL clubs in Queensland's three biggest cities, as well as an expansive state competition which stretched from Tweed Heads to Papua New Guinea.

In Queensland, the economy, politics, and rugby league were driven by the regions just as much as the capital city.

When Peter Parr first arrived in Townsville to work for the North Queensland Cowboys, he observed that town and regional rivalries tended to be casual and fluid. Parr, a New South Welshman who once worked for the Brisbane Broncos, also appreciated the friendly rivalry that had developed between the Broncos and the Cowboys. 'A lot of rivalries are built on dislike or hatred,' he said. 'This rivalry has been built on respect. I think that's what I like most about it.

The clubs essentially get on. The Broncos still like to dominate us, I'm sure, but we get on as clubs, a lot of the players have played State of Origin together, a lot of the players are friends.'

And therein lay a fundamental difference between rugby league in the two states. In New South Wales, Origin was just one event in the rugby league calendar. In Queensland, Origin was *the* foundational story: the big bang that had acted as a catalyst for all the changes in the state's rugby league infrastructure. Without Origin there would be no Broncos, no Cowboys, no Gold Coast Titans.

Brian Canavan, in his 2011 review of the New South Wales Origin set-up, found that the NRL clubs down south were not particularly enamoured with Origin as a concept. 'Whereas in Queensland, they dropped everything,' he recalled. 'They dropped everything to play Origin – that was the absolute pinnacle.'

Following the Maroons' eight-year winning streak in State of Origin, outsiders began to associate Queensland with its rugby league team just as much as it did the cattle and cane farms, the Bundaberg Rum and the Fourex beer, the rainforests and the Great Barrier Reef, and the maverick right-wing politicians.

Meninga understood this better than anyone. In the three and a half decades he had been involved, either as a player or a coach, in no less than 25 campaigns. He knew that Origin was the heartbeat of the state, the centrifugal force driving the continued popularity of rugby league. 'The best byproduct of Queensland's winning Origin run since 2006 has been the lift in participation numbers of rugby league players across all levels of the game – juniors, men and women,' Meninga later explained in a column for the *Courier-Mail*.

'They have been inspired to play the sport they love because of their connection to the success of the Maroons. What this means is that over the next 10 years, Queensland will have a much deeper talent pool to draw on, meaning better players working through the ranks, and eventually more quality players available for Queensland.'[4]

Before kick-off in Game III, as the players went through their final pre-game drills in the dressing sheds, more than 50,000 fans sat in darkness at Suncorp Stadium. Beams of blue light strobed the turf. A visual tribute to Justin Hodges, playing in his 24th and final Origin match, was projected onto the big screens. Then, alongside flashes of Maroon, the strained voice of Billy Moore rang out through the night: 'QUEEENSLANDAAH ... QUEEENSLANDAAH ... QUEEENSLANDAAH ...'

At fullback was Greg Inglis, the adopted Queenslander from down south, and on the wings were Darius Boyd from the Gold Coast, and Dane Gagai from Mackay. In the centres were Will Chambers from Nhulunbuy in the Northern Territory, and Hodges from Cairns. From Logan City came Cameron Smith, Corey Parker, and Josh Papalii, while Matt Gillett hailed from Bribie Island, and halves pairing Johnathan Thurston and Cooper Cronk were from Brisbane. In the front row was Matthew Scott from Longreach, and Nate Myles from Gordonvale. Second-rowers Sam Thaiday and Aidan Guerra both played junior football for Townsville Brothers, as did substitute Michael Morgan. Jacob Lillyman was from Richmond, a small outback town on the long road to Mount Isa.

Two-thirds of the squad was from the bush and one-third were of Aboriginal or Torres Strait Islander descent. Together, they were a visual symbol of Queenslanders working together and the latest custodians of a long tradition of diverse Origin representatives. It had been that way since 1980.

Queensland was nearing a state of rugby league nirvana. In the NRL, the Broncos were top of the competition ladder, the Cowboys had moved to second, while the Melbourne Storm – a kind of surrogate Queensland club by Smith, Cronk, Chambers, and Slater – were third. Tellingly, three-quarters of the 17 players on the field at Suncorp Stadium were drawn from those three high-flying clubs. Yet several key players – Slater, Cronk, Thurston, Smith,

Parker, and Hodges – were all on the wrong side of 30, and there was concerns that Queensland's dynasty was coming to an end.

Hodges, 33, was the elder statesman of the side and the quintessential Queensland State of Origin player. He had overcome early career dramas with the Broncos and a calamitous Origin debut – not to mention numerous setbacks, injuries, and depression – to become the captain of the Broncos and one of the first picked for the Maroons. He wore the hate directed at him by New South Welshmen as a badge of honour. 'Hodgo was really passionate about Queensland,' explained Kevin Walters, who coached him at both club and representative level. 'His first Origin wasn't his greatest, but he took ownership of his performance and finished as one of the great Queensland centres.'

In Hodges' final game, the Maroons scored first and then ran in seven more tries in a flawless display of Origin football. Queensland racked up 50 points for the first time in the history of the series. What's more, there had been eight different try-scorers – Gagai, Papalii, Inglis, Gillett, Morgan, Boyd, Chambers, and Guerra – while Thurston had kicked a record nine goals from nine attempts.

In a show of respect, Hodges was handed the ball to kick the final conversion of the match. In the coach's box high up in the stands, birthday boy Meninga felt the stars aligning, not least because Hodges was wearing his old No. 4 jersey. Down went a playful message from Mal – 'I want to see him toe-poke it over' – in reference to the old front-on style he employed in the very first Origin match in 1980. Ignoring his coach's request, Hodges placed the ball on the plastic tee and side-footed it through the uprights to make it 52 points to six. He wheeled away, arms outstretched like a celebrating soccer player, to the welcoming roar of a Queensland crowd.

'You don't play the game for individual honours,' remarked Thurston after the match. 'It's a team effort, and there's no better way to send out our boy Hodgie in his last series, to send him out the way he deserves. He's been a great servant for this state and this jersey. We couldn't have done it without him – he's a champion.'

With seven rounds to go in the NRL, the Brisbane Broncos, captained by Hodges, and the North Queensland Cowboys, captained by Thurston, were still in first and second place respectively. For both men, and for Queensland itself, the biggest moment was still yet to come.

★

For three years Australian rugby league had been run by an independent commission, established – in theory, at least – to rise above the tensions that existed between the ARL and News Limited; between New South Wales and Queensland; and between the 16 NRL clubs.

The inaugural chairman of the ARL Commission was John Grant, a former Kangaroo who could recall what it was like to be a 'token Queenslander' in a Sydney-dominated game. By late 2015, however, Grant was hinting that future NRL grand finals would be held in Brisbane and that the next expansion teams would likely come from Southeast Queensland. It was a sign of the state's growing influence off the field as well as on.

No sport is ever a flawless reflection of its host society – whether it be soccer in Brazil, baseball in the United States, or Gaelic football in Ireland. But for more than 40 years, rugby league has embodied all the hopes and dreams, contradictions and tensions of life in the Sunshine State. The game speaks to Queenslanders' sense of being the underdog and the outsider – a powerful undercurrent that sweeps through politics, business, the arts, and sport. The enduring appeal of State of Origin is that it allows Queensland to balance the scales, at least for 80 minutes.

Rugby league was there during the transition from the old to the new Queensland – a transformative period of history that began during the 1980s. As Queensland grew up, rugby league was completely refigured to meet the demands of the modern age. The interstate series became State of Origin. The bush football competitions, the Brisbane Rugby League, and the Winfield State League gradually morphed into the Queensland Cup. And where there were once community clubs embedded in small-time competitions, now there were three multi-million-dollar national sporting organisations based out of the Gold Coast, Brisbane, and Townsville.

There had been winners and losers along the way, of course. Communities of people lost teams, traditions, even entire competitions. Perhaps the changes were best exemplified by the divergent fates of the Confraternity of Brothers Clubs, and the Brisbane Broncos.

Brothers, although it had lost its mothership club in Brisbane, remained the engine room of Queensland rugby league. In places like Logan, Ipswich, Toowoomba, Bundaberg, Gladstone, Rockhampton, Mackay, Townsville, Innisfail, and Cairns, there was a Brothers club that had survived into the 21st century. These clubs, at essence, were community organisations that pursued community objectives. Most of all, they provided a space for young players to develop: in 2015, around half of the Queensland squad had played junior football for a Brothers club in Logan, Toowoomba, Mackay, Townsville, Innisfail, or Cairns.

'I'm still attached to Brothers,' said Tom Cranitch. 'It does make me proud that guys like JT, Billy Slater, and Cameron Smith all came from a Brothers club in Queensland. But in another sense, it makes me sad. In the days of old, those guys would have actually come into our system; those guys would have got channelled to the mothership club in Brisbane and would have played for us.'

Where Brothers survived on the strength of its grassroots network, the Brisbane Broncos thrived on on-field success, clever marketing, relentless promotion, and constant visibility thanks to its majority owners, News Limited. By 2015 it was one of the most successful and the most profitable sporting clubs in Australia with a fanbase that stretched the entire state of Queensland; a thoroughly modern franchise with business principles woven into its DNA.

Some traditionalists continued to sneer at the Broncos. And yet, since its foundation in 1988, no club had done more than the Broncos to advance Queensland sport. It was the first sporting organisation to deliberately reach out to women, the first to pursue a proper corporate strategy, and the first Queensland club to win something of note. It was the first club to face up to the reality of modern sport in Australia.

'I think, in retrospect, the Broncos were the best thing to ever happen to the city,' explained league writer Steve Ricketts. And the benefits weren't only accrued in Brisbane and the southeast – for all its faults, the Broncos were a chief driver in promoting rugby league throughout country Queensland, particularly in those early days between 1988 and 1995. 'All our trials were played in country Queensland,' recalled the Broncos' first chief executive, John Ribot. 'Our view was if we go to Townsville, or Mackay, or Gladstone, or Toowoomba, they picked up our expenses and kept the rest. It was a good thing for the leagues. I remember once going to Mackay, and we left something like $100,000 in town. We made a conscious effort, in the early days, to be Queensland's team.'

How fitting it was, then, for the 2015 NRL grand final to bring together the Brisbane Broncos and the North Queensland Cowboys. For two decades the clubs had an almost symbiotic relationship stemming from shared history, geography, and identity.

If State of Origin begat the Broncos, the Broncos laid the platform for the creation of the Cowboys. Those who knew their history could remember that autumn day in 1989, when the Broncos beat Parramatta at a sold-out Townsville Sports Reserve, in the process raising the possibility that North Queensland could one day have a team of their own competing in a national league. Now, 26 years later, the first all-Queensland grand final of any sport was about to take place. According to *Courier-Mail* reporter Paul Malone, the occasion, following on from Queensland's record win in the State of Origin decider, 'makes 2015 Queensland's greatest year in rugby league'.[5]

For 32-year-old Johnathan Thurston, who had spent a decade with the Cowboys, it was a final opportunity to win a premiership for North Queensland. Not only had he helped the Cowboys square up to the Broncos on the field, his mere presence in Townsville was a symbol of the changing of the guard in Queensland as sponsors, supporters, media interest, and general goodwill followed him up north.

Thurston had an uncanny ability to connect with North Queenslanders from Mackay to Mount Isa to Mapoon. Midway through the 2015 season, he joined forces with Apunipima, a health organisation in Cape York, to combat the spread of the drug ice in Indigenous communities. 'Having JT out there was great,' recalled Dr Mark Wenitong, an adviser for Apunipima. 'We could have the best academics, the best lawyers, the best whatever – I'm probably the fourth or fifth Aboriginal doctor to graduate, and I can go up there and tell those kids to stop smoking, and they'd just go, "Piss off." But JT goes up there and they listen to him.'

Thurston also gave North Queensland tremendous profile and publicity down south. After he inspired the Cowboys to a 20-point win over the Melbourne Storm in the preliminary final, the *Sydney Morning Herald* predicted that grand final week 'will all be about Thurston's dreams'.[6]

And so began seven days of intense focus on JT. In Sydney, Thurston's former club, Canterbury-Bankstown, began selling Cowboys jerseys at its club store, while thousands of sets of imitation JT headgear were distributed at an NRL function in Darling Harbour. In Townsville, cupcakes bearing his likeness were baked, while the District Court was draped in blue and gold with a large sign that read: 'a thurstin for a try from Thurston's almighty troops.'[7]

Journalists stretched the limits of hyperbole. One reporter declared Thurston to be 'less athlete than an alchemist. More miracle than man.' Another claimed that he was 'on the verge of being ordained as the new King of North Queensland', while a Sydney sportswriter declared that he would be backing the Cowboys for a few reasons: 'One, I love Townsville – beautiful tropical environment – and I love the tropics. Two, it's about time NRL history was created and the Cowboys get their first win. Three, Johnathan Thurston. Four, Johnathan Thurston. Five, Johnathan Thurston. Six, Johnathan Thurston … you get the drift.'[8]

Former players, too, were swept along in the unfolding fairytale. A grand final win for Thurston, declared Matthew Johns, 'will cap the greatest season any individual player has enjoyed in my time watching rugby league'.[9]

Thurston himself did all he could to focus on the football match ahead. On the night of the Dally M Awards, where he won halfback of the year and player of the year, he stayed in Townsville to nurse a sore calf. 'Apart from the birth of our two children, this is the most emotional I've seen him,' his wife, Samantha, told the *Sunday Telegraph*. 'He would give up this and his other three Dally Ms to win this grand final.'[10]

Although the occasion was far bigger than any individual, it did seem as if Thurston was made for this particular moment in time. Here, in a historic grand final contest between the two most popular sporting clubs in the Sunshine State, was the glorious culmination of the State of Origin era – the high point of Queensland's rugby league renaissance. 'As the past decade of State of Origin has demonstrated, God is a Queenslander,' joked Roy Masters.[11]

As Sydney prepared for its first all-Queensland grand final, Gene Miles, the chairman of the Former Origin Greats, wondered if there would be empty seats at ANZ Stadium. 'Because here we've got Brisbane and North Queensland playing,' he later admitted, 'and I'm thinking, *Are they going to fill the joint up?*'

He needn't have worried. Even despite the expensive airfares – which moved Bob Katter, a foundation member of the Cowboys, to accuse airline companies of 'price gouging' – an estimated 30,000 Queenslanders found a way to get to the game. Those who couldn't secure a flight had either hopped on an overnight bus or train, or hot-footed it down the east coast by car. So-called rival fans travelled to the game together, many of them wearing a piece of Maroons memorabilia. 'Everyone I spoke to reckoned Johnathan Thurston was such a great player, it'd be unreal to see him win a premiership,' recalled Alf Abdullah, who made the trip from Sarina. 'I desperately wanted the Cowboys to win that day, even though I am a Broncos supporter.'

The captains told the story of one the friendliest grand finals ever witnessed. Hodges, raised in the far north, led out the team from Brisbane, while Thurston, born and raised in the southeast, led out North Queensland's team. 'Two young men who are so strong in their Aboriginality – you go back five or ten years and you and I would not be having this discussion,' Linda Burney, the chair of the Australian Rugby League Indigenous Council, told a reporter from the *Australian*.[12]

By 2015 rugby league could rightly claim to be Australia's Indigenous game. One-third of the Australian team and 12 per cent of players in the NRL identified as Aboriginal or Torres Strait Islander, compared to 9 per cent in the AFL. And while AFL supporters were booing Adam Goodes – one of the code's great Indigenous players – into early retirement, rugby league fans were preparing for what Linda Burney called the game's 'Cathy Freeman moment'.

'Rugby league is a game we all associate with in Queensland and New South Wales,' later explained Preston Campbell, the founder of the Indigenous All Stars. 'It's great to be able to get together over a game that we all love and, at the same time – without even knowing it – getting along with each other! It's small, but it's a productive way of reconciliation.'

Before kick-off, one of the ARL commissioners, Dr Chris Sarra, spotted Prime Minister Malcolm Turnbull in the corporate area of the stadium. A mad Cowboys fan, Sarra was nervously focused on the 80 minutes that lay ahead. 'I don't like pressing the flesh with people and doing the corporate scene – I'm just there to watch the game, frankly,' he recalled. 'But on this occasion I thought I'd go out of my way and say g'day to the prime minister. So I went and said g'day … I'm Chris Sarra … I do this, that … blah blah blah. And he says, "So Chris, what are three things we can do to make a difference in the Indigenous policy space?"'

It was too big a question for the small-talk of the corporate box. 'I'll get back to you,' Sarra promised. And with that, he took his seat and settled in to watch one of the most profound, spine-tingling grand finals in the history of rugby league.

It began with two tries in ten minutes. The Broncos registered the first points with a penalty goal, and then broke free down the left wing on the very next set of six. Corey Oates ran 70 metres to score, and Corey Parker nailed the conversion to make it 8–0. Before the Broncos could settle into the lead, however, Cowboys hooker Jake Granville ghosted through a gap around the ruck and laid on a try for Justin O'Neill to make it 8–6. It was a scintillating opening act in an end-to-end performance characterised by fast, positive football; the kind of entertainment fans of the Queensland derby had become accustomed to. By halftime, the Broncos led 14 points to 12.

The second half started much like the first, with the Broncos winning an early penalty and electing to take the two points. As the match turned into a battle of attrition, the stars aligned for a late Johnathan Thurston special. Although he had not had a brilliant first half – his loose carry had led to the Broncos second try – a four-pointer here for the Cowboys would set the stage for JT to win the match with the resulting conversion.

The little general took up the challenge. He won the Cowboys a repeat set of six and then put Kane Linnett through for what seemed like a certain try, only for the usually reliable centre to drop the ball over the line. It seemed, for a moment, as though Linnett had dropped the Provan-Summons Trophy itself.

The Broncos held on. Halfback Ben Hunt began to kick for touch, looking to slow the game down and grind out the result. It was Brisbane's game to lose. In the Broncos corner was Wayne Bennett, who had coached the club to a remarkable six premierships in six attempts. Winning grand finals was what the Broncos did under Bennett. The Cowboys, on the other hand, was chasing its first premiership. When Kerry Boustead established the club all those years ago he never expected to win a grand final. Then again, he didn't see Super League coming either, and he certainly hadn't envisioned resigning from his post just a few games into the club's first season in 1995.

But he was back now. Earlier in the year, Cowboys chairman Laurence Lancini had repatriated Boustead to the board after two decades of estrangement. Perched high up in a corporate box and surrounded by football novices, before kick-off Boustead had told them that the Cowboys would start slowly but take the game to the final siren. 'A couple of minutes before the end, they'll do something brilliant and we'll win the game,' he predicted.

Boustead had learned to expect the unexpected from the Cowboys. Yet with only a minute and a half remaining, and the Broncos in possession, even he was starting to have doubts.

With 60 seconds left on the clock the Cowboys regained possession, 55 metres out from the try-line. The ball swept left to Kane Linnett, who juggled nervously and surrendered in the tackle with no metres gained. Antonio Winterstein made a strong run to advance to the 40-metre line. Jason Taumalolo did likewise to bring the Cowboys to within 30. On the fourth tackle Matthew Scott was brought to heel 15 metres out, directly in front.

With exactly 15 seconds left, this, surely, was the final play of the game. And Thurston, who was forced onto the back foot after collecting a loose pass off his bootlaces, was surrounded by Broncos and heading in the wrong direction. Back to goal, he turned to his right and saw no option. So he darted left, looped a pass to Michael Morgan, and hoped for the best.

Time no longer mattered. There were now only two possible outcomes: score a try, or lose the grand final. Morgan assessed his options as he drifted towards the right corner. Three on three. Needing to create the overload, he drew two defenders into a tackle and executed a perfect flick pass outside to Kyle Feldt.

Now there was only noise. The growing hubbub morphed into an excited, guttural roar as Feldt shimmied along the touchline, planted the ball down and wheeled away in celebration. As Feldt was met by ecstatic teammates the clock ticked over to 80 minutes – Broncos 16, Cowboys 16.

In that final, decisive minute Thurston had touched the ball no less than four times. And now he had a sideline conversion to win the game. He placed the kicking tee on the turf, and then reluctantly adjusted it at the referee's request. He picked his target behind the goal and wiggled his toes. Five steps back, three to the left, and another half a step back. Another wiggle of the toes, a roll of the shoulders, and he was ready. All the colour and noise of the occasion was suddenly irrelevant. It was just JT, the ball, and a shot at goal – the kind of set-shot he had been practising since he was a little kid. These moments, he later explained, 'are what dreams are made of'.[13]

He took four steps forward and on the fifth swung his right boot. The kick travelled low, with his customary right-to-left draw.

To Thurston, it looked almost as good as it felt. Just as he raised his right arm to celebrate, however, it straightened a little, struck the post, and bounced out.

Before he could dwell on the miss he was surrounded by teammates. A chant of 'COW–BOYS' echoed around the ground as the players switched ends for golden-point extra time. And then, from the restart, Broncos halfback Ben Hunt inexplicably dropped a high ball five metres out from his own line. Here was a second chance the Cowboys could not afford to waste.

Under immense pressure, the players took their time to set up the shot at goal. After four tackles the ball was fed to JT – 20 metres out and right in front. He had already scored a career-best five field goals that season. But this winning drop-kick, which soared high and straight between the uprights, would come to define his football career.

And what happened next – after the players embraced and the premiership rings were handed out – would transcend rugby league and push JT even further into the realm of celebrity. Thurston sat down on the turf and cradled his daughter Frankie and her little black doll.

Following more than two decades of recurring rugby league atrocities – the seemingly never-ending rampage of drunkenness, sexual assault, and violence – this was a gentle image to soothe a thousand hearts. According to the NRL, the photo of Thurston with his daughter and her doll was the most popular social media image in the history of the game. In England, the BBC reported that it had 'captivated Australia'.[14]

Professor Gracelyn Smallwood, a Cowboys fan and registered midwife, loved that image and every minute of the evening. 'I watched all the Foley Shields – never missed a game – and I always thought the Foley Shield was simply the best,' she recalled. 'But the 2015 Broncos and Cowboys final has to take precedence …

we were just in awe when the Cowboys won. That's how football should be played.'

★

The Provan-Summons Trophy had never been on a tour quite like it. First, the Cowboys took it to Townsville, where the players and coaching staff were swamped by an adoring crowd at the airport. Then, after a raucous party at the club's home ground, the Cowboys management announced a sweeping Trophy Tour of North Queensland. Several players led by co-captains Johnathan Thurston and Matthew Scott took the trophy on chartered flights to Mackay, Mount Isa, and Cairns. In an all-day round-trip that covered more than 2000 kilometres, they were met by ticker-tape parades and civic receptions and hundreds of requests for photos and autographs.

'North Queensland's been battered throughout the years by natural disasters – droughts, cyclones and the like – so taking that trophy up to those communities and seeing the smiles on their faces is something that I'll never forget,' Thurston later explained.[15]

And that was only the beginning. Greg Tonner, the Cowboys chief executive, believed the achievement belonged to supporters in little country towns as well as the major centres. After all, those fans had travelled further than any other to lead the club to a premiership.

Now it was the club's turn to hit the road. Over the next two months, the Provan-Summons Trophy would be ferried more than 30,000 kilometres around North Queensland – from Rockhampton to the Torres Strait Islands and even Papua New Guinea – to unite the region in success. 'We'd finally got to the top of the mountain,' recalled Doug Kingston, the former sports editor of the *Townsville Bulletin*, who'd been there from day one. 'There was a feeling of nostalgia, a sense of history about it. I think it got everyone in North Queensland together on one page. I think it stuck, and North Queensland is a closer community because of it.'

The trophy was taken through fishing villages in the Gulf of Carpentaria, Indigenous communities in Cape York, and mining towns along the Flinders Highway. It hopped from islands in the Pacific Ocean to the Torres Strait, and road-tripped past cane fields and cattle farms.

In Winton, 600 kilometres west of Townsville, Cowboys media man Tim Nugent needed to reattach the base of the trophy with superglue after it melted off onto the airport runway. 'There were a number of people who said, "You're kidding … you're losing the plot here,"' recalled Nugent. 'But I have to say, it was without doubt the right thing to do. Even if we didn't have a player with us, we had the goddamn trophy and it had Cowboys on it.'

The weird, wonderful, and sometimes whacky Trophy Tour seemed to capture all the finest aspects of rugby league in Queensland. One, it was a timely acknowledgement that distance and decentralisation were no hindrance to Queenslanders. Two, it showed that a modern franchise, even with just two decades of history, could still create moments rich in meaning and intense belonging. And three, it was proof that Queensland was at its best when it embraced the full diversity of its population.

In November, Cowboys fan Dr Chris Sarra took the tremendous symbolism of the grand final – and his pre-game chat with the prime minister – all the way to Federal Parliament. 'It occurred to me that the answer to Prime Minister Turnbull's question was being played out right before us on that epic NRL grand final night,' he said in an address to the Senate.

What we watched that night was nothing less than a festival of positive thinking about the relationship between Indigenous and non-Indigenous Australia. On a level playing field we saw the humanity of Indigenous Australians authentically acknowledged, embraced with enthusiasm, and celebrated with passion. […]

We saw Indigenous leadership working with non-Indigenous leadership together in an elite and honourable, high expectations relationship.

'This,' concluded Dr Sarra, 'is the perfect analogy for the Australian society we can develop.'[16]

The soaring oration marked a fitting end to a landmark year in Queensland rugby league. Not only were the Cowboys the best team in the country, the Ipswich Jets had been crowned NRL state champions, and the Maroons were perhaps the finest representative side Australia had ever seen. And in the women's game – the next chapter of rugby league – Queensland had already won the first 16 interstate challenges over New South Wales since its inception in 1999.

Johnathan Thurston was the best player in the game and Jenni Sue-Hoepper, a North Queenslander, won the inaugural Dally M award for women's player of the year. Cameron Smith was the captain of the national team and Mal Meninga, after ten years of dominating the Origin arena, was preparing to take over as coach of Australia.

The story of rugby league in Queensland since the 1970s had been one of dramatic upheaval, enormous loss, and constant reinvention. A feeling of perpetual struggle permeated the state – whether it be to level the playing field in State of Origin, to have more Queenslanders selected in the Kangaroos, or to establish brand new clubs in a national competition. Essentially, the struggle was for better representation in Sydney's game.

And now, despite the fact that power and money remains in New South Wales, the soul of rugby league is firmly embedded in Queensland. It's there in the faith of the travellers, in the men and women on the margins, from Cape York to Cunnamulla and all along the coast, who trek further than anybody to stay in the game.

ENDNOTES

INTRODUCTION

1   Dan O'Neill, 'The Revolution can wait: radical Brisbane and rugby league', *Footy Almanac*, 1 July 2012. www.footyalmanac.com.au/the-revolution-can-wait-radical-brisbane-and-rugby-league/

2   Tony Collins, *Rugby's Great Split: class, culture and the origins of rugby league football*, 2nd ed., Routledge, London, 2006: p. xiv.

3   Andrew Moore, 'Jimmy Devereux's Yorkshire Pudding: reflections on the origins of rugby league in New South Wales and Queensland', *1st Annual Tom Brock Lecture*, University of New South Wales, 2000: p. 17.

4   Barry Dick, 'Origin is league's lifeblood', *Courier-Mail*, 31 May 1982: p. 16.

5   Roy Masters, 'Maroons are masters of subterfuge and dirty deeds come origin time', *Sydney Morning Herald*, 26 May 2012: p. 7.

6   Lawrie Kavanagh, 'Origin league forced Queenslanders to face "big boys"', *Courier-Mail*, 11 February 1990: p. 71.

7   Roy Masters, '"And I awoke, and found me here on the cold hill side": rugby league and the decline of working class culture', *Meanjin*, vol. 54, iss. 3, 1995: p. 403.

8   Ross Fitzgerald, Lyndon Megarrity & David Symons, *Made in Queensland: a new history*, University of Queensland Press, Brisbane, 2009: p. 236.

9   Mike Colman, 'Maroons make us true believers', *Courier-Mail*, 7 July 2006: p. 111.

1   THE DEFEATS WE SUFFERED: 1974–1980

1   'Flood rain hits city', *Telegraph*, 25 January 1974: p. 1.

2   Max Howell, *The Centenary of the Greatest Game Under the Sun*, Celebrity Books, Brisbane, 2008: p. 296.

3   Howell, *The Centenary of the Greatest Game Under the Sun*, 2008: p. 301.

4   Ron McAuliffe & Pat Shaw, Department of the Parliamentary Library 1985, Ronald Edward McAuliffe interviewed by Pat Shaw in the Parliament's Bicentenary oral history project.

5   Bill Mordey, 'Muir declares war on NSW', *Daily Mirror*, 20 May 1975: p. 52.

6   Silvia da Costa-Roque, 'There's lots of fire left in Big Artie', *Courier-Mail*, 13 July 1980: p. 6.

7   Jack Reardon, 'Muir's "boys" keen to get on with job', *Courier-Mail*, 20 May 1975: p. 17.

8   Bob Bax, 'Muir Queensland's trump', *Courier-Mail*, 25 May 1975: p. 42.

9   Jack Reardon, 'Queensland down by 8–9; fluke try to NSW', *Courier-Mail*, 20 July 1975: p. 44.

10   Bill Mordey, 'COCKROACHES!', *Daily Mirror*, 19 May 1976: p. 104.

11   Steve Ricketts, *Lang Park: the first 36 years*, Queensland Rugby League News, Brisbane, 1994: p. 86.

12   Lawrie Kavanagh, 'State win will take a "miracle"', *Courier-Mail*, 21 May 1977: p. 36.

13   Geoff Prenter, 'Boustead blow-up', *Rugby League Week*, 8 March 1979: p. 1.

14   Lawrie Kavanagh, 'ANOTHER NSW ROUT', *Courier-Mail*, 30 May 1979: p. 23.

15   Humphrey McQueen, 'States of the Nation: Queensland – a state of mind', *Meanjin*, vol. 38, no. 1, April 1979: p. 41.

16   Jackie Ryan, *We'll Show The World: Expo 88*, University of Queensland Press, Brisbane, 2018: p. 37.

17   Hugh Lunn, *Joh: the life and political adventures of Johannes Bjelke-Petersen*, University of Queensland Press, Brisbane, 1978: p. 213.

18   Raymond Evans, *A History of Queensland*, Cambridge University Press, Melbourne, 2007: p. 229.

19   *Rugby League Week*, 11 September 1980: p. 32.

20   Lawrie Kavanagh, 'No stopping that mighty Valleys machine', *Courier-Mail*, 17 September 1979: p. 17.

21   Steve Haddan, *Our Game: the celebration of Brisbane Rugby League 1909–1987*, Steve Haddan, Brisbane, 2016: p. 283.

22   Frank Hyde, 'Take a bow, J.L.!', *Rugby League Week*, 29 May 1980: p. 5.

23   Ray Kershler, 'A trial – but no football', *Daily Mirror*, 28 May 1980: p. 44.

24   Jack Gallaway, *Origin: rugby league's greatest contest 1980–2002*, University of Queensland Press, Brisbane, 2003: p. 8.

25   Hugh Lunn, 'Origin of the Origin', *League of a Nation*, edited by David Headon & Lex Marinos, ABC Books, Sydney, 1996: p. 8.

26   'What every Queensland fan wanted ... Play NSW state of origin side', *Courier-Mail*, 29 May 1980: p. 17.

27   'Hands off the State matches, stars vote', *Daily Mirror*, 22 May 1980: p. 50.

28   Bob Fulton, 'Origin game hits Roosters cup hopes', *Daily Mirror*, 7 July 1980: p. 26; Bob Fulton, 'This state of origin match is useless', *Daily Mirror*, 23 June 1980: p. 26.

29   Ron Casey, 'Stop the big panic John, we're not all out to trip you up', *Daily Mirror*, 27 June 1980: p. 65.

30   John McCoy, 'The Real McCoy', *Rugby League Week*, 5 June 1980: p. 30.

31   Geoff Prenter, 'The Prenter Report', *Rugby League Week*, 19 June 1980: p. 2.

32   Paul Crawley, 'The Crow raises a glass to the big bloke', *Daily Telegraph*, 1 December 2011: p. 111.

33   Murray G. Phillips & Brett Hutchins, 'From independence to a reconstituted hegemony: rugby league and television in Australia', *Journal of Australian Studies*, vol. 22, no. 58, 1998: p. 141.

34   Thea Astley, 'Being a Queenslander: a form of literary and geographical conceit', *Southerly*, vol. 36, no. 3, 1976: p. 254.

35   Lawrie Kavanagh, 'It's official: Artie will come home', *Courier-Mail*, 20 August 1980: p. 27.

2   OUT OF THE HICKSVILLE DAYS: 1981–1982

1   Barry Dick, '"Marked men" of league', *Courier-Mail*, 26 August 1980: p. 1.

2   Lawrie Kavanagh, 'Devils hold off gutsy challenge; diehards to the letter', *Courier-Mail*, 15 September 1980: p. 15.

3   Tony Durkin, 'Lewis for Test spot!', *Rugby League Week*, 14 May 1981: p. 39.

4   John Lang, 'State league to provide bonanza for country', *Courier-Mail*, 20 May 1981: p. 27; John McCoy, 'The real McCoy', *Rugby League Week*, 14 May 1981: p. 38.

5   'A day for Queensland', *Courier-Mail*, 5 June 1981: p. 4.

6   Peter Peters, 'The senator', *Rugby League Week*, 26 March 1981: p. 13.

7   David Landers, 'QRL bursts from the ruck in the business of sport', *Courier-Mail*, 20 April 1982: p. 25.

8   John Lang, 'Lewis now out for 3 weeks', *Courier-Mail*, 19 March 1982: p. 21.

9   John McCoy, 'When justice makes no sense', *Rugby League Week*, 25 March 1982: p. 38.

10   Tony Durkin, 'Violence: we all suffer!', *Rugby League Week*, 18 March 1982: p. 39.

11   Betty Collins, *The Copper Crucible*, University of Queensland Press, Brisbane, 1996: p. 1.

12   Jim Crawford, 'Just a little larger than Switzerland ...' *Courier-Mail*, 24 September 1980: p. 24.

13 Arthur Beetson with Ian Heads, *Big Artie*, HarperCollins, Sydney, 2004: p. 208.

14 John McCoy, 'How the diehards won the west', *Rugby League Week*, 29 April 1982: p. 39.

15 Keith Lawrie, 'Barry praises State League "experience"', *Rugby League Week*, 7 April 1983: p. 26.

16 Tony Durkin, 'Lewis', *Rugby League Week*, 27 May 1982: p. 33.

17 Peter Peters, 'Showdown', *Rugby League Week*, 10 June 1982, p. 36.

18 Adrian McGregor, *King Wally*, University of Queensland Press, Brisbane, 1987: p. 111.

19 Peter Peters, 'A selection stunner!', *Rugby League Week*, 17 June 1982: p. 11.

20 Barry Dick, 'Sportsview', *Courier-Mail*, 19 September 1982: p. 74.

21 Kate Dennehy, 'Seagulls support in full flight', *Courier-Mail*, 20 September 1982: p. 1.

22 Keith Dunstan, 'Putting Games Brisbane on map', *Courier-Mail*, 25 September 1982: p. 25.

23 'Not all fun and Games', *Courier-Mail*, 29 September 1982: p. 4.

24 Paul Bird, 'Bonner blasts "autocratic" Joh', *Courier-Mail*, 28 September 1982: p. 9.

25 'Police blast "drunken disorderly southerners"', *Courier-Mail*, 1 October 1982: p. 3.

26 'Queenslanditis', *Cane Toad Times*, 1 September 1983: p. 5.

3 THE BEACON ON THE HILL: 1983–1986

1 Leon Pearce, 'Video replay will spot league club brawlers', *Courier-Mail*, 7 March 1983: p. 3.

2 Jane Cadzow, 'Captain colossus', *Courier-Mail Weekend*, 28 March 1992: p. 2.

3 John McCoy, 'Please ... not here', *Rugby League Week*, 10 March 1983: p. 13.

4 Jack Craig, 'The spectator', *Courier-Mail*, 9 March 1983: p. 24.

5 Tony Durkin, 'It's Mal the model!', *Rugby League Week*, 31 March 1983: p. 12.

6 Arthur Beetson, 'The clash others are judged by', *Rugby League Week*, 2 June 1983: p. 16.

7 Peter Badel, 'Aussie Test selectors told me to take out Maroons', *Sunday Mail*, 8 July 2007: p. 104.

8 John Brady, 'Lewis would flop!', *Sun*, 2 June 1983: p. 56.

9   McGregor, *King Wally*, 1987: p. 139.
10 Lawrie Kavanagh, 'Hail the conquering heroes', *Courier-Mail*, 14 May 1984: p. 32.
11 Tony Price, *More than the Foley Shield: a history of rugby league in North Queensland 1908–2014*, CPX Printing and Logistics, Brisbane, 2014: p. 317.
12 Wayne Lindenberg, *Toowoomba Chronicle*, 28 March 1984: p. 72.
13 Lawrie Kavanagh, 'Vikings prepare to go national', *Courier-Mail*, 3 March 1983: p. 17.
14 Arthur Beetson, 'Don't make the bushies go poor', *Rugby League Week*, 17 May 1984: p. 17.
15 Roy Masters, *Inside League*, Pan Books, Sydney, 1990: p. 16.
16 Glen Stanaway, 'Wally puts in the boot on coach selection', *Courier-Mail*, 31 May 1984: p. 1.
17 Ian Heads, 'You're a wonder, Wally!', *Rugby League Week*, 23 August 1984: p. 6.
18 Ian Heads & Tony Durkin, 'McAuliffe: Colourful, caustic, controversial …' *Rugby League Week*, 4 October 1984: pp. 22–23.
19 Lawrie Kavanagh, 'I reckon the axeman deserves the axe', *Courier-Mail*, 6 July 1985: p. 96.
20 Ian Heads, 'Flashpoint Fearnley', *Rugby League Week*, 11 July 1985: p. 5.
21 Terry Fearnley, 'Don's party', *Rugby League Week*, 27 February 1986: p. 9.
22 Gallaway, *Origin*, 2003: p. 78.
23 'Maroons special', *Rugby League Week*, 25 July 1985: p. 15.
24 Tony Durkin, 'The last chant … Ribot! Ribot! Ribot!', *Rugby League Week*, 1 August 1985: p. 3.
25 Barry Dick, 'Mal heads south with his eyes on England', *Courier-Mail*, 5 September 1985: p. 32.
26 Ian Heads, 'Hero Mal … heroic Magpies', *Rugby League Week*, 26 September 1985: p. 29.
27 Jack Gallaway, *The Brisbane Broncos*, University of Queensland, Brisbane, 2001: p. 13.

4   A CHANGE OF CULTURE: 1987–1989

1   Tony Durkin, 'The baby-faced thriller', *Rugby League Week*, 11 June 1987: p. 13.
2   Roy Masters, 'Bucks, bread and Broncos', *Good Weekend*, 13 March 1993: p. 14.
3   Bob McCarthy, 'Sign up these superkids now', *Rugby League Week*, 21 March 1986: p. 8.

4   Peter Frilingos, 'The tragedy of little Laurie', *Daily Mirror*, 22 May 1987: p. 78.

5   Peter Jackson, 'Small in stature, big in heart', *Super League*, vol. 1, no. 13, 1997: p. 15.

6   Gallaway, *The Brisbane Broncos*, 2001: p. 27.

7   Tony Durkin, 'The Origin operation', *Rugby League Week*, 29 July 1987: p. 17.

8   Wallace Brown, 'Joh factor key in ALP win: chiefs', *Courier-Mail*, 13 July 1987: p. 1.

9   Matthew Condon, *All Fall Down*, University of Queensland Press, Brisbane, 2015: p. 8.

10 'The Spirit of Past Brothers', courtesy of Steve Ricketts.

11 Paul Malone, 'Brothers favoured to reverse loss', *Courier-Mail*, 18 September 1987: p. 44.

12 'Last tango in Brisbane', *Rugby League Week*, 16 September 1987: p. 1.

13 Tony Durkin, 'Leprechauns last laugh', *Rugby League Week*, 23 September 1987: p. 5.

14 Stan Correy, 'Same game ... different attitude', *Background Briefing*, ABC Radio National, 10 March 1996. www.abc.net.au/radionational/programs/backgroundbriefing/same-game-different-attitude/3563850

15 McGregor, *King Wally*, 1987: p. 236.

16 Adrian McGregor, 'Broncos make it a family affair', *Courier-Mail*, 16 July 1987: p. 9.

17 Tony Durkin, 'The Maranta connection', *Rugby League Week*, 13 May 1987: pp. 11–13.

18 Paul Malone, 'Sawn off "Alf" is a natural', *Sunday Mail Magazine*, 29 May 1988: p. 5.

19 Ray Price, 'Dump the stadium – and go to Parramatta', *Rugby League Week*, 25 May 1988: p. 7.

20 Tony Durkin, 'Sam's blue', *Rugby League Week*, 25 May 1988: p. 4.

21 Janice Caulfield & John Wanna, *Power and Politics in the City: Brisbane in transition*, Macmillan Education Australia Pty, Melbourne, 1995: p. 44.

22 Ken Arthurson, *Arko: my game*, Ironbark Press, Sydney, 1997: p. 185.

23 Wayne Bennett, 'Broncos had a successful first season', *Courier-Mail*, 16 August 1988: p. 44.

24 'McAuliffe went out his way – with jazz', *Courier-Mail*, 20 August 1988: p. 72.

25 'Ron McAuliffe: Mr Rugby League', *Australian*, 18 August 1988: p. 4.

26 Lawrie Kavanagh, 'Farewell to a wizard', *Courier-Mail*, 22 August 1988: p. 33.

27 A.G. Stephens, *Why North Queensland Wants Separation*, North Queensland Separation League, Townsville, 1893: p. 5.

28 'A team phenomenon unites Queensland', *Townsville Bulletin Magazine*, 13 May 1989: p. 2.

29 Doug Kingston, 'North Qld gets league boss' vote for team', *Townsville Bulletin*, 18 May 1989: p. 1.

30 Doug Kingston, 'Humble pie for doubting crowd', *Townsville Bulletin*, 20 May 1989: p. 55.

5 THE COPERNICAN REVOLUTION: 1990–1992

1   Tony Durkin, 'A salute to the cream of Queensland', *Rugby League Week*, 14 February 1990: p. 18.

2   Steve Ricketts, 'ARL sticks with Wally as captain', *Courier-Mail*, 7 February 1990: p. 64.

3   Steve Ricketts, *Bennett's Broncos: the story of the Brisbane Broncos' golden era, 1992–2000*, New Holland, Sydney, 2014: p. 11.

4   Wally Lewis, 'A curse on a rotten season', *Rugby League Week*, 23 May 1990: p. 29.

5   'Who said that?', *Rugby League Week*, 23 May 1990: p. 14.

6   Adrian McGregor, *The Emperor – Wally Lewis*, University of Queensland Press, Brisbane, 1993: p. 63.

7   'Letters', *Courier-Mail*, 19 September 1990: p. 8.

8   Wayne Bennett, 'Broncos thrilled at bush support', *Sunday Mail*, 25 February 1990: p. 70.

9   Kate Collins, 'So-oo EXcellent', *Sunday Mail*, 25 February 1990: p. 8.

10 Wayne Bennett with Steve Crawley, *The Man in the Mirror*, ABC Books, Sydney, 2008: p. 74.

11 Kerry Boustead, 'QRL unethical in launching own Winfield Cup team', *Townsville Bulletin*, 22 March 1991: p. 26.

12 Tony Durkin, 'Origin exit', *Rugby League Week*, 4 April 1991: p. 7.

13 Ross Fitzgerald, *From 1915 to the early 1980s: a history of Queensland*, University of Queensland Press, Brisbane, 1984: p. 252.

14 John Jiggens, *The Cane Toad Times Warts and All Best of Collection, 1977–1990*, Cane Toad Times Collectives, Brisbane, 2005: p. 2.

15 Mark Lewis, *Cane Toads: an unnatural history*, Ronin Films, Sydney, 1987.

16 John Gardiner, 'Toads and Cockies', *Courier-Mail*, 9 June 1991: p. 13.

17 Brian Williams, 'Trust the toad to turn iconic', *Courier-Mail*, 9 June 2006: p. 7.

18 Roy Masters, 'The new Wally', *Sydney Morning Herald*, 6 June 1992: p. 72.

19 Lawrie Kavanagh, 'King Wally, the peerless player', *Courier-Mail*, 14 June 1991: p. 44.

20 McGregor, *The Emperor – Wally Lewis*, 1993: p. 172.

21 Paul Malone, 'Farewell King Wal', *Courier-Mail*, 30 March 1992: p. 26.

22 ibid.

23 Alan Ramsey, 'A Labor mayor but his own man', *Sydney Morning Herald*, 17 May 2003, p. 37.

24 Neil Cadigan, 'Gilly toasts a grand season', *Rugby League Week*, 23 September 1992: p. 29.

25 'The Broncos, the bold new face of rugby league', *Courier-Mail*, 26 September 1992: p. 30.

26 Joel Gould, 'Renouf recalls the try that became his calling card', *NRL Podcast*, 26 July 2018. www.nrl.com/news/2018/07/26/nrl-podcast-steve-renouf-recalls-the-try-that-became-his-calling-card/

27 Robert Craddock, 'Lewis lauds gutsy Gilly', *Courier-Mail*, 28 September 1992: p. 27.

28 'Our finest week', *Sunday Mail*, 4 October 1992: p. 57.

29 'Grand final wrap-up', *Courier-Mail*, 30 September 1992: p. 8.

30 Tony Currie, 'Broncos have set the standard', *Courier-Mail*, 29 September 1992: p. 36.

6 ON THE SHELL OF A MUDCRAB AND THE SKIN OF A MANGO: 1993–1996

1 Denis Watt, 'Peter Jackson: out of Meninga's shadow', *Rugby League Week*, 21 June 1984: p. 38.

2 Tony Durkin, 'In the footsteps of The King', *Rugby League Week*, 11 March 1992: p. 13.

3 Jason Gagliardi, 'Alfie's army happy in their new home', *Courier-Mail*, 29 March 1993: p. 2.

4 Roy Masters, 'Ribot a victim of campaign', *Sydney Morning Herald*, 5 February 1994: p. 53.

5 'League ready to take legal action against the Broncos', *Sydney Morning Herald*, 22 April 1993: p. 47.

6 Tony Durkin, 'A dozen on the trot', *Rugby League Week*, October special 1993: p. 18.

7 Steve Ricketts, 'Jacko goes out a true winner', *Courier-Mail*, 27 September 1993: p. 28.

8 Stephen Gray, 'Bronco chiefs buy London team', *Courier-Mail*, 21 January 1994: p. 1.
9 Tony Durkin, 'Marlins' boost for Cup hopes', *Rugby League Week*, 19 June 1991: p. 30.
10 Doug Kingston, 'On the shell of a mudcrab and the skin of a mango', *Cowboys Round Up*, iss. 1, February 1995: p. 8.
11 'Cowboys primed for big time', *Courier-Mail*, 24 January 1995: p. 37.
12 Mike Colman, *Super League: the inside story*, Ironbark Press, Sydney, 1996: p. 87.
13 Paul Malone, 'Selectors eye Bartrim for Origin', *Courier-Mail*, 6 May 1995: p. 96.
14 Paul Malone, 'Maroons regain hunger', *Courier-Mail*, 21 May 1994: p. 96.
15 Mike Colman, 'Call of the tribe', *Courier-Mail*, 27 May 2017: p. 9.
16 Mark Coyne, 'Queenslander catch-cry was enough to make a difference', *Courier-Mail*, 17 May 1995: p. 62.
17 'The Unforgettables', *Queenslander Magazine*, ed. 27, Autumn 2015: p. 15.
18 Daniel Lane, 'Simply the best of the best', *Rugby League Week*, 15 June 1995: p. 18.
19 Mal Meninga address at the National Press Club, 19 September 1995. https://catalogue.nla.gov.au/Record/2490218
20 Norman Tasker, 'The judgement', *Rugby League Week*, 28 February 1996: p. 16.
21 ibid.
22 Paul Crawley, 'The Raging Bull; new "tactful" Tallis puts a sock in it', *Sun Herald*, 17 May 1998: p. 117.
23 Patrick Stack, 'Episode Six – Gorden Tallis', *The Stack Report*, 8 May 2017. player.whooshkaa.com/episode?id=99791
24 Adrian McGregor, 'New paddock for Raging Bull', *Weekend Australian*, 4 September 2004: p. 21.

7 I'LL MISS THAT FEELING: 1997

1 John Ribot, 'Battle of the Heavyweights', *Super League*, no. 8, 1997: p. 4.
2 Tony Durkin, 'PAYDAY', *Rugby League Week*, 21 May 1997: p. 27.
3 Joe Gorman, *The Death and Life of Australian Soccer*, University of Queensland Press, Brisbane, 2017: p. 214.
4 Peter Jackson, 'Even if it's bloody, fix it', *Super League*, no. 26, 1997: p. 13.
5 'Tough guy Tallis man on mission', *Illawarra Mercury*, 17 September 1997: p. 64.

6   Andrew Moore, 'Super League and "the decline of working class culture"',
      Overland, iss. 149, Summer 1997: p. 70.

7   Norman Tasker, 'Ribot: the man and his vision', *Rugby League Week*,
      24 May 1995: p. 8.

8   K.V. McElligott, 'For love, not money', *Rugby League Week*, 12 April 1995:
      p. 29.

9   Bernie Pramberg, 'For the love of the game: Steve McEvoy', *Courier-Mail*,
      28 January 2012.

10   Colman, *Super League*, 1996: p. 229.

11   'Tossa's best 10 memories', *Courier-Mail*, 20 June 1994: p. 30.

12   Peter Jackson, 'As always, it's great to be a QUEENSLANDER!', *Rugby
      League Week*, 29 April 1993: p. 10.

13   Natalie Poyhonen, 'Jackson's widow welcomes royal commission into child
      abuse', *The World Today*, 23 November 2012. www.abc.net.au/worldtoday/
      content/2012/s3639386.htm

14   'League in mourning for larrikin Jacko', *Age*, 8 November 1997: p. 24.

8   MY OLD LANG PARK: 1998–2001

1   'Chilling out with Darren Lockyer', *Super League*, no. 20, 1997: p. 41.

2   Mike Colman, 'His brilliant career', *QWeekend*, 27 August 2011: p. 14.

3   Tony Durkin, 'Boy wonder!' *Rugby League Week*, Summer special 1997:
      p. 21.

4   Darren Hadland, 'Night of nights', *Rugby League Week*, 10 March 1999:
      p. 12.

5   Roy Masters, 'League's year of living dangerously; starring Neil Whittaker
      in the Mel Gibson role', *Sydney Morning Herald*, 1 March 1999: p. 25.

6   Tony Durkin, 'Sprucing up a Queensland icon', *Rugby League Week*,
      4 August 1999: p. 27.

7   David Leser, 'Skinned', *Good Weekend*, 13 November 1999: p. 21.

8   Greg Mallory, *Voices from Brisbane Rugby League: oral histories from the 50s
      to the 70s*, Greg Mallory, Brisbane, 2009: p. 160.

9   Tony Durkin, 'Time for the tough decisions', *Rugby League Week*,
      11 March 1998: p. 10.

10   Trevor Gillmeister, 'Pride fires up rivals', *Sunday Mail*, 27 May 2001:
      p. 122.

11   Howell, *The Centenary of the Greatest Game Under the Sun*, 2008: p. 487.

12   David Malouf, *Johnno*, University of Queensland Press, Brisbane, 1975:
      p. 52.

13   Matthew Franklin & Sean Parnell, 'Beattie denies "Hinze tactics"',

Courier-Mail, 14 June 2001: p. 4; Sean Parnell, 'Minister to make stadium decision', *Courier-Mail*, 13 June 2001: p. 3.

14 Bruce Wilson, 'Stadium stays close to our hearts', *Courier-Mail*, 10 November 2003: p. 8.

15 Bennett with Crawley, *The Man in the Mirror*, 2008: p. 225.

16 Paul Kent, 'It was even a surprise to mum and dad', *Daily Telegraph*, 26 June 2001: p. 4.

17 Martin Lenehan, 'State of Origin Top 5: selection masterstrokes', NRL website, 22 June 2018. www.nrl.com/news/2018/06/22/state-of-origin-top-5-selection-masterstrokes/

18 Ray Chesterton, 'Let's have Joh on the wing as well', *Daily Telegraph*, 26 June 2001: p. 4.

19 Allan Langer, 'For Alfie, fairytales can come true', *Courier-Mail*, 30 June 2001: p. 1.

20 Paul Kent, 'Enchanting stuff – coach cuts loose to lead Alf's cheer squad', *Daily Telegraph*, 3 July 2001: p. 60.

21 Peter Frilingos, 'BLOODY ALF', *Daily Telegraph*, 2 July 2001: p. 1.

9 BLACK AND WHITE BROTHERS: 2002–2005

1 Astley, 'Being a Queenslander', *Southerly*, 1976: p. 252.

2 'Storm boy: Billy Slater on hard knocks, family love and future plans', *Domain*, 11 September 2017. www.domain.com.au/domain-review/storm-boy-billy-slater-on-hard-knocks-family-love-and-future-plans-489431/

3 Sam Broughton, 'Same old Cowboys, same old result', *Rugby League Week*, 3 April 2002: p. 44.

4 Murray Hurst, 'The Cowboys took away my dream but I'll keep supporting them', *Courier-Mail*, 10 April 2002: p. 46.

5 ibid.

6 'Young guns a big plus for Cowboys', *Rugby League Week*, 20 March 2002: p. 29.

7 Robert Rachow, 'Nothing short of brilliant', *Rugby League Week*, 8 May 2002: p. 24.

8 *2001 Census of Population and Housing, Aboriginal and Torres Strait Islander Peoples Demography*, Office of Economic and Statistical Research, Queensland Government. www.qgso.qld.gov.au/products/reports/atsi-demography-c01/atsi-demography-c01.pdf

9 Evans, *A History of Queensland*, 2007: p. 257.

10 'Pauline Hanson's maiden speech to parliament: full transcript', *Sydney Morning Herald*, 15 September 2016. www.smh.com.au/politics/federal/

pauline-hansons-1996-maiden-speech-to-parliament-full-transcript-20160915-grgjv3.html

11 Cameron Bell, 'Nathan says he's not good enough', *Sunday Telegraph*, 5 May 2002: p. 61.

12 Will Swanton, 'Laurie Daley never made a big deal about it, but he's comfortable in his own skin – Aboriginal and proud of it', *Sunday Telegraph*, 22 August 2010: p. 66.

13 Stuart Honeysett, 'Hodges replays the hazards of Duke', *Australian*, 6 June 2002: p. 18.

14 Gorden Tallis with Mike Colman, *Raging Bull*, Pan Macmillan, Sydney, 2003: p. 65.

15 Glenn Jackson, 'Childhood dreams become reality for Smith', *Sydney Morning Herald*, 20 April 2012: p. 26.

16 Steve Ricketts, 'Wesser and Smith in frame to spark Maroons – are these men our secret weapons?', *Courier-Mail*, 4 July 2003: p. 51.

17 Robbie Kearns, 'Smith debut softens Origin blow', *Herald Sun*, 19 July 2003: p. 73.

18 Matt Marshall, 'Sweet revenge', *Rugby League Week*, 23 July 2003: p. 21.

19 Cameron Smith, 'The day I met Billy', *Players Voice*, 11 August 2018. www.playersvoice.com.au/cameron-smith-the-day-i-met-billy/#tYdWpduvHVrhx8rL.97

20 Nick Walshaw, 'From the sheds', *Rugby League Week*, 23 June 2004: p. 34.

21 William Stamer, *Recollections of a Life of Adventure*, vol. 2, Hurst & Blackett Publishers, London, 1866: p. 98.

22 Johnathan Thurston with James Phelps, *Johnathan Thurston: the autobiography*, HarperCollins Publishers, Sydney, 2018: p. 35.

23 Joel Gould, 'When dogs cry', *Rugby League Week*, 25 May 2011: p. 17.

24 Thurston with Phelps, *Johnathan Thurston*, 2018: p. 138.

25 Wayne Bennett, 'Switching Queensland derby to Townsville has everyone buzzing', *Courier-Mail*, 18 September 2004: p. 46.

26 Michael Madigan, 'Cowboys walk on air ... and on water', *Courier-Mail*, 20 September 2004: p. 1.

27 Matt Bowen, 'The rise and rise of Ratboy', *Players Voice*, 1 September 2018. www.playersvoice.com.au/matt-bowen-rise-of-ratboy/#yCxjY1WfVjulyQJ6.97

28 Joel Gould, 'The untold story of how Cowboys roped in JT', NRL website, 19 February 2018. www.nrl.com/news/2018/02/19/the-untold-story-of-how-the-cowboys-signed-johnathan-thurston/

29 Wayne Smith, 'Small man a giant for his people', *Weekend Australian*, 4 June 2005: p. 56.
30 Jessica Johston, 'All aboard glory train: supporters urged to lap up excitement', *Townsville Bulletin*, 26 September 2005: p. 4.
31 Jordan Baker, 'Cowboys or Tigers, they're riding on black pride', *Sydney Morning Herald*, 1 October 2005: p. 7.
32 Tony Mooney, 'Cowboys v Tigers, The Big One: messages from the mayors', *Townsville Bulletin*, 30 September 2005: p. 60.
33 Alicia Newtown, 'Thurston still haunted by '05 grand final nightmare', NRL website, 5 May 2018. www.nrl.com/news/2018/05/05/johnathan-thurston-still-haunted-by-05-grand-final-nightmare/

10 A SENSE OF BELONGING: 2006–2010

1   Steve Ricketts, 'Origin essence at stake – Keep it Queensland, says Close', *Courier-Mail*, 29 July 2005: p. 3.
2   Greg Inglis, 'Greg Inglis on why he chose to play for Queensland over NSW', Triple M website, 30 May 2018. www.triplem.com.au/story/greg-inglis-on-why-he-chose-to-play-for-queensland-over-nsw-95699
3   Tom Cranitch, 'Erosion of tribalism leads to Origin trouble', *Eureka Street*, 26 June 2006: p. 28.
4   Mal Meninga, 'It's an honour', *League Queensland*, iss. 13, 2018: p. 16.
5   Adam Gardini, 'Thurston oozes class: NQ halfback sparks team as Maroons clinch series', *Townsville Bulletin*, 6 July 2006: p. 46.
6   Chloe Hooper, *The Tall Man: Death and life on Palm Island*, Jonathan Cape, London, 2010: p. 160.
7   Tony Koch & Patricia Karvelas, 'Dead man's son the forgotten one', *Australian*, 2 December 2004: p. 7.
8   Stephen Hagan, *The 'N' Word: one man's stand*, Magabala Books, Broome, 2005: p. 194.
9   Louise Willis, 'Controversy over racist language', *PM*, ABC Radio, 23 April 2003. www.abc.net.au/pm/content/2003/s838767.htm
10 Neil Brown, 'Big Artie backs "Nigger"', *Toowoomba Chronicle*, 13 July 1999: p. 1.
11 ibid.
12 A. Marshall, 'Long live the stand', *Toowoomba Chronicle*, 20 July 1999: p. 14.
13 Stephen Hagan, *The 'N' Word*, 2005: p. 194.
14 Daniel Lane, 'Bush roots wither where Boomerangs can't come back', *Sydney Morning Herald*, 7 September 2002: p. 11.

15 Martin Flanagan, 'We need to follow footprints of Barcaldine', *Age*, 3 November 2007: p. 12.

16 Joel Gould, 'United we stand', *Rugby League Week*, 19 August 2009: p. 43.

17 Joel Gould, 'Racist Blues', *Rugby League Week*, 16 June 2010: p. 11.

18 'Johnathan Thurston backs calls for conversation on changing Australia Day date', ABC News, 25 January 2018. www.abc.net.au/news/2018-01-25/johnathan-thurston-backs-australia-date-conversation/9362520

11 HEARTLAND: 2011–2014

1 Anna Bligh, press conference transcript, 13 January 2011. statements.qld.gov.au/Statement/Id/73282

2 Vanessa Dunne, 'Families, not Suncorp, are the real tragedy', *Sunshine Coast Daily*, 15 January 2011: p. 37.

3 Zane Bojack, 'Tully Tigers toothless after Yasi', ABC North Queensland, 23 February 2011. www.abc.net.au/local/stories/2011/02/23/3146518.htm

4 Ben Dorries, 'NQ see silver lining in storms', *Courier-Mail*, 17 February 2011: p. 84.

5 Matt Marshall, 'There's no room in here for big heads', *Courier-Mail*, 14 May 2011: p. 106.

6 Phil Lutton, 'Maroons prove to be jewels of Emerald', *Sydney Morning Herald*, 8 June 2011. www.smh.com.au/sport/nrl/maroons-prove-to-be-jewels-of-emerald-20110608-1fsgx.html

7 Billy Slater with Richard Hinds, *Billy Slater Autobiography*, Ebury Press, Sydney, 2017: p. 220.

8 Phil Rothfield, 'What's the buzz?' *Daily Telegraph*, 26 June 2011: p. 56.

9 Mal Meninga, 'Queensland's triumph a victory over the dirty rats of Origin', *Sunday Mail*, 10 July 2011: p. 12.

10 Anna Bligh, media statement, 18 December 2011. statements.qld.gov.au/Statement/Id/78219

11 Lee Rhiannon, 'Speech: Tribute to Mr Arthur Beetson AO', The Greens website, 7 February 2012. greensmps.org.au/articles/speech-tribute-mr-arthur-beetson-ao

12 Steve Ricketts, 'League greats praise Tosser', *Courier-Mail*, 24 June 2008: p. 83.

13 'Beetson spirit to be with Maroons in 2012', *Sydney Morning Herald*, 15 December 2011. www.smh.com.au/sport/nrl/beetson-spirit-to-be-with-maroons-in-2012-20111214-1ous3.html

14 Ewen Jones, 'Adjournment: State of Origin rugby league', 21 May 2012. parlinfo.aph.gov.au/parlInfo/search/display/display.w3p;query=Id:

%22chamber/hansardr/abc2c0c8-7187-4566-b4d3-a8f9194f0813/
0224%22

15 Brent Read, 'Artie's spirit in the sky leads Maroons', *Australian*, 4 July 2012: p. 36.

16 Russell Gould, 'State of Zen', *Herald Sun*, 3 June 2013: p. 58.

17 Scott Ellis, 'Origin clash smashes ratings records', *Age*, 5 July 2012. www. theage.com.au/entertainment/tv-and-radio/origin-clash-smashes-ratings-records-20120705-21iiz.html

18 Peter Badel, 'An era as battlers not to be forgotten', *Courier-Mail*, 1 June 2013: p. 100.

19 Ray Warren, 'Ray's wrap', *Men of League*, August 2013: p. 15.

20 Glenn Jackson, 'Meet Johnathan Thurston, most misunderstood man in game', *Sydney Morning Herald*, 5 May 2011: p. 21.

21 Dan Koch, 'Cowboys on a high after Johnathan Thurston re-signs', *Australian*, 11 March 2013: p. 35.

12 GOD IS A QUEENSLANDER: 2015

1 Joel Gould & Tony Adams, 'Join the club, JT', *Rugby League Week*, 2 March 2015: p. 3.

2 Evans, *A History of Queensland*, 2007: p. 219.

3 John Wanna, 'In the Sunshine State, the winds of electoral change can hit with cyclonic force', *Weekend Australian*, 7 February 2015: p. 20.

4 Mal Meninga, 'Great to be a Queenslander', *Courier-Mail*, 6 October 2015: p. 22.

5 Paul Malone, 'This week soak up the elation of rare all-Queensland decider', *Courier-Mail*, 28 September 2015: p. 59.

6 Michael Carayannis, 'Thurston leads the way as Cowboys charge into grand final', *Sydney Morning Herald*, 27 September 2015: p. 46.

7 Victoria Nugent, 'City court up in finals fever', *Townsville Bulletin*, 3 October 2015: p. 5.

8 Trent Dalton, 'Fairytale of north meets reality in the south', *Weekend Australian*, 3 October 2015: p. 1; David Riccio, 'This is the one JT has waited a decade for', *Daily Telegraph*, 4 October 2015: p. 2; Jamie Marcuson, 'Canterbury Bulldogs selling North Queensland Cowboys jerseys in lead-up to NRL grand final', *Sydney Morning Herald*, 30 September 2015. www. smh.com.au/sport/nrl/canterbury-bulldogs-selling-north-queensland-cowboys-jerseys-in-leadup-to-nrl-grand-final-20150930-gjy3zs.html

9 Matthew Johns, 'An immortal Cowboy to outgun Clint Eastwood', *Daily Telegraph*, 2 October 2015: p. 124.

10 David Riccio, 'This is the one JT has waited a decade for', *Sunday Telegraph*, 4 October 2015: p. 2.

11 Roy Masters, 'Brisbane Broncos v North Queensland Cowboys NRL grand final proves God is a Queenslander', *Sydney Morning Herald*, 27 September 2015: p. 42.

12 Brent Read, 'The game's "Cathy Freeman moment"', *Australian*, 1 October 2015: p. 35.

13 Stan Grant, 'S2015 Ep16 – Johnathan Thurston', *Awaken*, NITV, 18 January 2016. www.sbs.com.au/nitv/video/569339971636/Awaken-S2015-Ep16-Johnathan-Thurston

14 'Johnathan Thurston: how rugby star daughter's doll captivated Australia', BBC, 5 October 2015. www.bbc.com/news/world-australia-34440600

15 Alan Jones, '"From that moment on I thought, this is what I want to be": what made Johnathan Thurston one of the greats', 2GB, 17 October 2018. www.2gb.com/from-that-moment-on-i-thought-this-is-what-i-want-to-be-what-made-johnathan-thurston-one-of-the-greats/

16 Chris Sarra, 'Chris Sarra's "Delivering beyond Indigenous policy rhetoric" lecture: full text and key quotes', SBS, 13 November 2015. www.sbs.com.au/nitv/article/2015/11/13/chris-sarras-delivering-beyond-indigenous-policy-lecture-full-text-and-key-quotes

INDEX

Brisbane Broncos (*continued*)
original team, 80–1
recruitment, 153
salary cap, 120
Super League, 125–6, 133, 139–41, 145
Brisbane Roar, 2
Brisbane Rugby League (BRL), 34–5, 44–5,
160, 242
collapse, 77–8, 87, 92
Brisbane Strikers, 138
Brohman, Daryl, 53–4
Brothers club, 20, 21, 74–8, 144, 159, 201,
243–4
Brown, Edward Stanley, 208
Bruton, Ray, 154
Buderus, Danny, 185
Burchett, Justice, 133, 135
Burney, Linda, 247
Butler, Terry, 56, 66
Buttigieg, John, 168, 177

Campbell, Preston, 210, 212–13, 215, 228,
247–8
Canavan, Brian, 33–4, 214–15, 225, 239
Canberra Raiders, 38, 79, 133, 139, 158
Cane Toad Times, 48, 74
cane toads, 103–5, 106
Cann, Alan, 112
Canterbury-Bankstown, 118, 192–3
Super League, 125, 126, 133, 139
Thurston signing, 189
Carlaw, Dane, 167, 168
Carne, Willie, 98, 107, 154
Carr, Norm, 42
Carroll, Tonie, 152
Carter, Steve, 77
Casey, Ron, 25
Castlemaine Perkins Brewery, 60, 82, 85, 121
Chambers, Will, 240–1
Channel 9, 125, 230
Channel 10, 219
Chesterton, Ray, 103, 166
Christensen, George, 237
Civoniceva, Petero, 7, 152–3, 163–4, 168,
199, 209
Clive Churchill Medal, 151, 160, 206
Close, Chris 'Choppy', 7, 22–3, 31, 35–7,
48, 59, 62, 83, 95, 128–31, 141, 149, 156,
184, 198–9, 203–4
'cockroach', 16
Collins, Tony, 54–5
Colman, Mike, 125, 130, 143
Comans, Jim, 53

Conescu, Greg, 57, 62, 70, 72, 80, 84, 95
Connell, Cyril Junior, 153–4
Cooke, Brad, 181, 207, 215
Coolwell, Adrian, 200
Costigan, Neville, 209
Courier-Mail, 5, 15, 32, 37, 40, 44, 72, 86,
102, 108, 111, 113, 117, 126, 157, 167,
175, 191, 194, 220, 239
Cowley, Ken, 120, 133
Coyne, Mark, 130–1
Cranitch, Tom, 8, 20, 29–30, 52, 78, 80, 110,
144, 201–3, 243
Cressbrook, Reggie, 172
Crocker, Mick, 185
Cronin, Mick, 27
Cronk, Cooper, 226–7, 230, 234–5, 240
Cronulla-Sutherland, 133, 139, 158
Currie, Tony, 7, 66–7, 83, 85, 95, 101, 113,
121, 180, 207
Cyclone Carlos, 220
Cyclone Wanda, 11
Cyclone Yasi, 219–20

Daily Mirror, 16, 25, 43, 70
Daily Telegraph, 166, 167, 180, 221
Dairy Farmers Stadium, 220
Daisy, Frank, 89, 90
Daisy, Vern, 89–90, 123, 207
Daley, Laurie, 133, 180
Daley, Phil, 84
Dallas, Brett, 131
Dally M Awards, 86, 97, 246
Davies, Jonathan, 174
Dick, Barry, 5, 44, 103
Dolan, Frank, 77
Dooley, Dr Tom, 33–4
Dore, Michael 'Micky', 5
Dowling, Greg, 56–7, 59–60, 62–3, 70, 72,
80, 90, 95, 97
Doyle, John, 177
Drake, Frank, 229
Duke, Phil, 44, 182–3
Durkin, Tony, 102

Eastern Suburbs (Easts), 20, 82, 100, 155
English Premier League, 120
E.S. 'Nigger' Brown Stand, 208–9
Eureka Street, 201–2
Evans, Raymond, 178, 237

Falkenmire, David, 103
Fearnley, Terry, 61–3
Feldt, Kyle, 250